TEMPLE
OF THE
COSMOS

TEMPLE

OF THE
COSMOS

The Ancient

Egyptian

Experience of

the Sacred

JEREMY NAYDLER

Inner Traditions
Rochester, Vermont

Inner Traditions International
One Park Street
Rochester, Vermont 05767

LIBRARY OF CONGRESS CATALOGING-IN-PUBLICATION DATA
Naydler, Jeremy.
Temple of the cosmos : the ancient Egyptian experience of the sacred / Jeremy Naydler.
p. cm.
Includes bibliographical references and index.
ISBN 0-89281-555-8
1. Egypt—Religion. 2. Spiritual life. I. Title.
BL2441.2.N38   1995
299'.31—dc20   95-34644
CIP

Printed and bound in the United States
10 9 8 7 6 5 4 3 2 1

Text design and layout by Virginia L. Scott
This book was typeset in Janson with Augustea and Weiss as the display typefaces

Distributed to the book trade in Canada by Publishers Group West (PGW),
Toronto, Ontario
Distributed to the book trade in the United Kingdom by Deep Books, London
Distributed to the book trade in Australia by Millennium Books,
Newtown, N. S. W.
Distributed to the book trade in New Zealand by Tandem Press, Auckland
Distributed to the book trade in South Africa by Alternative Books, Randburg

CONTENTS

PREFACE

The title of this book is taken from a passage in the *Corpus Hermeticum*, a collection of mystical texts attributed to Hermes Trismegistus, the "thrice-great Hermes," whom the Egyptians knew as Thoth, the wisest of the gods. He is in dialogue with his pupil Asclepius, describing to him in bold terms the symbolic significance of Egypt in the spiritual history of the world. He says:

> Egypt is an image of heaven, or to speak more exactly, in Egypt all the operations of the powers which rule and are active in heaven have been transferred to a lower place. Even more than that, if the whole truth be told, our land is the temple of the entire cosmos.[1]

Trismegistus says these words by way of introducing a prophecy, which falls into two parts. First, he tells Asclepius that a time will come when Egypt, "the temple of the cosmos," will be left desolate. Human beings will become weary of life and will cease to regard the universe as worthy of reverence or wonder. Religion will be felt as burdensome, and people will "prefer darkness to light." In that time the gods will depart from humankind, and their voices will no longer be heard. The soil will turn barren, the very air will sicken and stagnate, and in this way old age will come upon the world.

Thus far the prophecy, although ostensibly to do with the fate of Egypt, clearly embraces a larger historical process than simply that of ancient Egyptian civilization. It is a historical process that we can recognize as extending into our own time; indeed, it seems to be describing the destiny of Western civilization. Perhaps his words imply that we make a mistake in regarding Egypt as belonging to an epoch essentially different from our own. As we struggle with a sense of weariness in a godless and polluted world, we might feel inclined to acknowledge that the first part of the prophecy has now been fulfilled: "Egypt" has been desolated.

But then comes the second part. When all this has come to pass, says Trismegistus, through God's grace there will be a renewal of human consciousness of the sacred. Wonder and reverence will once again fill human hearts. There will be a general reawakening to the divine, which will cause human beings once more to sing unceasing hymns of praise and blessing. This will amount to a new birth of the cosmos, "a holy and awe-striking restoration of all nature." All of this is stated still within the framework of a prophecy about Egypt, but it has become apparent that the fate of Egypt incorporates at the same time the fate not only of Western civilization (from which no part of the modern world has remained immune), but also of all nature.

We are presented here with the idea of a vast cosmic cycle, within which Egypt has a special symbolic importance, but which also includes our own time in a particularly significant way. For we live today at that juncture when the first stage of the cycle—the desolation of the temple—has been virtually accomplished, but the second stage—the restoration of the temple—is only just beginning. In the terms of the prophecy, "Egypt" in some respect represents all of humanity and all of nature. In the civilization and spiritual life of ancient Egypt, something was brought to expression that stood for us all at a particular moment in our evolution. Ancient Egypt crystallized in itself a peak of human spiritual attainment and relatedness to nature that has become part of our cultural biography.

Today, we are all brought up to believe that our own era began with the Greeks on the one hand, and the Israelites on the other. The Greeks gave us science and reason; the Israelites gave us monotheism. Thus the soul of the West was forged by means of a heroic antipathy toward a previous epoch of irrational superstition and rampant paganism. This is, however, a picture of our cultural identity that carries less and less conviction with the passage of time.

The Greeks did not so much inaugurate a new epoch of science and rationalism as let slip from their grasp an older dispensation. It was a dispensation of which the Egyptians were the chief guardians in the ancient world, and according to which knowledge of the spiritual powers that pervade the cosmos was assiduously cultivated. As the Greeks slackened their grip upon this older, more attuned mode of consciousness, they had increasingly to orient themselves by reference to the narrower human faculties of logic and sense perception. Similarly, the Israelites did not found their monotheistic religion in a spiritual vacuum, but in the teeth of the ancient polytheistic consensus. From the polytheistic point of view, the religion of the Israelites was an incomprehensible minimalism that even the Israelite people could scarcely understand, and that they only came to accept through a painful, often violent, process of readjustment.

The traditional biography of the Western mind that sees our roots in Greece and Israel does not give us the complete picture. The complete picture must include the world that the Greeks and the Israelites turned away from. The soul of the West is older and wiser than we have been given to believe. In the effort today to reclaim the depth-dimension of the soul, it is necessary, therefore, that we shift our perspective to the blazing culture that lies the other side of the Judeo-Greek horizon. In so doing, not only do we begin to recover a sense of our larger identity, but we also gain a more accurate perspective on the developmental path that we have slowly but inexorably taken since those times.

Egypt calls to us like a lost part of ourselves. As we strive to achieve a new sensitivity toward the spiritual powers that pervade our lives, Egypt comes increasingly into focus for us. We find that there is a new and lively dialogue between the unfolding spirituality of modern times and that of the ancient, pre-Greek and pre-Judaic world. Perhaps we recognize that we are beginning to enter, in our modern way, areas of experience with which the Greeks and Israelites felt uneasy, but with which the Egyptians were entirely familiar. For this reason, it is of inestimable value to pursue this dialogue with the ancient Egyptians. For although their era has now passed, they can nevertheless become our companions and guides as we venture toward our own future.

This is not to advocate some New Age revamp of ancient Egyptian religion. Our modern consciousness is not the same as the ancient consciousness. It has been through a long developmental process that we should honor. Simply to embrace ancient Egyptian spirituality today would be to deny the very meaning implicit in the extraordinary historical process that is the cultural biography of the West. The importance of ancient Egypt today lies in its being a reminder that our modern culture has deeper roots than we may have suspected, deeper not only historically but also spiritually. In tapping these roots we go to a profound source of inspiration and guidance. But at the same time we should recognize that the restored temple will not have the same form as the temple that was desolated. There should be no question, therefore, of our "going back" to Egypt. We have the opportunity today of entering into dialogue with the Egyptian experience, and hence with our own spiritual foundations. Recognizing these foundations, the real challenge is to build toward the future.

This book has owed much to many different people, and it would be impossible to mention them all by name. But grateful thanks are especially due to the following, without whose help and encouragement the book may never have come to the light of day. To Sam Betts and Alison Roberts for reading through early chapters and offering much useful advice and feedback; to Vicky Yakehpar for essential aid with typing; to Barry Cottrell for many perspicacious comments on the completed manuscript and for the beautifully rendered line drawings done specially for this book. I have been most fortunate in having such a sensitive and painstaking editor as Cannon Labrie at Inner Traditions, to whom I am gratefully indebted. Finally, I would like to thank my friends Louanne Richards and Ajit Lalvani for being willing to listen to crucial sections of the book and for their unflagging support.

1 A METAPHYSICAL LANDSCAPE

Radiant Sun

The first thing that strikes one in Egypt is the sun. It is truly majestic, far more so than our northern sun, which too often is limp and cloud defeated. The Egyptian sun commands the lower atmosphere, permeating it with its brilliance. It is a regal presence that dominates the whole country. So pure, so radiant is the light that issues from the Egyptian sun that the ancient Egyptians perceived in it the divine presence of a god they named Shu, of whom it was said that "he fills the sky with beauty."[1]

The nearest equivalent to the dazzling beauty of Shu's light is the atmosphere above the clouds, which one can experience on high mountaintops, or glimpse from airplane windows. The Greeks called this upper atmosphere the "ether." It is heavenly air that is so much more refined and translucent than mundane air that the gods were felt by the Greeks to live and move in it. One can experience this ether on Mount Olympus, when suddenly one breaches cloud level. But in Egypt, the whole country seems to exist in this godlike atmosphere. One feels that much closer to the heavens, to the divine source that proclaims itself in the all-pervading brilliance of the sun. And so one understands how this country was once known to its inhabitants as *ta neteru*, "the land of the gods."

The influence of the sun spreads even into the night. The sun-inebriated air retains a purity that draws the stars close to the earth. Out of the towns, the Egyptian nights belong to the stars. The whole body of the heavens arches over the earth, covering it with a glittering embrace. This body belongs to Nut, daughter of Shu.

By night, the star-studded daughter of Shu is as powerful a presence as her father is by day. Indeed, it is Nut who gives birth to the sun each morning. Mythologically, there is a reciprocity in the relationships of Shu to Nut and of Nut to the sun god Ra who, though he is the father of Shu, is also born of Nut. The pervasive quality of luminescence that characterizes both day and night links these deities in a circle of interdependence.

But there can be no question of the ultimate supremacy of the sun. It is the sun that is the source of life and emblem of the creative spirit that permeates the whole world. From the earliest times, hymns of praise were addressed to the sun god Ra:

Splendid you rise, O living sun, eternal Lord!
You are radiant, beauteous, mighty,
Your love is great, immense.
Your rays light up all faces.
Your bright hue gives life to hearts,
When you fill the Two Lands with your love.

Mighty God, who created himself,
Who made every land, created what is in it,
All peoples, herds and flocks,
All trees that grow from the soil;
They live when you dawn for them,
You are mother and father of all you made.

When you dawn, their eyes observe you,
As your rays light the whole earth;
Every heart acclaims your sight,
When you are risen as their lord.[2]

Such feelings do not come readily to dwellers of the cloud-covered, mist-laden north. We have little experience of the realm beyond the clouds, and we breathe a denser atmosphere than that of the Egyptians. Perhaps it would have been impossible for our modern, secular, scientific civilization to have arisen in the climate of Egypt, for civilizations, like plants, belong to and grow out of a certain soil; they unfold and develop in a specific ambience of light and air. In Egypt the quality of light alone acts as a refining influence on spiritual life, and the ancient culture that developed there was profoundly aware of its indebtedness to the source of this light that "filled the Two Lands [Egypt] with love."

River and Desert

But it is not just the quality of light that has such a profound influence on the character of Egypt. There is also its unique landscape, which is made up of dramatic polarities closely juxtaposed, if not intertwined. Were it not for the Nile, Egypt would be desert. Yet because of the Nile, Egypt is a long, lush oasis with an exuberance of vegetation. It is true that the sun is the source of life, but the life-giving warmth and uplifting light of the Egyptian sun can only be appreciated in the region of the Nile valley. Once beyond the ambit of the river, the lord of life burns the land with the merciless heat of the desert. Egypt is, as Herodotus said, "the gift of the Nile."[3] It is the fertilizing waters of the Nile that transform the sun's intrinsic fierceness into a generous benevolence.

The Nile valley is a wonder for the northern traveller. Plants that we see only in the heated greenhouses of our botanical gardens grow luxuriantly there: the banana and date palm, mango and pomegranate, guava and *soff-saff* tree. There is an abundance, a profusion of greenery. But one is always aware that it is but an oasis. The desert is always at hand: a few miles away, sometimes just a few yards. The desert is a presence one feels even in the midst of the oasis. In Egypt, one becomes acutely aware of the precipitousness of life. Life flourishes on the precipice; it flourishes through the grace of geographical circumstance.

Thus Egypt plays host equally to the extremes of the overflowing life of the oasis and the intractable hostility of the barren desert. There is such a concentration of life, and at the same time such an unequivocally sterile expanse surrounding it, that one wonders at the peculiar destiny of this landscape that has to bear within itself, in such extreme degrees, both fecundity and desolation. It is as if here, in this unique physical environment, one comes closer than anywhere else in the world to an experience of the universal forces of life and death, playing out their mutually antagonistic yet complementary roles. They vie with each other, they contend with each other, but there is also a kind of harmony in this perpetual tension and conflict of each within the other. Neither can drive the other one out, and so they exist in a state of dynamic equilibrium.

The ancient Egyptians called their country the Two Lands. This is usually taken at its face value to refer to the Delta region on the one hand, and the rest of the Nile valley on the other. But the broad and fertile plain of the Delta—Lower Egypt—and the long, confined valley of Upper Egypt were themselves a reexpression of a deeper, underlying polarity. From the beginning, the Delta was the domain of Horus while Upper Egypt was the province of Seth, the great opponent from whom the imperiled life and fecundity of the Nile valley had annually to be won. Seth ruled the desert; the desert was Seth's land. And Seth was eternally opposed by Horus; eternally combatted and defeated. As much as the Two Lands of Egypt are the North and the South, they are equally the fertile Black Lands of the Nile valley, and the barren Red Lands of the encompassing desert.

But the concept of Two Lands goes further than any merely geographical distinction. In Egypt, the physical landscape has a metaphysical resonance of which the ancient Egyptians were keenly aware: the Two Lands are the two contending yet mutually interpenetrating realms of life and death, of the spiritual or heavenly world on the one hand, and the world of lifeless matter on the other.[4] It is not without significance that the name Horus—in Egyptian, Heru—meant "He who is Above." Horus was representative of Heaven, while the domain of Seth was that of unspiritualized matter, chaos, and death. And so this landscape is both paradise and hell, at war with each other yet united in precarious balance and reciprocity.

The Egyptian sun, with its life-giving, translucent light and its searing desert heat contains the same polarity. The sun that shines benevolently upon the flourishing Nile valley is the same sun that scorches the desert. And so the deity whose visible manifestation is the sun, Ra, contains within himself all duality. He is source and progenitor both of the Above and the Below, of Heaven and Earth, and of Horus and Seth. Each night Ra acknowledges this by entering into, passing through, but finally overcoming, the domain in which the forces of Seth are rampant—the Underworld. Here Seth's power manifests as a life-denying opposition to spirit, but—as such—it is also the necessary precondition of the renewal of life and spiritual rebirth. Even Seth, who in so many respects is the archetype of negativity, embodies a certain duality; he was never thought of as unequivocally bad or evil, but rather as a necessary component of the cosmos viewed as a totality.

This ambivalence of Seth can be experienced in the Egyptian desert. It is indeed mercilessly hot, and there is nowhere to find shelter from the sun. But in this landscape of rock and silence, where no bird flies and no animal save the desert viper moves, there is a solitude that the Nile valley cannot offer. The Nile valley has an intensely social, as well as natural, fertility. In ancient as in modern times, it must have been virtually impossible to experience being alone in the entirely humanized landscape of the valley; for there are no wild places there, no woods, heaths, moorlands or craggy hills to offer retreat.

The valley is in its entirety given over to cultivation. There the human and natural spheres of existence are blended into a harmonious unity, as if all partake of the same social fabric. Men, women, and children work together with their donkeys and oxen, sit with their cows or herds of sheep and goats under trees. Even the egrets that gather—as they have always gathered—in the fields mingle with the workers as if they were domestic fowl. The gods of Egypt were the spiritual denizens of the cultivated land. They were part of the social fabric of the Nile valley. All of them, that is, except for Seth. Seth was always the outsider god, encountered when a person stepped outside the socially cohesive fertile land into the desert. In the eerie, fearful wastes of the desert, the wanderer might or might not stumble upon a venomous snake. But there was no avoiding meeting one's own solitude. It was here, in Seth's domain, far from the reassuring presence of the company of gods, that one could experience the utter deprivation of spirit that is the precondition of inner renewal.

In Egypt, one is constantly impressed by the balance and interplay of the opposites: life and death, abundance and barrenness, light and dark, day and night, society and solitude. Each is so clearly described that one sees that the ancient Egyptians could not but understand the world in dualistic terms. Their landscape teaches the metaphysics of the equilibrium of opposing principles.[5] To maintain this balance of the Two Lands, of Horus and Seth, of the Above and the Below, was the central preoccupation of the Egyptian people, which devolved specifically upon the king. One of the titles of the king was "The Two Lords." In the office of kingship, and thereby throughout the whole country, Horus and Seth were embodied and held in equilibrium.[6]

Flood and Drought

As much as the landscape was—and still may be—experienced as resonating with metaphysical import, so equally was the seasonal cycle that transformed the landscape each year. Today, because the flow of the Nile has passed out of the hands of the gods and into the control of human beings, we can only reconstruct this experience in our imaginations. The Egyptian year used to be governed by the influx and reflux of the Great River, as the Nile was called. The Great River was itself regarded, like virtually all landscape features of ancient Egypt, as the body of a god. His name was Hapi, and he was usually depicted as androgynous, for he was the nurturing mother of the abundant life of the Nile valley. Hapi was not merely a "personification" of the river; it was as if, in those days, people *saw through* the vivid landscape in which they lived to the energies, forces, and beings of which it was an expression.[7]

The country on each side of the river was modified by the ancient Egyptians to accommodate and make maximum use of the annual inundation. Many dikes were constructed both parallel to the river and at right angles to it, dividing the valley into a vast network of basins descending in terraces from Upper Egypt in the south to Lower Egypt in the north. Each great basin formed the frame of a whole agricultural district, which in turn was subdivided into a crisscross of ditches and embankments, canals and dikes. The cycle of inundation and retreat thus acted as a principle of organization and division of the land as a whole; it conditioned the agricultural and political ordering of the Nile valley into a series of mutually dependent districts.[8]

Beginning at the time of the summer solstice, when Sirius rose above the horizon, the floodwaters slowly worked their way north to the Delta. The advance wave of the flood turned the waters of the Nile green with a mass of vegetable detritus floating in the river from the equatorial swamps farther south. For several days the Nile would smell so foul with this decaying vegetable matter that gods, men, and demons stood aghast.[9] In the green Nile came Osiris the purifier, who with this stench drove out all evil before the oncoming flood.

A few days later there came a second wave, colored red with ferruginous mud brought down from the soils of Ethiopia. It came on in a spate, and the inundation followed rapidly. The Nile rose forty to forty-five feet in the south, and weeks later about twenty-five feet in the Delta region. These rich, red, humus-filled waters were remarkably sweet. In the ancient festival celebrating the inundation, the people would ritually wash themselves in and drink from the floodwaters.[10] The waters submerged the whole country, giving it the appearance of a vast lake or sea. This is how Diodorus described the inundation in the first century B.C.: "Since the country is flat, and towns, villages and rural dwellings are built on earthworks made by the hands of men, the appearance of the whole recalls the Cyclades islands."[11] This description echoes that of Herodotus several hundred years earlier:

> When the Nile overflows, the whole country is converted into a sea, and the towns, which alone remain above water, look like the islands of the Aegean. At these times water transport is used all over the country, instead of merely along the course of the river, and anyone going from Naucratis to Memphis would pass right by the pyramids instead

of following the usual course by the Cercasorus and the tip of the Delta.[12]

Such a phenomenon aroused emotions of both apprehension and joy. In one of the ancient Pyramid Texts, we read how "They tremble, they who see the Great River when it surges; but the meadows smile, and the river-banks blossom."[13]

The tremendous force of the oncoming flood destroyed everything in its path, disintegrating long stretches of riverbank and obliterating boundaries. In the event of too great a flood, whole villages might be swept away, cattle and people drowned. On the other hand, an insufficient inundation—which was more common—carried with it the threat of starvation. Normally, inadequate inundations could be compensated for by the storage of food supplies from previous years of abundance. But a succession of low inundations threatened the whole land with starvation.

Unlike the rivers of Mesopotamia, however, the annual inundation of the Nile was both predictable and for the most part entirely benevolent. Occurring at the hottest time of the year, the inundation was yet another confirmation of the wise ordering of the universe that caused there to be equilibrium between opposing forces. In the months preceding the flood, the power of Seth would visibly grow. The land became increasingly parched, the earth turned to dust, the vegetation shrivelled. Animals and human beings became listless from the heat, and the Nile shrank ever smaller. It seemed as if the country would soon become absorbed into the surrounding desert.[14] At the very moment in the year when the life-sapping, destructive power of Seth seemed closest to victory, then the Nile waters would miraculously begin to swell, "a wave spreading over the orchards which Ra made to nourish all who thirst, you [Hapi] give drink to the desert places."[15] It was an event that never ceased to cause the visiting Greeks to marvel

the rising of the Nile is a phenomenon which astounds those who see it and appears quite incredible to those who hear of it. For whereas other rivers shrink about the time of the summer solstice, and grow smaller and smaller from that point onwards, the Nile alone begins to swell, its waters rise, day by day, until in the end they overflow almost the whole of Egypt.[16]

The annual cycle of the three seasons: of Deficiency (Shomu) from April to June, of Inundation (Akhet) from July to October, and of Coming Forth

7

or Emergence (Proyet) from November to March, dramatically represented the myth central to the Egyptian religious consciousness—that of the death and resurrection of Osiris. During the drought, Osiris was "lost" or "dead." It was at this time that his son Horus battled with Seth, the inundation betokening Horus's victory and Seth's defeat. It was on account of this that Osiris, the divine source of fertility and reproductive power, was enabled to rise from his condition of unconsciousness and impotence. The surge of plant life that followed the retreat of the waters was the physical corollary of the resurrection of Osiris's soul.[17]

The seasonal cycle, however, did more than act out the phases of the Osirian myth. It recalled the very process of the creation of the universe. For when Egypt was submerged under the floodwaters, the whole land returned to the primordial condition of formlessness that prevailed before creation began. The sinking back of the waters and the reemergence of the land was a quite obvious reenactment, in the world of space and time, of what occurred (and eternally occurs) in the very Beginning, in the very first stages of the emanation of the spatiotemporal world from the non-spatiotemporal, spiritual realm. The seasonal transformations that the landscape of Egypt underwent were—like the landscape itself—a reflection on the physical plane of metaphysical realities.

Orientations

In Egypt, the directions of east and west, north and south, are never in any doubt. Through the whole six-hundred-mile span of the Nile valley, there is an almost unbroken constancy in the northward flow of the river. It thus divides the land equally into a western and an eastern half. This physical division of the country by the Great River is given symbolic meaning by the cosmic and divine event of the daily birth of Ra in the east, his journey across the heavenly Nile (of which the earthly Nile is but an image), and his senescence and descent into the realm of the dead beyond the cliffs of the western desert. East and west are thus not simply physical directions, they are mythical and metaphysical orientations. The symbolism of the sun's diurnal cycle deeply impresses itself upon the Egyptian landscape. The western side of the Nile valley *has* to be the side of the funerary complexes and mortuary temples, for it is there, beyond the western desert, that Ra descends into the Underworld. The east *has* to be the side of rebirth, of new life, for every morning the whole country turns east as it awakens to the enlivening rays of the newborn sun.

But just as the country is divided into easterly and westerly realms, as much mythographical as geographical, so also is it divided into the northern, low-lying expanse of the Delta, and the narrow Nile valley to the south. Looking southward, one can have the sense of gazing into another mysterious, metaphysical zone where, as with the east and west, physical geography blends into mythography. The source of the life-giving waters that flowed through the land was essentially mythic: the Egyptians said the sacred river came to the earth from the Underworld or Dwat.[18] Now the Dwat (for which our "Underworld" is a somewhat misleading translation) was a region midway between the earthly and the spiritual worlds, and— as will be described later—was the source of all life, health, and fertility for the physical realm. Hence the connection of the Lord of the Dwat— Osiris—with the fertilizing power of the Nile's flood. And indeed not only Osiris but the whole Osirian myth rises up before one when looking to the south.

The ancient Egyptians quite literally saw Osiris appear in the southern sky in the constellation of Orion, in the period immediately preceding the flood. But the flood itself was directly heralded by the appearance of Isis in the iridescent star Sirius, some time after the first reemergence of Orion from below the southern horizon. The Nile's inundation was said to be caused by the tears of Isis for her stricken lord, tears that, as it were, came streaming from the rainbow hues of this star down into the emaciated river.

If in looking south one gazes toward the Dwat, then behind one are the stars of the north, the pole stars that never set and that for the Egyptians constituted a cosmic image of eternity. It was the uninterrupted circuit of these stars that the most blessed dead would join, the realm beyond the Dwat, the realm of pure spirit.

A person standing and facing south is in the "archetypal" position by which the ancient Egyptians oriented themselves in "the Beloved Land" (ta-meri). One of the terms for "south" is also a term for "face," while the word usually used for "north" is related to a word that means "back of the head." The word for "east" is the same as that for "left"; likewise the word for "west" and "right."[19] In no other country are directions in space so clearly defined in the landscape. One feels "held" by this landscape as one does nowhere else in the world. In the fact that the directions in space were each felt to correspond to sides of the human body, one glimpses something of the rootedness, the absolute *belonging*, of the ancient Egyptian to this landscape. One understands how this landscape must have nurtured a great confidence in the orderliness of the universe: *there* is the Great River, *there* is the fertile Black Land, *there* is the desert, and *there* is the sun journeying from east to west each day. No matter where a person stands in the Nile valley, he or she is at the center of a cross whose axes are described by the Nile and its embankments on the one hand, and by the sun's course on the other. Wherever one is in the Nile valley, one can imagine how the ancient Egyptians must have felt to be always at the center of a metaphysical universe.

It is an interesting fact that the Egyptians regarded their land not only as being at the center of the world but also as being, in a certain sense, the *whole* world. Thus they called their country "that which the sun encircles," with the implication that it stood for the whole planet. It was not through ignorance of other countries beyond Egypt's frontiers; neither was it through a condescending or dismissive attitude toward the "foreign lands." Rather, it was due to a feeling that characterized the relationship of all ancient peoples to the earth: the feeling that in the part of the earth that they inhabited, the *whole* was present.[20] But more than in any other country, because of its unique qualities of climate and landscape, in Egypt such a feeling could arise with the force of a self-evident truth.

2 INTERPENETRATING WORLDS

The modern traveller to Egypt has an awareness of the natural world, and of personal selfhood as well, that is essentially alien to that of the ancient Egyptian. The most that we can achieve is to experience but an echo of what was once a powerfully resonant landscape; it is like coming into a concert hall just after the final notes of the symphony have been sounded, with the difference that it is our entry upon the scene that causes those notes to die away. The gods are no longer present for us as they were for the ancients, and it is important that we understand why.

In ancient times, people had the feeling that in the part of the world they inhabited, the whole was experienced as present. Each country was apprehended macrocosmically. In this macrocosmic experience of landscape people saw universal, spiritual forces active and immanent in the desert and flood, the course of the sun, the dome of the sky, and throughout the phenomenal world. The physical universe had a "vertical dimension"; it reached up into, and included within itself, spiritual realities that for the modern consciousness are no longer a living experience. But for the ancient Egyptian, a metaphysical world poured into the physical, saturating it with meaning.

The modern consciousness has developed in such a way that access to this vertical dimension has become more or less closed off to it. For the ancient Egyptians, awareness of the vertical dimension was a condition of their experience of life. But today we are, to a large extent, shackled to a "horizontal" mode of perception from which the illuminating presence of the gods has been excluded. The corollary of this development is that we are now that much more aware of how the part of the world in which we live is but a part—one segment of the whole. And if our landscape becomes imbued with symbolic value, we are only too ready to dismiss this as merely subjective, as merely the product of sentiment. Modern rationality asserts that the only objective value a landscape can have is economic value; aside from this, each part of the world is equal to any other part. And so we arrive at our concept of the whole by putting together all the parts. Wholeness is for us simply totality. No longer does it come naturally to us to apprehend the whole as an indwelling presence within the part, for each part of the world has come to be experienced as but a fragment of a whole conceived purely quantitatively. Modern geography operates only on the "horizontal" plane; it is a "democratized" geography from which all metaphysical and mythical elements have been expunged.

Though it may be beyond our powers to recapture the ancient Egyptians' experience of their world, it is nevertheless worthwhile at least to make the attempt. What this experience entails is no less than a completely different relationship to space.

Outer and Inner Space

Despite the sustained efforts of modern physicists to alter the way in which we think about space, most of us still think of it as a kind of container that physical objects are "in." Space is assumed to be a neutral and uniform medium, lacking any qualities, and within which objects exist. It is thereby relegated to the background of our thought. We focus on the objects that are "in" space rather than the space itself.

If we turn our attention to this space, however, it proves to be particularly difficult to apprehend. To have an experience of space emptied of objects—to experience sheer "empty space"—is quite impossible.[1] It seems that we are simply grasping at an abstraction. In order to experience space, we must experience a world of objects. And so we find that rather than objects being "in" space, space is "in" the relationship of one object to another.

Our modern experience of spatially related objects is an experience of their being external one to another, and also external to ourselves. When we refer to the abstraction that we call "space," what we are really referring to is a condition of our modern experience of the world, namely, the condition of its "out-there-ness," it's being external to us. And if we experience the spatial world as one conditioned by externality, then this is because we experience ourselves as external observers of the world.

But spatiality does not necessarily have to be experienced in this way. It is evident that in ancient times space was experienced not simply as the condition of the outwardness of objects in the world but also as disclosing varying degrees of internality. There were vast and important regions of the cosmos that existed entirely inwardly, in which quite different conditions prevailed, but from which the externalized world derives, and in which it partakes. By implication, human beings did not experience themselves simply as observers of an external world. By virtue of objects having an inner dimension, people were able to enter into them in a way that has become quite unfamiliar to us today.[2]

This inner dimension is, of course, the symbolic or vertical dimension. What belongs to this dimension is not physical. Within it are located the nonphysical aspects of objects that have an external mode of existence, and also nonphysical forces, energies and beings that may or may not become manifest in external space.

In modern times, there is a strong tendency to regard such an internal dimension as *within us*. It tends to be located within human subjectivity, either conscious or unconscious. In ancient times, by contrast, inner space was regarded as objective and as existing independently of the human psyche. It was a realm that people perceived or into which they ventured, rather than a realm confined to the individual, or even collective, human psyche. If we were to point to one outstanding difference between the modern and the ancient consciousness, it would be this: that whereas the modern consciousness feels that it contains within itself an inner world, the ancient consciousness felt itself to be *surrounded* by an inner world. And whereas the modern consciousness feels that objects are contained in external space, or at least separated from each other by a space that is "between" them, the ancient consciousness felt that objects contained, and therefore could reveal, an inner, metaphysical space. It was this experience of a non-subjective, inner dimension to the world that nourished and sustained the ancient symbolic worldview. The decline of this mode of experiencing the world, which led to objects becoming increasingly opaque and incapable of transmitting any transcendent value, lies behind the development of the secular, materialistic worldview of modern times. Let us now turn to the cosmos as the ancient Egyptians experienced it.

The Manifest Cosmos

The Egyptian cosmos was conceived primarily as consisting of three realms: the flat mountain-rimmed earth; the sky above the earth; and the atmosphere between the earth and the sky. None of these realms was thought of as being simply physical, each one manifested an inner, divine presence. To describe the Egyptian cosmos is also to describe a world of divine beings whose nature is expressed in their respective cosmological domains. These domains are only marginally physical, and insofar as they are physical they are also symbolic.

For the Egyptians, the lower realm of the earth was represented in its entirety in the image of the Beloved Land. It was pictured as a wide alluvial plain, through the center of which the Great River flowed; on either side it was bounded by a range of mountains. Beyond these were located the other Middle Eastern countries, which throughout Egyptian history existed on the periphery of the Egyptian universe. Egypt was the country that focalized in itself the macrocosmic whole; the countries beyond Egypt failed to attain the metaphysical status as "an image of the heavens," and hence were not assigned any cosmic centrality.[3] They all merged into the general blur of "foreign lands" that had only peripheral significance in a world picture that was essentially symbolic.

The earth itself was identified with the divine being Geb. In one text, it is described literally as the body of Geb, on whose back vegetation grows, and from whose ribs the barley springs forth.[4] Figure 2.1 shows Geb the earth god, his body covered with plants and reeds. The earth was thus alive and ensouled. To tread upon the earth was to tread upon a god.

This image of the earth as god is clearly not based simply on sense perception, nor is it based upon logical reasoning. It is an imaginative vision that *sees through* the physical landscape into its interiority. Ancient Egyptian theology was to a large extent the product of this higher type of perception, which one might easily misinterpret as an imaginative construct, or some kind of psychological projection. But it actually consists in an imaginative *insight* into the invisible forces and beings that exist in "inner space," and that we grasp hold of in symbolic images. Such a mode of awareness might seem to lose sight of the earth altogether, but it would be more accurate to say that our perception is augmented by an experience that resonates at a deeper level of the soul. It is at this deeper level of "soul perception" as distinct from sense perception that, as Henry Corbin says, "the universe of archetype-Images is experienced as so many personal presences."[5]

In figure 2.1, we see Geb in a typical pose. He is nearly always represented in this manner when he is portrayed as the spirit of the earth. We see him in a similar posture in figure 2.2. His right leg (and often his right arm, as in figure 2.1) is usually raised, and he rests on his left elbow and

Fig. 2.1. The earth god, Geb. New Kingdom papyrus.

left buttock. His face is turned toward the earth, seemingly in a gesture of resignation to a fate that entails having become ensnared in the realm of matter. Geb is rarely shown looking up. It is as if, with a mixture of surprise and sadness, his gaze is arrested by what is below rather than by what is above him. What is above him is his beloved consort Nut, the goddess of heaven.

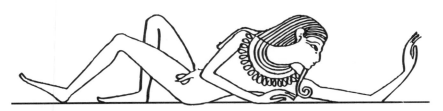

Fig. 2.2. The earth god, Geb, in a posture that suggests surrender to the world of matter. Papyrus of Nisti-ta-Nebet-Taui. New Kingdom.

Geb always seems to lack vitality, and looks as if he is unable to raise himself up. Or is it that he has just landed, having fallen from a great height? Whichever way one sees him, Geb symbolizes the energy that lies behind the world of matter, which is traditionally passive in relation to the world of spirit. In most mythologies the divine being associated with the earth is feminine and is regarded as passive or receptive in relation to a sky god. It is interesting that in ancient Egypt not only is the earth god male, but there are no passive goddesses in ancient Egyptian theology. Geb's partner, the sky goddess Nut, is a far more energized presence than he. Geb appears in these illustrations like a man exhausted from lovemaking,

Fig. 2.3. Geb as cosmic goose. Papyrus of Userhet. Eighteenth Dynasty.

which, as we shall see, is indeed one way in which he can be understood.

Geb was also pictured in other forms. Most usually, he had the form of a goose, which was the main domestic egg-laying bird in Egypt up until the reign of Thutmosis III. Figure 2.3 shows Geb as "the Great Cackler," or cosmic goose. As such, his place in the total scheme of things is different from the Geb of the previous illustrations. For it is from the cosmic goose that the world egg comes into being. The cosmic goose would appear to be an image of the androgynous Creator of Worlds, whom we shall meet in the Heliopolitan creation theology as Atum-Ra. Just as it is from the goose's egg that life arises, so it is from the god Geb at the beginning of time that life emerges and takes on material form.

In these two different ways of imaging Geb we are not only presented with two different aspects of the god; we also come face to face with the paradoxical nature of polytheistic thinking, which is that any single god with apparently limited functions or sphere of operation can at the same time be apprehended as the ultimate Godhead and source of all existence.

Above the earth, and looking down upon the earth god Geb, the Egyptians pictured the heavenly goddess Nut. She is usually represented as a naked woman, her body covered with stars, as in figure 2.4. Her fingertips and toes reach out and down to touch the four cardinal points of the earth, over which her star-spangled body is outspread. This can be seen more easily in figure 2.5, which shows the goddess from the side. It is interesting that both Geb and Nut are nearly always represented naked, which is not normally the case with other deities of the Egyptian pantheon. Perhaps this is because they were thought of primarily in their role as lovers. Or perhaps it is because these two deities—more than any others—show themselves without reserve to the imaginative eye. For they have given themselves utterly to the world of manifestation, and hide nothing from those able to see beyond the outer surfaces of the sense-perceptible world.

With these images of Nut we have only marginally to do with the sensory phenomena of the blue sky of the day or the dark, star-filled night. But this way of representing the dome of the sky is not simply an imaginative construct projected onto the heavens. It is rather a vision of the great cosmic being through whom the stars, the planets, and the sun all come into existence. In figure 2.4, two white circles of the sun disk can be seen on Nut's body, marking the stages in its journey, having been swallowed by her at sunset, and then being born from her at dawn. Nut is naked as a woman is naked who is giving birth. Nut is eternally giving birth to the world of spiritual forms, symbolized by the stars and planets. It is in this sense that she is the overarching divine presence, in whose cosmic embrace the whole world rests. To her, the following words were sung:

> *O Great One who has come into being in the sky,*
> *you have achieved power,*
> *you have achieved strength,*
> *and have filled every place with your beauty,*
> *the entire land is yours,*
> *you have taken possession of it,*
> *you have enclosed the earth*
> *and all things within your embrace.*[6]

Nut is the cosmic correspondent to Geb the earth god. If she is the great mother who clothes all beings in their spiritual forms, then it is Geb who gives them material embodiment. The two deities can be seen as two principles: the heavenly or spiritual and the earthly or material source of forms. In figure 2.6, Geb takes the shape of a snake-headed man underneath the figure of Nut. This may be an allusion to the primordial nature of the god, or perhaps to the fact that snakes are the creatures that live closest to the earth. However we understand his snake form, we notice how Nut does indeed "enclose the earth" in her all-encompassing embrace.

Heaven and earth alone, though, do not comprise the universe. Between them, there exists a third principle that both holds them apart from one another and also mediates their respective energies. This is the atmosphere, which, as we have seen, was also apprehended by the ancient Egyptians in the form of a divine presence—Shu. It is Shu who provides the conditions for the manifestation of the world by creating an ambience

Fig. 2.4. The goddess Nut looks down upon the earth. Painted coffin. Twenty-first Dynasty.

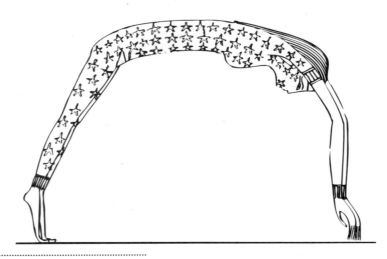

Fig. 2.5. The goddess Nut overarching the earth. Papyrus of Nisti-ta-Nebet-Taui. New Kingdom.

in which plants can grow, animals move, and birds fly. It is through his intervening presence that light and the breath of life enter into the universe. Hence Shu's characteristic gesture is that of the *ka* sign, the sign of animating or vital energy, formed by the arms being held aloft either side of the head, as in figure 2.7. In this illustration Shu has a stripped palm branch on his head, which is the hieroglyph for youthful vigor.

The emblem that Shu normally wears upon his head is an ostrich feather, which as a hieroglyph carries the sound value *shu*. Shu is in fact (like the goddess Maat, who shares the same emblem) sometimes depicted as winged. Figure 2.8 shows him in androgynous form, merged with the god of infinite space, Heh. He kneels with outstretched wings between the figures of the south wind (winged, multiple-headed lioness) and the north wind (double-headed bull).

> "I am Shu," he says, "child of Atum.
> My clothing is the air of life,
> which gathers around me from the mouth of Atum,
> and opens the winds on my path.
> I am the one who makes possible
> the sky's brilliance after darkness . . .
> My strides encompass the length of the sky.
> The breadth of the earth is my foundation."[7]

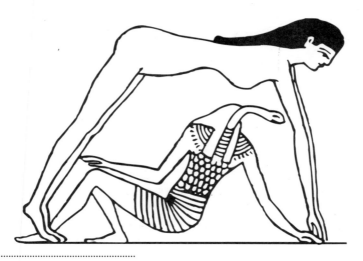

Fig. 2.6. Geb and Nut. New Kingdom papyrus.

Shu is the cause of the polarization of heaven and earth into an Above and a Below. His *ka* gesture is the means by which the sky is held apart from the earth, thus ensuring that a separation between spiritual and material existence takes place. Shu's posture suggests the need for his constant intervention: were he to relax his pose for one moment, the duality that characterizes manifest existence would cease, and heaven and earth would once again unite. In figure 2.9, the relationship between the three deities who constitute the three spheres of the manifest universe is shown. The goddess Nut dominates the scene, while a diminutive Geb lies prostrate below her. Between them, Shu stands, his upraised arms supported by two ram-headed spirits.

Nut, the heavenly goddess, is invariably depicted as a bigger and stronger presence than either Shu or Geb. Shu's arms are only apparently raised in order to support her, for the goddess can quite easily support herself with her own arms and legs, as we have seen in figure 2.6. Sometimes Nut takes the form of a cow, her four legs the four pillars that hold up the sky (figure 2.10). It is then quite clear that Shu's gesture refers less to any need of the goddess for support, and more to his own impulse to fill the space between her and the earth. In figure 2.10, Geb is no longer present. According to one myth, Shu separated Geb and Nut because of his own love for his daughter Nut. Looking again at figure 2.9, could it be that Shu's arms are drawn upward by the sheer magnetism of Nut's breasts and

vulva? Shu steps into the space that is created through Geb's separation from Nut. He stands there like a pillar, stretching the full length between earth and sky, and totally dominating the intermediate zone between them.

In comparison to both Shu and Nut, Geb is feeble. He is sometimes shown ithyphallic, and hence potent, as in figure 2.11, but he is nearly always recumbent and seemingly without active energy. He is usually much smaller than his consort Nut, so one has the feeling of his being enveloped by her. It was believed that Geb and Nut were originally united in a primordial embrace, but it is hard to imagine that their respective positions were different, save that Geb was then conjoined to her rather than she to him. Hence their separation must have involved Geb *falling away* from Nut. That this was the case can be seen in figure 3.5 of the next chapter.

The cosmological images of the three deities suggest an obvious hierarchy in which the goddess of the heavens is the dominant figure. Shu and Geb seem to belong to a lesser mode of being, subsidiary to that of the great mother who arches over them. But of the two, it is clear that Shu has a more active and a more significant role than the prostrate Geb. It is as if Geb has dis-

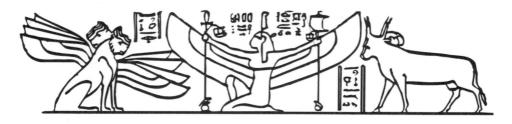

Fig. 2.8. The god Shu-Heh, with outstretched wings, between two wind deities. New Kingdom.

Fig. 2.9. The manifest cosmos comprising the gods Nut, Shu, and Geb. Papyrus of Nesitanebtashru. Twenty-first Dynasty.

gorged his divine vitality into the material world. As god of the earth, Geb is most connected with the realm of external, physical existence. Shu stands between this realm and the heavenly or spiritual world. He is dependent both on the earth to support his feet and on the heavens toward which his arms reach out. Shu represents the "in-between" realm that as much as it separates heaven from earth, also ensures contact between them. Thus in the relationship of these deities to each other, and in the way in which they are characteristically portrayed, a metaphysical scheme is revealed. Egyptian cosmology is based on the division of the manifest cosmos into three qualitatively distinct domains. These domains are not simply physically distinct but also metaphysically distinct. They are three *orders of being* to which the physical regions approximate and by which they are symbolized. In order of priority, they are:

1. The spiritual or heavenly (Nut)
2. The intermediate (Shu)
3. The physical or earthly (Geb)

The psychic nature of Shu's intermediate realm is hinted at by the fact that Shu's arms are often portrayed as being supported in their life-giving gesture by ram spirits. These can be seen both in figure 2.9 and in figure 2.12. In figure 2.12, the ram spirits take the form of *ba* birds, or soul birds.

21

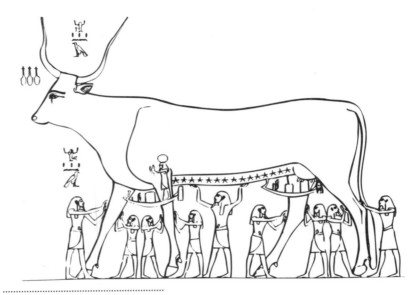

Fig. 2.10. Nut as heavenly cow. Her four legs are the four pillars that hold up the sky. From the outermost shrine of Tutankhamon. Eighteenth Dynasty.

Fig. 2.11. Geb, Nut, and Shu. Twentieth Dynasty papyrus.

Fig. 2.12. Shu's arms supported by two ram-headed ba *birds. New Kingdom coffin.*

The hieroglyph of the ram in fact has the sound value "ba." Their frequent depiction in the intermediate region occupied by Shu is an indication that this was understood on one level as symbolizing the realm of soul, which is intermediate between spirit and matter.

Through a consideration of these cosmological images alone, it becomes evident that to the ancient Egyptians, the physical universe was still to a certain extent transparent to the spiritual world that lay beyond it. It would be a mistake, therefore, to think of them as imaginatively interpreting the physical cosmos. Rather, through the symbolic image and the power of imaginative perception, the spiritual order was made accessible in and through the physical. If the flat-earth cosmology of the ancients appears to the critical modern mind as physically naive, we should remind ourselves that it related primarily to the inward, or vertical, dimension of existence. Flat-earth cosmology was the product of a fundamentally different intention from that of our own modern cosmology. It was not meant to chart precisely the physical cosmos but to represent symbolically a metaphysical order of being. For all its physical naiveté, it had a spiritual profundity that is totally absent from the physically sophisticated but metaphysically barren modern cosmography. The ancients lived in a world that could be entered into and experienced in its inward depth; the moderns, oblivious of this depth dimension, are content to map in interminable detail the outer surfaces of a godless universe.

The Unmanifest Cosmos

The cosmology of the ancient Egyptians so far described is, however, not yet complete because the flat-earth cosmology also included defining further, more subtle areas of the "vertical dimension" that we must also consider. In figure 2.13, the sky goddess Nut is once again depicted. But now both Geb and Shu are absent. There is a new focus in this figure, in relation to which Geb and Shu are no longer strictly relevant. The focus is on the relationship between the heavenly goddess and the sun god Ra. On the left, Nut can be seen about to swallow the sun as it reaches the western horizon. Instead of going down beneath the horizon, the sun is thus taken up into the body of the sky goddess. Nine star gods stand in adoration before this event. The sun then traverses the whole length of Nut's body through the hours of the night, and is born again in the east, a much larger and more imposing presence (on the right). Below, it is shown how the barge of the sun god is towed by jackals with attendant gods.

Figure 2.13 is a detail from the New Kingdom Book of Day and Night, which appears in some tombs of the Valley of the Kings and in various papyri of the same period. It is of particular interest because it shows another, further dimension to the cosmos, beyond those that we have so far considered. For within Nut's body is a region that is entirely invisible, entirely beyond the range of sense perception. When the sun enters this region it can no longer be seen, for it has entered a world that exists purely internally. Here there is no "external space" in which it becomes manifest.

From our modern perspective we may feel tempted to say: "But we know that when we can no longer perceive the sun, it can nevertheless be perceived by other people in another part of the world. It therefore still exists in external space, and anyone who says that it has entered a realm beyond the range of sense perception is simply deluded." From the point of view of the ancient Egyptians, we would, however, be seriously missing the point about the fate of the sun after it has reached the western horizon. From their spiritual and cosmological perspective, the cycle of the sun is not simply the cycle of a physical object but is essentially a mythological process that the apparent journey of the physical sun symbolizes. Their

Fig. 2.13. The journey of the sun through Nut's body. Detail from the Book of Day and Night. Sarcophagus chamber of the tomb of Ramesses IX. Twentieth Dynasty.

whole relationship to the sense world was such that the outwardly percep-tible surfaces of phenomena were constantly breached in order to concen-trate on the noumenal or mythological core of the events that engaged them. For the Egyptians, what is occurring in the sun's journey, even as it is perceived by the senses, has an aspect that is deeper than what is simply sense-perceptible, for the sun is the outward manifestation of a god. It is the life-process of this god that for them was the reality determining the cycle of the sun. And this life-process involved an alternating rhythm of manifestation and retreat. In the inwardness of the Dwat, the god under-went a renewal that enabled him once more to be born into the world of manifestation.

Our problem today is that, in the name of "objectivity," we treat sense-perceptible events in isolation from their mythological components, which we regard as merely subjective. In so doing we cut out the living heart of reality, and satisfy ourselves with the empty husk that is left when the gods have been banished from our experiential world. If we should feel tempted to dismiss the ancient Egyptian perspective as a fantasy that they elaborat-ed through ignorance of physical facts, we would be wise to ask ourselves how deep our knowledge really goes. For our failure to appreciate the epis-temological premises of the ancient Egyptian worldview not only results in our misunderstanding it, it also helps to perpetuate our ignorance of the metaphysical aspect of reality of which they were so intensely aware, and toward which the limited outlook of naive empiricism is totally uncompre-hending.

The region within Nut's body, in the interior of the sky, is the Dwat. As we have already seen, to translate this word as "Underworld" is somewhat misleading. It should now be clear why. The Dwat is not represented in this illustration as under the earth, where one expects to find the Underworld; it is, rather, within the body of the heavens. It is less an Underworld than an *innerworld;* it is a deeply interior world.[8] If we think of Nut, the goddess of the sky, symbolizing the spiritual order of being, then in passing from the stars that cover her flesh to the invisible interior of her body, we enter into this spiritual order that the visible stars merely gesture toward. And entering into it, all outwardly observable conditions fall away.

Just as the sun ceases to be physically perceptible when it enters the Dwat, so do all creatures when they die. For like the sun, all creatures lose their outwardly manifest forms when they enter the Dwat. Though the Dwat may be conceived of as a kind of place, it is in reality less a place than a "condition of being" that things have when they pass out of physical existence, and before they pass back again into physical existence. So it is where the dead go, and equally where the living come from. Just as the sun, when it rises in the east, is in fact born from the womb of the great goddess, so too are all creatures the children of her womb, the Dwat. All things that come into being in the manifest world come from the Dwat. That is where they preexist, before they are born into the light of day, and that is where they return having relinquished their physical forms.

The god who presides over the Dwat is not Nut, however, but her son Osiris. It is Osiris who is the Lord of the Dwat and who governs the cycles of generation and destruction, of coming into being and passing away to which all creatures are subject. The relationship between Nut and Osiris is shown in figure 2.14, which is taken from the mystical New Kingdom Book of Gates. Osiris's body arches round in a circle, so that his toes touch his head, while his arms reach up to the top of his head to lend support to Nut, who stands holding the disk of the sun. The inscription beside Nut reads: "This is Nut, she receives Ra." The text that the figure of Osiris encircles states: "This is Osiris, he encircles the Dwat."[9]

In figure 2.14, which is a detail from a larger picture, we have the sense that Osiris encloses a secret region, of which Nut is on the outside. She in fact seems to be in a relationship of dependency upon Osiris, for it is on his head that her feet are placed, and it is his hands that support her legs. Here, then, we glimpse a region that is interior to Nut in the sense that it seems to have a more profound and mysterious mode of existence. The Dwat is formed by the god Osiris, who encircles it, and appears almost like

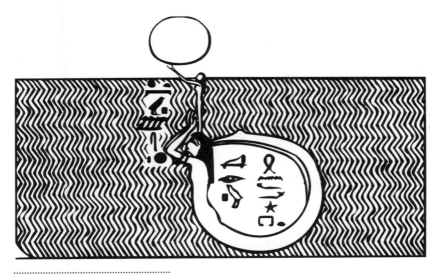

Fig. 2.14. Nut and Osiris. From the Book of Gates, division 12. Tomb of Ramesses VI. Twentieth Dynasty.

an image of the unconscious of the goddess; it has both a wholly internal manner of existence—which means that it does not belong to the world exteriorized in space and time—and yet it is the foundation on which the goddess stands. Here, of course, the perspective we must take is no longer that of the deities of the manifest cosmos—Geb, Shu, and Nut. It is not that Osiris is an alternative or substitute for Geb. Rather, we are contemplating spiritual forces more profound than those that the deities of the manifest cosmos can represent. The Dwat that Osiris encompasses is the spiritual powerhouse that is the source of all forms, and the creative and destructive forces to which all forms are subject. As we shall see in later chapters, the Dwat, as the Underworld of the dead, is also a realm of psychic energies.

One more feature in figure 2.14 should be noted. This is the fact that Osiris is surrounded by water. So also is Nut, up to her head, which apparently rests on the surface of the ocean in which Osiris is submerged. She holds the sun above the water, so it exists in a different element. We can now turn to figure 2.15, from which figure 2.14 is a detail. The detail is taken from the top, and in the context of the whole picture, the correct orientation of the detail is upside down. Beneath it, the space occupied by the sun disk extends to the whole length of the sun barge. Nut can be seen to

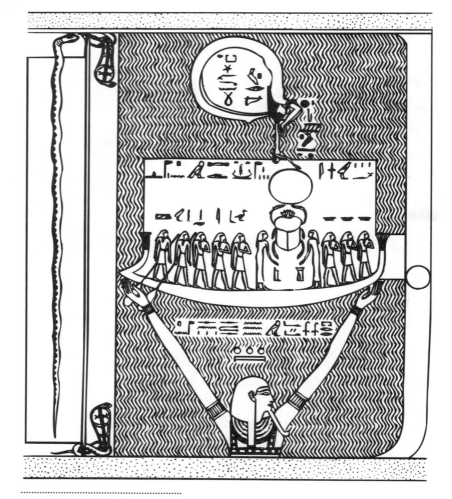

Fig. 2.15. Nun, the primordial ocean, raises up the sun boat. From the Book of Gates, division 12. Tomb of Ramesses VI. Twentieth Dynasty.

be actually receiving the disk from Kheprer, the scarab beetle, which is the form Ra takes as he comes into manifestation. Either side of Ra-Kheprer are Isis and Nephthys, who watch over his birth, and either side of them is the crew of the sun boat.

The sun boat itself makes a space, a kind of air bubble, in the ocean that now appears to be of infinite extent. The sun boat ensures that a world comes into being within this ocean. The ocean is in fact personified in the

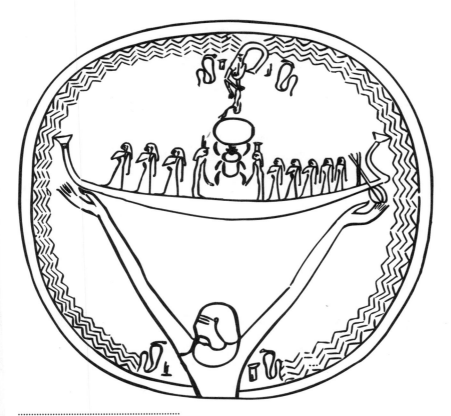

Fig. 2.16. In lifting up the sun boat, Nun creates a space in the cosmic waters. Papyrus of Khonsu-mes, New Kingdom.

figure who holds the sun boat aloft, thus indicating a further level of dependency, a deeper foundation for the manifest universe. This figure is called Nun. The text states: "These arms come up out of the water. They lift up this god [i.e. Ra]."[10] In lifting up the god and the retinue of gods upon his sun boat, the arms of Nun lift up the whole cosmos, which lives in and through the life-giving and light-imparting god, Ra.

The same scene is depicted in figure 2.16, but with one important difference. Nun's gesture—so similar to that of Shu in previous figures—now itself seems to create a space in the waters, which are forced back to the boundaries of the world. And this positioning of the cosmic ocean at the outer circumference of the world would seem to correspond best to the way in which the ancient Egyptians conceived it.

What, then, is this ocean? How are we to understand it? Of one thing we can be certain: the ancient Egyptians did not *literally* believe there was an ocean of water somewhat like the Mediterranean Sea defining the outermost boundaries of their cosmos. For the waters of Nun have an altogether more subtle mode of existence than the waters that we meet with in the physical world. In both figures, Osiris and the invisible realm that he encircles are shown to be submerged in these waters, which suggests that the waters have a more mysterious mode of being than even they have.

Nun's nature is indeed so ineffable that it is usually described in negative terms—Nun is dark, formless, inert.[11] Nun is the unrealized potentiality for existence, symbolized by the formless fluidity of a vast expanse of water. Water best symbolizes the qualities of Nun because although it is the source of life, it is in itself without shape or definition; hence, it exists prior to all forms, whether manifest or unmanifest. Nun exists prior to the gods, prior to Osiris, prior to the Dwat, and prior to the familiar world externalized in space and time. As one Pyramid Text puts it, Nun exists "before the sky existed, before the earth existed, before that which is made firm existed."[12] Because of Nun's essential unknowability, Nun is located at the boundaries of the known world. Nun is not a god, but is rather "the substance and father of the gods."[13] Hence not even the gods can be said truly to know Nun, for Nun is the ineluctable foundation and source of existence itself.

In figure 2.17, the relationship between Nun and the whole cosmos is portrayed. The illustration is from the cenotaph of Seti I, and is the product of the mature theology of the New Kingdom (ca. thirteenth century B.C.). It shows Nut the sky goddess in her usual position, with Shu beneath

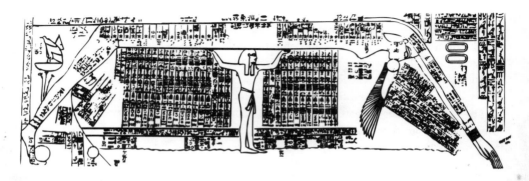

Fig. 2.17. *The cosmos, manifest and unmanifest. Tomb of Seti I. Nineteenth Dynasty.*

her, standing on the earth (here referred to simply as "sands"). The sun disk is swallowed by Nut on the right and enters her body. In passing through her body, it traverses the regions of the Dwat and is finally reborn. The newborn sun disk is shown on the left by Nut's foot. Here, then, are all the main features of the ancient Egyptian cosmological picture: heaven, earth, intermediate region, sun, and the Dwat. But something more.is included in this picture that is normally absent from similar representations, which gives it a completeness the others lack. In the top right-hand corner, outside of and above Nut's body, a text describes Nun. The text is evidently placed here quite deliberately. It is outside the compass of Nut's embrace, just as it is an area quite distinct from the Dwat within her body. This is what the text says:

> The uniform darkness, fount of the gods . . .
> How the upper side of this sky exists is in uniform darkness,
> the southern, northern, western and eastern limits of which are
>   unknown,
> these having been fixed in the Waters [Nun], in inertness,
> There is no light of the Ram [i.e. the sun god Amon-Ra] there:
> he does not appear there—
> a region whose south, north, west and east
> is known neither by the gods nor Spirits,
> there being no brightness there.[14]

If the Dwat is the first degree of nonmanifest reality, Nun is yet more remote from the familiar world of sense-perceptible forms. For whereas the Dwat harbors spirit forms, all form dissolves in the dark waters of Nun. Insofar as Nun is the utterly formless void or "abyss" (as it is often translated), it is beyond all categories of knowledge. Hence it can only be described in the negative terms to which mysticism universally reverts when contemplating the source of existence. In order best to appreciate the significance of Nun in the cosmological and metacosmological theology of the ancient Egyptians, and in order to understand more fully the wider significance of everything that has so far been discussed, we must now turn to the myths that tell of the creation.

MYTHS
OF
COSMOGENESIS 3

Given the nature of the ancient Egyptian worldview with its qualitatively and metaphysically distinct orders of being (signified by the gods), we should expect that the myths about how this world comes into existence would largely be concerned with expressing the relationship of these different orders of being to one another, rather than with attempting to give a simply physical account of the origin of the cosmos. The creation myths describe a "vertical" ontology that extends from the most exalted divinities far removed from the physical world, through gods that are ever more implicated in the earthly realm, to the creatures that inhabit this realm. That is, the creation myths delineate a hierarchy of being from the Godhead or Absolute Spirit to material creatures. But this is by no means a static hierarchy. It is portrayed as a succession of gods or godlike conditions of the universe, which lead to the world as we know it becoming manifest. The way in which this occurs is described in images depicting the relationship of the gods to each other: images of generation, birth, union, and splitting apart.

The creation myths, therefore, can be read in at least two ways. On the one hand, they outline an ontology in which the relationship between the eternal world of the gods and the spatiotemporal world of ordinary human experience is described. Hence, they invite us to look beyond the physical to the metaphysical order upon which the physical is founded, and from whose source it eternally emerges. Were the activity of the spiritual beings who dwell in these higher spheres to cease, then the world would return to its original primordial state. There is a constant and necessary relationship between the spiritual and spatiotemporal orders, the latter being utterly dependent on the former.

On the other hand, since the process of creation is a process of emanation of the eternal world of spirit into the spatiotemporal matrix, this process is one in which spatiality and temporality are necessarily implicated, but not—at least "in the beginning"—as the spatiality and temporality with which we are familiar. The creation myths describe an evolutionary process—an evolution of predominantly spiritual conditions in a prespatial spatiality and pretemporal temporality. How are we to understand this?

For the ancient Egyptians who looked back into the distant past, the conditions of existence were perceived to be fundamentally different from the conditions that prevailed at that time in ancient Egypt. The further back they gazed, the more *internal* did the universe seem. Spatiality itself dissolved into an increasingly inward and "fluid" modality in which external reference points simply did not exist. The original state of the universe was entirely inward; it comprised none other than the spiritual beings by whom it was composed and who constituted its different qualities. If these beings were described as having an external aspect (for example, Ra as the source of life-giving light, Shu as the radiant, light-filled air, or Shu's consort, Tefnut, as moisture), this external aspect should be understood as the manifestation of qualities that were originally unmanifest. In other words, light, air, and moisture existed in a wholly spiritual or godlike manner. They were not the light, air, and moisture that we know, for the world itself had yet to come into being.

In the same way, the nature of time was felt by the ancient Egyptian to alter as it was traced further and further back. Time, like space, shed its externality. In the distant past, time was not determined by the annual cycles of the Nile, sun, moon, and Sirius. It had not yet acquired these external reference points, and was measured solely in relation to the succession of gods who ruled over a "heavenly" Egypt. This age of the gods was called the First Time. It was a "time" before time in an earthly sense had come into existence. As much as they define an ontology, therefore, the creation myths also describe a "metaphysical history" of the outpouring of the Godhead or Absolute Spirit into external manifestation. Through this outpouring, the world of space and time came to assume its present form. The ancient Egyptian creation myths are therefore quite dissimilar to modern scientific cosmogony from which all reference to the vertical dimension is omitted, and which—because it attempts to explain the generation of the cosmos from purely materialistic premises—is unable to conceive of the cosmos existing in a prior spiritual state.[1]

In ancient Egypt there were many different creation myths, as many as there were cult centers of different gods. Our focus will be on the three most important creation myths that acted, to a large extent, as the archetypal models on which other variant cosmogonies (for example, that of Amon at Thebes) based themselves, and together they provide a fairly complete account of the way in which the interrelationship between the nonmanifest and the manifest worlds was understood. These three cosmogonies were developed at the cult centers of the three gods Ra, Thoth, and Ptah, which were located at Heliopolis, Hermopolis, and Memphis, respectively. They are usually referred to as the Heliopolitan, Hermopolitan, and Memphite creation myths or cosmogonies, but one should always remember that what distinguishes them is not so much the fact that they emanated from different places as that they expressed the different perspectives of the cults of the gods worshiped in these places. Each of these gods served a specific function in the whole pantheon of gods, and this was reflected in the position they held in the unfolding of the divine into externality. While it is not possible to determine the precise dates of origin of these creation myths, their formulation and formalization in specific texts can be dated. The first references to the Heliopolitan cosmogony occur in the Old Kingdom Pyramid Texts, while the chief source for the Hermopolitan cosmogony is from various Middle Kingdom Coffin Texts. Our knowledge of the Memphite cosmogony is derived from a text dating from the Late Period, which is widely believed to have been copied from an earlier New Kingdom source. Thus the three creation myths we shall be considering span the whole of ancient Egyptian history.

While it could be argued that they each held ascendency during the respective periods of their formulation, this is not the reason for choosing to focus on them here. Rather, it is because there is a deeper metaphysical significance in the three different emphases of the creation myths. The Heliopolitan cosmogony focuses on the original act of divine self-definition through which the creation of the world became possible, but it hardly concerns itself with the creation of the world as such, concentrating entirely on the spiritual events that preceded it. The Hermopolitan cosmogony, by contrast, emphasizes the way in which the divine creative energy is channelled into the world. Again, it pays little attention to the physical level, but focuses on the ordered transition from the unmanifest to the manifest. Finally the Memphite cosmogony concerns itself primarily with the embodiment of the divine in material form, paying considerable attention to the details of the incarnation of spirit in matter.

As we have seen, the central protagonist of the Heliopolitan cosmogony was Atum-Ra, a god preeminently associated with the sun. More than any other cosmic body the sun was, for the Egyptians, an image of the concentrated power of the heavenly realm. At Hermopolis it was Thoth the moon god about whom the cosmogony turned. The moon, reflecting the light of the sun in measured degrees, can be understood as the cosmic body representing the realm intermediate between heaven and earth. The Memphite cosmogony features the god Ptah, whose association was primarily with the earth and the material realm. The three cosmogonies should not therefore be regarded as antagonists or rivals but rather as articulating the drama of the unfolding of spirit into matter, as this occurs in the three great cosmological domains. Viewed in this way, the three cosmogonies together form a sublime imaginative metaphysics, comparable to that of the Upanishads.

Heliopolis

The cosmogony that evolved at Heliopolis focused on the creation of the universe from the specific perspective of the priesthood of Ra. From the Fifth Dynasty, Heliopolis was the chief center of worship of Ra. The Greek Heliopolis means "City of Helios," the sun god Helios being the Greek equivalent to Ra. In Egyptian, the name given to Heliopolis was Yunu (often written as "On" or "Onnu") and it was represented by the hieroglyph of a pillar or column. In the early Old Kingdom sun temples, this cult object was placed right at the center of the large open courtyard in which the god was worshiped. The Heliopolitan cosmogony, then, is a cosmogonic and theological scheme in which Ra is given a pivotal position.

In this cosmogony, the description of the outpouring of the eternal world of pure spirit into materiality begins with Nun. In the Beginning, there exists only Nun, the dark and abyssal waters that stretch everywhere to infinity. There is no distinction of any one form from another within this primordial ocean; there is only a pervasive formlessness that amounts to nothingness, as all things merge together in this great sea of Nun. One has to imagine a quality of existence that is prior to space and time, up and down, before and after. Nothing lies outside anything else, for everything is intrinsic to every other thing; hence, there are no separate things. Here there is a primordial unity, of which it is impossible to speak save in terms of negatives. And yet the image of water conveys the positive notion of Nun as the source of life. Nun, though nothing in itself, nevertheless contains everything that is to be. Nun is the whole diverse and varied universe existing in a state of potentiality.

This primordial condition to which the name of Nun is given was sometimes pictured as a great serpent. But already, the image of the serpent of many coils must be seen as a first manifestation of *something* from out of the ocean of potentiality. This serpent is called Nehebkau, which means "Provider of Life-Energies." In the Pyramid Texts, Nehebkau says:

> *I am the Outflow of the Primeval Flood [Nun],*
> *the one who emerges from the waters.*
> *I am Nehebkau, the serpent of many coils.*[2]

Nehebkau has a similar ambivalence to Nun, in that the snake's coils both entrap the life energies of all existence in a state of unrealized potentiality, and at the same time provide a secure home, a protective embrace from which these life energies can flow forth. Within the coils of the serpent, and also swimming within the waters of Nun, resides a creative principle that is the spark of life; it alone can release the life-energies held in potential within Nun. The Egyptians referred to this creative principle as Atum, which means "to be complete."[3] Atum and Nun are both aspects of the supreme Godhead, containing the manifold potentialities of existence within themselves. But Atum is the principle that initiates the movement from potentiality to actuality, or from internality to externality. It is Atum who activates the life-potential of Nun, and brings this into actuality. Initially, Atum rests in the waters in a state of passivity or inertness, for he has nowhere to place his feet:

> *I was alone in the waters,*
> *in a state of inertness,*
> *before I found anywhere to stand or sit,*
> *before Heliopolis had been founded.*[4]

In figure 3.1, the waters are shown as having taken the form of the great encircling serpent, in which Atum languishes, his face turned down.

Atum is not originally distinct from Nun. Neither is he distinct from the serpent. In the Coffin Texts, for instance, Atum says:

> *I bent right around myself,*
> *I was encircled in my coils,*
> *one who made a place for himself*
> *in the midst of his coils.*[5]

But insofar as he makes a place for himself within the serpent's coils, Atum begins to define himself as something distinct from them; likewise, within the waters of Nun, Atum begins to differentiate himself from these waters. The self-definition of Atum within the primordial ocean is the first cosmic deed, which initiates a series of creative acts by which an ordered world emerges from out of the original ocean or abyss.

In the act of self-definition, Atum's nature changes; no longer is Atum simply the totality of everything that is, held in solution in the waters of Nun; Atum is the act by which everything

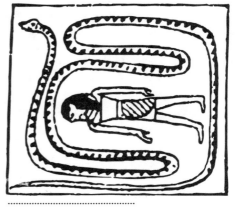

Fig. 3.1. Atum within the coils of the encircling serpent. Nineteenth Dynasty papyrus.

that is comes into being. And since everything that is is no different from Atum, its coming into being is Atum's coming into being. Hence, Atum's act of self-generation is simultaneously an act of world generation. In this act the principle of Becoming is born and Atum is called Kheprer, "the Becoming One." From a state of sheer Being, Atum takes on the mode of Becoming, and it is at this moment that process and change (though not process and change in time as we conceive it) begin.

Kheprer, "the Becoming One," is symbolized by the scarab beetle, renowned in ancient Egypt for its apparent capacity to spontaneously generate itself from balls of dung. In figure 3.2, Atum—still in the coils of the serpent that has now sprung many heads—with his face turned upward, draws to himself the scarab beetle. In so doing he draws to himself the power of generation, thus assimilating to himself the energy of Becoming. In this way Atum emerges from the waters of Nun, and frees himself from the coils of the primeval serpent.

The emergence of Atum is pictured in two ways. In the first, it is represented as land surging forth from the waters. In this symbol of the First Land or the "Primordial Hill," something solid forms itself in the midst of the all-pervading fluidity of the great ocean.

> *"Hail to you, Atum!" says a hymn in the Pyramid Texts,*
> *"Hail to you, Kheprer, the self-created!*
> *You rose up in this your name of High Hill.*
> *You came into being in this your name of Kheprer."*[6]

Fig. 3.2. Atum, still in the serpent's coils, draws Kheprer to himself. From the Book of
What Is in the Underworld, division 6. Eighteenth Dynasty.

This emergence of Atum as the High Hill was symbolically repeated each
year when the first land reappeared as the Nile floodwaters (symbolic of
Nun) receded.

The second picture of Atum's emergence is of his freeing himself from
the serpent's coils. He has to take on the serpent in a battle, in the course
of which Atum changes his form into that of a cat or a mongoose in order
to kill the serpent. This can be seen in figure 3.3. As the cat Atum kills the
serpent, a tree springs up outside the serpent's folds. This tree is a persea,
which for the ancient Egyptians was the World Tree in the branches of
which the whole world came to exist.

Now, the springing into existence of the World Tree at the moment
when Atum defeats the primeval serpent corresponds to a further event
that follows the rising up of the First Land from the abyssal waters. This
is the washing up of a reed on the shores of the Primordial Hill. The reed
takes root and grows. And from out of the surrounding darkness flies a bird
of light, a luminous wide-winged bird that settles upon the reed. This
wondrous bird that brings light into the darkness is the primeval form of
the god Ra. In some versions, the light bird settles upon the sacred Benben
stone. The Benben stone (the word *benben* in ancient Egyptian carries the
connotation of "outflow") is the original pillar or column that came to be
the cult object of Ra in the Old Kingdom. The light bird perching on the
reed on top of the First Land can be seen in figure 3.4.

What is described here, then, are two successive epiphanies of Atum:
the first is as solidity within fluidity, definition within the indefinite mass
of the Primordial Ocean. The second is as the light that shines into the
darkness of nonbeing. Just as the appearance of the Primordial Hill was
reenacted every year when the Inundation receded, so the illumination of

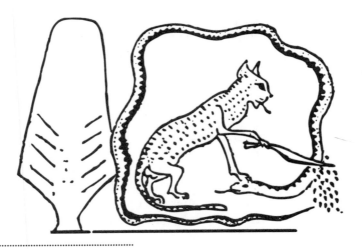

Fig. 3.3. Atum, in the form of a cat, kills the serpent. New Kingdom papyrus.

the world was symbolically repeated every morning with the appearance of light after the darkness of the night. Kheprer is involved as much with the dawning of light as in the emergence of land. But it is especially in connection with the first light that Kheprer is associated with Ra, the Godhead made visible in the sun. Insofar as Atum draws to himself the energies of Kheprer, Atum shows himself to be Ra. Hence in the Book of the Dead we read:

> *I am the divine soul of Ra*
> *who issued from Nun. . . .*
> *I came into being of myself*
> *in the midst of Nun*
> *in this my name of Kheprer.*[7]

Thus Atum is trinitarian: Atum-Kheprer-Ra. This transformation of the One into the Three—strictly speaking, the One into the Four, if we include Nun—is not susceptible to strict logical analysis. We must resist our desire to clarify further, for example, the relationship between Nun and Atum, or Kheprer and Ra, or Ra and Nun, and so on. Surrendering to this desire, we would only move further away from, rather than closer to, the fluid mode of thought of the Egyptians themselves, and thereby from the truth as they experienced it.

The subject matter of ancient Egyptian cosmogony is so far from the

Fig. 3.4. The light bird, Ra, perches on the reed that grows upon the pyramid-shaped Primordial Hill. Papyrus of Anhai. Twentieth Dynasty.

gross physical reality that has tutored the modern scientific consciousness that to attempt to fit this subject matter into a neat logical system would be to cut ourselves off from its living content. We must adopt a more organic way of thinking in which thought-contents flow into one another rather than stand rigidly outside each other. Nun is Atum; Atum is Ra; Atum-Ra is Nun; and yet Nun and Atum are evidently distinguishable. Indeed, it is the very fact of their implicit difference, one from the other, that causes Atum to differentiate himself from Nun. But in this act of self-differentiation, Atum moves on, and becomes Kheprer—a movement whose completion is in Kheprer "becoming" Ra. Ra, we could say, is the end of this process: the fourth hypostasis of the One Godhead. But Ra has in reality been present and active in the process of his own self-unfolding. In the following passage, the beautifully enigmatic relationship of the four to each other is expressed:

I am Atum in rising up.
I am the only One.
I came into existence [Kheprer-na] in Nun.
I am Ra in his rising in the beginning . . .
I am the Great God who came into existence
by himself (Kheprer t'esef)
Nun, that is, who created his name
"Substance [or Father] of the Gods," as god.[8]

A text such as this deserves our deepest contemplation. This is high metaphysics, cast in a mythical rather than an abstract form, but metaphysics all the same.

The one Godhead having become four (Nun-Atum-Kheprer-Ra), the scene is set for the creation of the gods. As creative principle, Atum's nature is such that he longs to express his creativity. The expression of creativity is crucial to his identity. Atum must be productive, he must pour out his essence into the world:

I am the one who came into being as Atum.
It was in Heliopolis that my phallus became erect.

I grasped hold of it, and came to orgasm.
Thus it was that the siblings, Shu and Tefnut, were born.[9]

The motif of masturbation indicates that Atum is androgynous. Atum is "the Great He-She" who is able both to fertilize and to conceive, and then to give birth.[10] In other words, the principle of duality is extrinsic to Atum. Atum himself exists in a nondualistic mode, in accordance with his intrinsically unitary nature.

Paralleling the masturbation motif is the image of expectoration:

You spat out Shu,
You expectorated Tefnut.
You put your arms round them
as the arms of a ka,
so that your ka *was in them.*[11]

Both images express a different kind of deed from Atum's original "becoming" as Kheprer. Here there is an act of creation rather than self-definition or self-differentiation. The gods Shu and Tefnut are separate enough from Atum for it to be necessary for him to put his arms around them so as to instill in them his *ka*. Nevertheless, it is Atum that makes them live, and hence their separateness from him is not total independence. To use the language of medieval Scholasticism, Shu and Tefnut are distinct essences dependent on Atum for their existence; their relationship to Atum is comparable to the relationship of angels to God in Thomistic theology. The image often used in ancient Egyptian sacred texts concerning the gods in general is that they are the "limbs" of the Godhead. Thus, in the beginning, when contemplating creating the universe,

Atum said to the Abyss [Nun]:
"I am in a relaxed state, and I am very weary,
my people are not yet formed;
if earth were alive it would cheer my heart
and enliven my bosom.
Let my limbs be assembled to form him,
and let this great weariness be settled for us."[12]

In order for the "earth" (the material world) and the "people" (all creatures) to come into being, Atum must first assemble his "limbs"—the company of the gods. It is only when Atum's limbs have been assembled that the earth can then be formed. In this text we also find reinforcement of the idea that the reason for creation lies in Atum's irrepressible creativity. The divine nature seeks to express itself, to overflow beyond its original state of aloneness with itself, for only then does it experience full joy.

The production of Shu and Tefnut is a crucial step in the process of world evolution. Shu, as we have seen, represents the principle of air or space. In one text, Shu says: "I am that space which came about in the waters,/I came into being in them, I grew in them,/But I was not consigned to the abode of darkness."[13] Shu is space, but not space as we experience it, for there is as yet no universe. Rather we must conceive of Shu as the principle through which form can arise out of the formlessness of the primordial unity. It is through Shu that Atum can express his creative will and bring the gods and the manifest universe into being. The goddess Tefnut was associated with moisture in the sense of the moist vulva; her significance in terms of the sequence of creation resides in her being the female partner of Shu. The androgynous or bisexual Atum, who is the principle of primordial unity, generates duality from himself. Shu and Tefnut represent the emergence of duality—in the form of sexual polarity—from unity. Not only are they Two (distinct from each other) but they are Two distinct from the original One. In this way the One becomes Three. In the late papyrus Nesi Amsu, this numerological aspect is made explicit: "I emitted from myself the gods Shu and Tefnut, and from being One I became Three."[14]

The first stage in the process of creation thus repeats the original process of self-differentiation within the One. Just as Atum differentiated himself from Nun (One = Two), and in so doing "became" Kheprer (One = Three), the principle of generation, so here Atum creates Shu-Tefnut (One = Two), who embody in themselves the principle of duality (One = Three) now expressed sexually, and hence as generative power.

It is through the sexual union of Shu and Tefnut that the next generation of gods is born. We thus come to a third distinctive phase in the creation process. The first phase was the self-differentiation of the creative principle within the primordial One. The second phase was the self-generation from this creative principle (Atum) of the Two (Shu and Tefnut) extrinsic to the One. The third phase is the creation of further gods in accordance with, or subject to, the principle of duality that the gods Shu and Tefnut embody. The creation process is now so far removed from the supreme Godhead for Atum not to be directly involved.

From the sexual union of Shu and Tefnut, Geb and Nut are born. Geb is the earth and Nut is the heavens, but we should not at this point think of them as heaven and earth as they later came to be experienced by human beings. For Geb and Nut are born together in loving embrace. Earth is originally united with heaven. There is no space in between them; they constitute a single being, an as yet undivided unity, and so we must imagine a condition that is still preworldly. There is not yet a manifest universe.

It can be seen that the universe of the gods in this phase, with the birth of Geb and Nut, now mirrors the fully explicated primordial unity of the Godhead, the united Geb-Nut corresponding to Ra:

```
        Nun                    Atum
       /   \                  /   \
 Atum - Kheprer         Shu - Tefnut
       \   /                  \   /
        Ra                  Geb - Nut
```

Just as when the original One becomes Four, the conditions were set for a further phase in the creative process (Atum's act of masturbation), so now the scene is set for the next major phase: the creation of the manifest world order. This occurs through an act, not of sexual generation, but of splitting apart. In figure 3.5 we see the image of Shu (holding his hands up on the right) separating Geb from Nut. This is a quite different image from previous images of One becoming Two. In the first—of Atum differentiating

Fig. 3.5. The sundering of Geb and Nut. Papyrus of Tameniu. Twenty-first Dynasty.

himself from Nun—we see Atum surging out of the waters in the form of a hill. Atum, celebrating his own creative power, defines himself as a distinctive hypostasis of the Godhead. In the parallel motif of the defeat of the serpent, there is an exultation in Atum's bloody triumph over the forces of inertia. In the further stage of the One becoming Two—Atum creating Shu and Tefnut—we see Atum masturbating or spitting out the Two from himself. Here the motif is, at least in part, of pleasurable procreation. But in the next image of One becoming Two in which Shu separates Geb and Nut, we have to picture the One (Geb-Nut) being divided by an external agency (Shu)—an act that is the source not of pleasure but of pain. For it is not willingly undergone by the loving couple who, it would seem, would have happily remained united for eternity.

It is through the sundering of Geb and Nut by Shu that the spiritual world at last enters into manifestation. With heaven raised above the earth, and with Shu taking his place between them, holding them apart, the conditions are set for that which is essentially spiritual to take on outward form. It is at this moment that the gods (who presumably subsisted within and as a part of the united Geb-Nut) acquire outer bodies; they take the form of stars, which shine on the upraised belly of Nut: "You [Nut] have taken to yourself every god who possesses his barque, that you may install them in the starry sky."[15]

Of particular significance is Ra's entering into manifestation as the sun. The birth of the sun is sometimes pictured as a hatching of the light bird from the cosmic egg produced by "the Great Cackler" (the cosmic goose). Once again, the event of the spiritual becoming manifest is portrayed as a rendering or splitting asunder of what originally was a unity. There is, then, a sense of disruption that accompanies the coming-into-being of the manifest world. The image of Geb and Nut's enforced separation in particular evokes the idea that the world comes into existence on the basis of pain. Pain and suffering are the condition of life in the manifest world.

This world is pictured in figure 3.6. Here we see Atum-Ra in his sun-boat, sailing over the body of Nut, and received on the right by the opened arms of the Dwat. Although Atum-Ra is creator of the gods, Nut is the mother of all that enters into manifestation. To the extent that Ra is manifest in the sun, his "daughter" (really his granddaughter) Nut is necessarily also his mother.

With the coming into being of the heavenly bodies above, the earth below also takes on existence as an entity in its own right. From henceforth it is the earth that is the stage for all further spiritual evolution. It is upon

Fig. 3.6. The manifest world comes into being. New Kingdom papyrus.

the stage of the earth that the subsequent drama of the gods is enacted, but now in relationship to the spatiotemporal conditions familiar to us. From the division of Geb and Nut, four children come into existence: Osiris, Isis, Seth, and Nephthys.[16] All these deities are essentially cosmic, each one having areas of the cosmos assigned to it. Most obviously, Osiris is associated with Orion and the moon; Isis with Sirius; Seth with the constellation of the Thigh (our Ursa Major); and Nephthys with the sphere of the sky below the horizon. Less obviously, they each mediate energies that were experienced by the Egyptians as emanating from the cosmos. Because we today think of the cosmos as somehow "outside" the earth, it is difficult for us to understand that the polar qualities of good and evil, fertility and barrenness, hatred and devotion, strife and reconciliation, and so on, could be cosmic. But for the Egyptians, all that happened on the plane of the earth was a literal image of universal forces. It is the nature of the Heliopolitan theology that it scarcely touches upon the world of sense-perceptible creatures. It focuses almost entirely on the gods, and on the ultimate question of how the many gods arise from the One.

With the genesis of the Nine gods from the One, the creation theology of Heliopolis is completed. The number nine is, numerologically speaking, a limit that cannot be surpassed without returning once again to the beginning. It is of significance that with the advent of Horus (the child

Fig. 3.7. Ancient Egyptian characters for one and ten.

of Isis and Osiris), the number of gods is raised to ten (which was in fact the sacred number attributed to Horus). The significance of the number ten is that, both in our own and in ancient Egyptian writing (fig. 3.7), it symbolizes a return to the beginning; for Horus is the microcosmic reflection of Atum, and is the god through whom the return to the One is accomplished.

Hermopolis

The cosmogony of Heliopolis was evolved in a city that was the center of the cult of Ra, the supreme Godhead made visible in the sun. It expressed the theology of the priesthood of Ra, according to which Ra was both Atum made explicit and Atum become creative. Hermopolis, on the other hand, was the chief center of the cult of Thoth, whose relationship to the moon is comparable to that of Ra's with the sun. In the Hermopolitan cosmogony, for which there survives no coherent text, there is a divergence of emphasis that reflects something of the difference between these two deities.

At Hermopolis, Thoth was the universal demiurge. One form that Thoth took was that of the sacred ibis (fig. 3.8), and it was as such that he hatched the world egg at Hermopolis.[17] But it is in his capacity as "Lord of the Moon" and "Master of the Word" that Thoth's nature is best revealed. It is in this capacity that the difference between Atum-Ra and Thoth, as representing distinct aspects of the divine creativity, is most clearly shown.

As moon god, Thoth (as is often the case with moon gods) was particularly concerned with the regulation and ordering of the universe. One of his titles was "He who reckons in heaven, the counter of the stars, the enumerator of the earth and of what is therein, and the measurer of the earth."[18] It is likely that the Egyptian name of Thoth, Djehuti, has the connotation "the measurer."[19] As such he can be thought of as the divine "mind," the universal principle that the Greeks were to call the Logos. Indeed, Plutarch was later to describe him as "the most Logos-like of the gods," for he is that aspect of the supreme Godhead that channels the effusion of divine energy according to principles of harmony and proportion, so that the world comes into being as an organized cosmos.[20] It is appropriate, therefore, that Thoth's feminine counterpart (or consort) is Maat, principle of order, truth, and justice. Like Maat, Thoth is the mediator of heavenly forces, directing their ordered expression in lower realms.

Fig. 3.8. Thoth as sacred ibis and as baboon with the moon on his head. New Kingdom.

Thoth is sometimes portrayed adjusting the balance in scenes showing the Weighing of the Heart. In this role he usually has the form of a baboon, as opposed to that of the ibis. In figure 3.9, the deceased person kneels in the left-hand scale nearest to Maat, while his heart (in a special jar) is in the right-hand scale nearest to Thoth. Between them squats the beast Ammit who devours the souls of those who fail the trial of the balance. Both Thoth's and Maat's roles here are consonant with their preoccupation with establishing balance, harmony, and proportion. Quite often Thoth (in his ibis form) is portrayed painting Maat's sacred emblem, the ostrich feather, as in figure 3.10. This beautifully expresses Thoth's intense engagement with, and devotion to, the qualities that Maat represents.

Another of Thoth's titles was "Lord of Divine Words." He is the divine mind whose creative instrument is the voice. It is through his voice that Thoth is creative. According to Maspero

> The articulate word and the voice were believed to be the most potent
> of creative forces, not remaining immaterial on issuing from the lips,
> but thickening, so to speak, into tangible substances; into bodies which
> were themselves animated by creative life and energy; into gods and
> goddesses who lived or created in their turn.[21]

The cosmos therefore came into being through Thoth, the universal intelligence, articulating creative sound. The universe is therefore sound made substantial. Thoth is the divine power that utters this sound. It is for this reason

Fig. 3.9. Thoth and Maat adjust the balance. Papyrus of Qenna. New Kingdom.

that Thoth was god of magic, crucial to which was the correctness of intonation in the chanting of incantations. Only if the voice was "true" could the magician gain command of the subtle formative forces of nature. Thoth is the god who governs the exact expression of creative energy so that it manifests as harmonious form, truly reflective of its spiritual source.

As the demiurge, Thoth was sometimes described as the "heart" and "tongue" of Ra[22]—the heart corresponding to intelligence, the tongue to the power of expression—which suggests that the Hermopolitan and Heliopolitan cosmogonies were not necessarily rival, but rather complementary to each other, each laying emphasis on a particular aspect of the divine creativity. As we have seen, the dominant images used in the Heliopolitan cosmogony stress the fecundity of the Absolute. Creation occurs through a superabundance and overflow of creative energy, expressed in the image of Atum ejaculating or expectorating. This aspect of the Godhead is perfectly symbolized by the constant overflow of life-giving light and warmth from the sun. By contrast, the Hermopolitan cosmogony stresses the containment and channelling of the divine superabundance so that it acquires, and becomes manifest in, ordered and harmonious forms. Central to this activity is number and measure. The moon, which measures out the amount of sunlight that it reflects toward the earth in its monthly cycle, is a natural symbol of this aspect of the divine. It is through Thoth's regulatory function that the gods, or universal principles that govern the world, are each allocated their proper sphere of activity. Thoth "opens a place" for each:

> Hail to you, Moon, Thoth,
> Bull in Hermopolis, dweller in Hesret,
> Who opens a place for the gods. . . .
> Nothing is done without your knowing.[23]

Fig. 3.10. Thoth paints the emblem of Maat. Papyrus of Taucherit. Twenty-first Dynasty.

As in all the creation myths, the Hermopolitan begins with Nun, with the great fluidity of nonbeing from which nothing can be distinguished. In the sequence of creation, Thoth, having sent forth the aboriginal creative sound, brings into being four gods and goddesses within the waters. The gods were pictured as having the heads of frogs, the goddesses as having the heads of serpents. These can be seen in figure 3.11, which comes from the temple of Philae. In the top register on the right, the god Ptah, standing on a plinth symbolic of Maat, regards four of the gods and goddesses, while below the ibis-headed Thoth does the same. The meaning of their reptilian and amphibian forms is open to conjecture. But, as we have already seen, the serpent was thought of as having the most primeval of forms, and hence was the creature closest to the conditions that prevailed "in the beginning." The frog was naturally associated with the teaming life that emerges from water, and so in a sense these two types of creature represent the life-potential of the precosmic state.

The eight gods, or Ogdoad, as they are called, come into being at Hermopolis—which was known to the ancient Egyptians as Khmunu or the "City of the Eight." The Ogdoad is not part of the created universe. Rather, they represent the different qualities of the unmanifest, as their names indicate:

Nun and Naunet: formlessness, or chaos.
Kuk and Kauket: darkness, or obscurity.
Heh and Hehet: unendingness, or limitlessness.
Amon and Amaunet: the hidden, or unmanifest.

Fig. 3.11. The Ogdoad of Hermopolis. Temple of Philae.

The earliest allusion to the Ogdoad is to be found in the Old Kingdom Pyramid Texts.[24] Later, in the Middle Kingdom, they are a constant refrain in a certain section of the Coffin Texts where they provide the background to the divine creative activity.[25] But in this case it is Shu who is given the role Thoth assumes in the Hermopolitan theogony. It has been argued that Shu may be an early form of the god Thoth,[26] and it is not unknown to have portrayals of Shu apparently baboon-headed, as in figure 3.12. A similar conflation of Shu and Heka, the god who personifies magic, is also made. So, for example, in figure 3.13 the figure between Geb and Nut is

Fig. 3.12. Baboon-headed Shu between Geb and Nut. Papyrus of Nisti-ta-Nebet-Taui. New Kingdom.

called "Heka, Great God, Master of the Sky." Upon his head is the hiero-glyph of a lion's hindquarters resting on a standard, which is the sign for "creative word."[27] All of this points to the notion that we have here to do with the divine creativity in the intermediate realm symbolized by Shu. It is in this respect especially that the "lunar" theogony of Hermopolis contrasts with the "solar" theogony of Heliopolis.

Returning to the Ogdoad, it would seem that none of the qualities symbolized by the four pairs of gods is in itself creative, but it is Thoth's skill to transform them into their opposites, turning them inside out, so that the world of form, light, and limitation becomes manifest. Presided over by Thoth, these eight primitive deities swim together in the Flood and together make the cosmic egg, from out of which hatches Ra, as the bird of light, heralding the creation of the universe. Alternatively, they mysteriously conjure forth a lotus from the waters, and when its petals open, it is seen to harbor the sun god as divine child. In figure 3.14 Heh and Hehet kneel on the surface of the Primordial Ocean, either side of the lotus, assisting the birth of the young sun god from the flower. Above the sun god's head, the scarab beetle Kheprer raises aloft the sun disk.

This event of the birth of the sun from the lotus is explained in a text inscibed at Edfu Temple as follows:

Fig. 3.13. Heka, the god personifying magic, in the place of Shu. Twenty-first Dynasty coffin.

Fig. 3.14. Heh and Hehet assist the birth of the sun god. New Kingdom.

You [the Eight] have made from your seed a germ,
and you have instilled this seed in the lotus,
by pouring the seminal fluid;
you have deposited in the Nun,
condensed into a single form,
and your inheritor takes his radiant birth
under the aspect of a child.[28]

Having hatched from the cosmic egg or lotus bud (fig.3.15), it is Ra who then assumes the role of creator, with Thoth as his heart and tongue or, as we would say, his mind and creative will. The theme of emergence from the primeval waters is thus (like that of Heliopolis) the basic context of the Hermopolitan creation theology, despite its divergence from the Heliopolitan cosmogony in other respects. At Hermopolis there existed a sacred lake called the Lake of the Two Knives, in the middle of which was an island called the Isle of Flames. It was here that the cosmic egg was hatched, here that the wondrous emergence of the god from the lotus took place, here that the world became manifest at the beginning of time.

Fig. 3.15. *The solar creative principle is born from the lotus. Papyrus of Ani. Eighteenth Dynasty.*

Memphis

The third major cosmogonic scheme is that of the priesthood of Ptah, and derives from his cult center at Memphis. Although it was possibly formulated comparatively soon after the Heliopolitan cosmogony, in the Old Kingdom, we know the Memphite cosmogony from a Twenty-fifth Dynasty granite block, onto which was inscribed an earlier text (probably dating from the Nineteenth Dynasty) on the orders of King Shabaka.[29] Unlike both the Heliopolitan and Hermopolitan cosmogonies, which dwell on different aspects of the premanifest Godhead, the Shabaka Text throws emphasis on the creative deeds of the Godhead or Absolute Spirit as Ptah, and thereafter affirms the immanence of the supreme deity in all earthly creation. The Heliopolitan cosmogony had carefully distinguished different phases in the outpouring of the divine substance, each phase indicating a further distancing of the creative process from the supreme Godhead. The end of this process was the creation of the quaternity of gods: Osiris, Isis, Seth, and Nephthys. The Hermopolitan cosmogony had stressed the premanifest qualities of divinity in the Ogdoad of primeval beings, which Thoth first brought into existence and then, in his role as orderer of the universe, transmuted into the foundations of the manifest cosmos. In the Memphite cosmogony, the emphasis is shifted further toward the active involvement of the Absolute Spirit or Godhead in the creation of the universe, for Ptah is personally engaged in creation right down to the emergence of "people, beasts, crawling creatures, and whatever else lives."[30]

Ptah is the Godhead conceived as formgiver or shaper of the material world. For this reason he was the chief god of craftsmen and all workers in metal and stone, and was later to be identified by the Greeks as the blacksmith god, Hephaistos.[31] The name Ptah probably means "sculptor" or "engraver," and so we may picture Ptah as God at work in the world, giving to all creatures their forms.[32] He is usually depicted wearing the skullcap of the craftsman, as in figure 3.16. Here he also stands on a chisel-shaped plinth, which is the special symbol of the goddess Maat, of whom Ptah was said to be the lord.[33]

The connection of Ptah with the material world is to be seen especially in his aspect as Ptah-Tatenen, which literally means "risen (or exalted) earth," a reference perhaps to the Primordial Hill. Tatenen was in fact a god, comparable in many respects to Geb, and often—like Geb—was painted with a green face and limbs. Conjoined with Ptah, Tatenen becomes a creator god, concerned specifically with the final phase of the outpouring of the Absolute into the inert but living matter of the earth. In a hymn to Ptah-Tatenen, we read:

> *Thou didst knit together the earth,*
> *thou didst gather together thy members,*
> *thou didst embrace thy limbs,*
> *and thou didst find thyself*
> *in the condition of the One who made his seat,*
> *and who fashioned the Two Lands.*[34]

It is significant that Ptah is usually represented as a mummiform god, like Osiris, with whom he eventually became identified. Much of the

Shabaka Text concerns the relationship of Osiris to Ptah. But Ptah was linked not only to Osiris but also to Sokar, the god who presided over the very deepest regions of the Underworld. The Memphite theology thus relates to that aspect of the divine that is most involved in matter, the aspect that has sacrificed a purely spiritual mode of being in order to become crystallized in materiality.

The identification of Ptah with the supreme Godhead is an assumption explicitly made in the Shabaka Text. We read how within Ptah both Nun and also the Primordial Hill came into being. But their origin within Ptah is asserted without referring to the mythic upsurge of the Primordial Hill from the waters of Nun; it is perhaps presupposed that this is already known. At this point in the text, there is no mention of explicit cosmogony, but rather brief theological or metaphysical statements concerning the necessary background to the cosmogony. The key affirmation is that Ptah is "the mighty Great One" the source of all that exists, and hence the equivalent of the Heliopolitan Atum. The cosmogony as such begins with these words: "There came into being as the heart and there came into being as the tongue something in the form of Atum."[35] This can also be translated thus: "In the form of Atum there came into being heart and there came into being tongue."[36]

Fig. 3.16. The mummiform god Ptah in a shrine. Papyrus of Ani. Eighteenth Dynasty.

Before this "moment," Ptah is wholly identified with the Absolute Spirit. It is thus in the first emanation of the Absolute Spirit that Ptah assumes the form of Atum. It is as Atum that Ptah becomes creative by bringing into existence the two organs of creativity: heart and tongue. The heart is the organ of thought, the tongue is the organ of speech. As we have seen, these organs were attributed to Thoth in the Hermopolitan cosmogony. In the Shabaka Text, only the tongue is associated with Thoth, the heart belongs to Horus. It is thus as the trinity

Atum-Horus-Thoth that Ptah sets about the work of creation:

> *The mighty Great One is Ptah,*
> *who transmitted life to all gods,*
> *as well as to their* kas,
> *through this heart, by which Horus became Ptah,*
> *and through this tongue, by which Thoth became Ptah.*[37]

The first beings brought into existence by this trinitarian Ptah are the company of gods that, the text states, are to be regarded as the teeth and lips of Ptah:

> *His divine company is part of him as his teeth and lips,*
> *which correspond to the seed and hands of Atum.*
> *[In that myth] the Divine Company arose*
> *through the action of his seed and fingers.*
> *But the Divine Company is really the teeth and lips*
> *in that great mouth which gave all things their names.*[38]

The Divine Company, or Ennead, is in this way distinguished from the Heliopolitan Ennead. For the Heliopolitan Ennead arose as a result of Atum's act of procreation, whereas the Memphite Divine Company is *identified with* the act of procreation. Just as Horus and Thoth are assimilated into the being of Ptah, so also is the whole company of gods. The spiritual world of gods is grouped together as one with Ptah the world creator. They are all instruments of the one supreme god's creative thought and deed. The significance of this is that whereas the Heliopolitan and Hermopolitan cosmogonies concentrated on the emanation of the Absolute through successive spiritual stages, with these represented by the gods who are the spiritual preconditions of the manifest universe, the Memphite cosmogony—insofar as it regards the gods simply as instruments of the creator—thereby relegates them to the background of interest. It is then able to focus all the more on the final stages of the emanation of the Absolute into materiality, and to assign responsibility for this wholly to Ptah.

> *And so the making of everything,*
> *and the creation of the gods,*
> *should be assigned to Ptah.*
> *He is the Primeval Hill which produced the gods,*

from whom everything has come,
whether food, divine sustenance or any other good thing.[39]

It is precisely because the gods, who in the Heliopolitan and Hermopolitan cosmogonies stood as intermediaries between the supreme Godhead and creation, are here assimilated into the Godhead that stress is laid on the immanence of the Godhead in creation. God is the "heart" and "tongue" of all creation:

> It happened that heart and tongue prevailed over [all other] members, considering that he [Ptah] is [as heart] in every body, [as tongue] in every mouth, of all gods, people, beasts, crawling creatures, and what-ever else lives, while he thinks [as heart] and commands [as tongue] everything that he wishes.[40]

Since it is "in the form of Atum" that "there came into being heart and there came into being tongue," it can be seen that from the Memphite per-spective Atum (or Ptah in the form of Atum) is brought down to earth, and regarded as immanent within all creation. Thus, in the hymn to Ptah-Tatenen we read:

> *The winds come forth from thy nostrils,*
> *and the celestial water from thy mouth,*
> *and the staff of life [i.e., wheat, barley, etc.]*
> *proceeds from thy back;*
> *thou makest the earth to bring forth fruit,*
> *and gods and men have abundance.*[41]

The emphasis on the immanence of Ptah extends beyond the natural world to the realm of human conduct. The Shabaka Text states:

> *And so justice is done to him who does what is liked,*
> *and evil is done to him who does what is hated.*
> *And so life is given to the peaceful,*
> *death to the criminal.*
> *And so are done all labour and all arts.*[42]

Ptah's involvement in the material world ramifies into the details not only of social but also of religious life, down to the determining of the shapes in which the gods are to be worshiped, and the materials from which their statues are to be made, since these "grow" upon him as the earth god:

> *He gave birth to the gods,*
> *he made the cities,*
> *he established the provincial divisions,*
> *he put the gods in their places of worship,*
> *he fixed their offerings,*
> *he established their shrines.*
> *He made their bodies according to the wishes of their hearts.*
> *And so the gods entered into their bodies*
> *of every kind of wood,*
> *of every kind of stone,*
> *of every kind of clay,*
> *of every kind of thing which grows upon him,*
> *in which they have taken form.*[43]

This kind of attention to detail is the special prerogative of Ptah, who is lovingly involved with the material world. The Memphite cosmogony presents us with the fulfillment of the divine creative process, the final embodiment of the divine substance in material form. Viewed in this light, the cosmogonies of Heliopolis, Hermopolis, and Memphis do not appear as rivals so much as complementary aspects of a greater cosmogonic scheme in which different phases of the emanation of the divine into material manifestation are given emphasis.

4 THE MARKING OF TIME

Modern and Ancient Experience of Time

As we have seen, for the ancient Egyptians space had an inner dimension. It conditioned the existence of objects not only in an external, physical world, but also in an inner, spiritual world. The objects and beings that existed in inner space were regarded as more real than those that existed outwardly. They were often the source and archetype of the latter. As with space, so also with time. For the Egyptians, time also had an inner dimension. But in order to understand the Egyptian experience of time, it is necessary first to examine our modern presuppositions about the nature of time.

Just as we talk of events happening "in" space, so we talk of them happening "in" time. The language we use misleads us into thinking of time, like space, as a kind of container within which events occur. There is no absolute "empty" time, however, in which events occur. Rather, time exists in the relationship of events to each other: without events, there could be no time. Time, like space, enables us to distinguish events from each other. The ordering of occurrences in a temporal sequence means that they achieve relative externality from each other. Each one has its distinct place in an "objective" time, conceived as a continuum flowing from ever receding "pasts" to ever approaching "futures."

The key to the externalizing function of time is that this continuum is numbered. Time is conceived by us on the analogy of an infinitely long tape measure, unrolling slowly but inexorably, and against which events are

Fig. 4.1. Eighteenth-century clockface, still showing reference to the sun (in the semicircle above). Made by Thomas Ogden, Halifax, 1750.

placed. We actually have a spatialized view of time; this is necessary in order to ensure that events are differentiated from each other, and to ensure that their externality one to another is maintained. But more than this, by quantifying time, we are able to "place" events against a continuum with which we feel absolutely no connection, no soul relationship. This has the consequence that not only are events distinguished from each other in a temporal sequence, but they are also—through being objectified in this manner—separated from us.

In the modern era, our conception of time has become deeply, perhaps inextricably, linked with the concept of something measurable, and the activity of measuring it. We live in the age of the clock, by means of which time is associated with a succession of numbers marked either by moving hands or by simply flashing up in a faceless digital display. Time has become for us something very abstract; it is neutral, and entirely uniform. We no longer regard time itself as something having qualities, and the numbers by which we "tell" the time have no intrinsic significance. If we experience, for example, 2 P.M. as being an especially important time, then we know that this is personal to us. It is due to a special event in *our* life, but does not objectively reflect the nature of that particular time. Everyone may experience 2 P.M. in an entirely different way, but it remains the same 2 P.M. Our common reference is to the unit or succession of units, stripped of qualities, which we regard as the objective time. This is the time we tell each other, the time that we hold in common. In order for time to be objective, it must be deprived of all quality.

The late-twentieth-century digitalization of clocks has only served to accentuate this experience of time as completely lacking in quality. With the old circular clockface and its moving hands the measurement of time still has a relationship to the cosmos. Looking at a round clockface, one can still feel, dimly, the connection between the progress of the hands and the progress of the sun. At midday, when the sun is overhead, the hour hand points upward; and the course of the hour hand through the morning and afternoon reflects the journey of the sun around the earth. In figure 4.1, which shows a rare eighteenth-century clockface, this cosmic quality is made explicit. The clockmaker has included in the design of the clockface a rotating sun, which indicates when noon is reached in the countries marked in the semicircle above (London is directly overhead). The modern digital clock, however, wrests from our experience of time even this last, dying echo of cosmic cycles. Time becomes a series of instants occurring in a vacuum. The faceless and limbless digital clock may tell us that it is 12 P.M., but it no longer reminds us that the sun is overhead (fig. 4.2).

Fig. 4.2. "Pulsar" electronic watch, made in 1970. Electronic digital watches like this were first developed in the 1950s in Switzerland. Hamilton Watch Company, United States.

The process by which time has been reduced to an abstract, qualityless succession of units, isolated from all other human experience, is part of a more general process in the development of human consciousness in which the experience of qualities has been gradually denied objective significance. This process was already well advanced by the time Galileo first formulated what later became the famous philosophical distinction between primary and secondary qualities.[1] The distinction gives ontological priority to that which is measurable: what cannot be measured is merely subjective. The instruments of measurement, therefore, become the major reference points for the Western psyche, which, schooled in modern scientific ways of thought, learns to distrust experiences that cannot be measured. It is now a kind of reflex of this psyche to assume that measurement in some way lays hold of objective reality. Our psychological security is founded on this ability to measure; this is what lies behind the drive to purge our measuring instruments (the clock for example) of any reference to the qualitative.

The tendency toward the abstraction of the quantitative from the qualitative in human experience has led to the modern feeling that the basis of reality is the smallest spatial or temporal unit. We now assume, for instance, that a week is "made up" of seven days, rather than being a quarter of a month.

61

Up until relatively recently, however, most Europeans still experienced the qualitative values of the different quarters of the lunar cycle. The weeks were felt to correspond to phases in this cycle rather than to be simply accumulations of days. How many people today are aware of the phases of the moon? How many believe such awareness to be important? For the modern consciousness, the experience of the passage of time is completely divorced from any reference to such cosmic events as the lunar cycle.

Just as we tend to think of a week being "made up" of seven days, so most people regard a day as "made up" of twenty-four hours, an hour sixty minutes, a minute sixty seconds. It is the second, ultimately, that we build our sense of time on. All other measures of time are but accumulations of seconds, rather than fractions of larger units. Thus the larger units are denied their intrinsic qualities, that is, their cosmic reference. In our modern age, time, like space, has become atomized. The second is the temporal equivalent of the spatial atom; in the second we reach the horizon of the realm of qualities. The second, and its fractions, are too small to bear any noticeable qualities.

It is necessary to reflect on our own assumptions about the nature of time in order to understand how different the experience of time must have been in ancient Egypt, where there were no clocks. That is not to say that there were no measuring devices at all, only that the clock as we conceive it did not exist. Time was less measured than *marked* by significant events that were of cosmic stature: the great cycles of the sun, the moon, Sirius, the thirty-six constellations of the southern sky (the so-called decans) and the season-determining cycle of the Nile. (In addition to this there was the regnal cycle that will be treated separately in chapter 5.)

In ancient Egypt the smallest formal unit of time was the hour. Anything smaller than that was imprecisely referred to as a "moment."[2] Each hour of the day had a recognizable quality and consequently was named and assigned to a god and goddess.[3] Figure 4.3 shows the twelve hour-goddesses of the night, six of whom stand on water, and six of whom stand on earth, indicating their connection with the two elements that predominate in the Underworld, to which they belong. Whether or not the twelve hours of the day and the twelve hours of the night corresponded to zodiacal constellations is uncertain. They did, however, relate both to the decans and to stages in the sun's diurnal journey. Since throughout the year the number of hours assigned to the day and night remained constant, the hours of the day must have expanded in summer and contracted in winter (the Season of Coming Forth), while the hours of the night contracted and expanded in reverse. Time breathed like a living organism.

Fig. 4.3. The Twelve Hours of the Night. Book of Gates, division 3. Tomb of Ramesses VI. Twentieth Dynasty.

Sun and Moon

The division of the day and night into hours was a priestly division made for religious purposes and not generally followed outside the temples. For the common people, the day was simply divided into morning, midday, and evening, according to the stage of the sun's journey. But if the sun was the ancient Egyptian equivalent of the modern clock, insofar as it regulated the daily activities of the people, then their whole relationship to time must have been radically different from ours. Far from displaying an abstract succession of numbers, the sun is experienced as going through different *qualitative* changes, from the apparent frailty of the dawn sun, to the magnificent power of the midday sun, to the mellowness of the evening sun that seems to draw back into itself the light it has distributed through the day. It was by these different qualities of the sun as it traversed the sky that the time of day was known.

But we must ask: what was the sun for the ancient Egyptians? For all of Egypt—for both priests and common people—the sun was no mere body of incandescent gases; it was the manifestation of a divine being of utmost splendor and radiance. The sun was not just an object in the sky, it was a spiritual subject. The journey of the sun from dawn to dusk was felt to express something of the nature of this spiritual entity who, for the Egyptians, was a very great god. It was in the sun that the supreme Godhead showed itself to the world; and through the sun's diurnal cycle, the life of the Godhead was symbolically enacted.

Just as in the creation myths, in the Beginning, before creation, the Great God was immersed in the darkness and formlessness of Nun, so

Fig. 4.4. The sun child, with the sidelock of youth, emerges from the lotus. New Kingdom.

before the sun rises, it is immersed in the dark, form-dissolving night. The sun's emergence from the night was a symbolic reenactment of the original outpouring of life-giving light at the beginning of the creation of the world. At dawn the sun manifests once again the qualities of the Becoming One, Kheprer, at the first dawn of time. The "newborn" sun was also pictured as a child, emerging from the opening petals of the mythical lotus that grows in the Primordial Ocean (fig. 4.4).

As he rises higher in the sky, the Becoming One sheds all youthful frailty and takes on the more defined, more powerful "adult" form of Ra, whose nature is no longer simply to become, but to *be*. The midday sun expresses the divine creativity of Ra, which irresistibly overflows into the world. It is through Ra that the world, in all its manifold forms, appears; the world owes its being to Ra. But at the end of time the world will return to its spiritual source—to Atum—just as each individual life, of every human being, every creature, returns at death to the spiritual source from which it originated. The "old" sun at the end of the day reenacts the last phase in the cycle of creation: the withdrawal of the light back into itself, the return of the divine to its own inherent internality. In figure 4.5, the morning sun is shown as Kheprer in his scarab beetle form, while the evening sun is shown as a ram-headed man. Both images of Kheprer and the aging Ra are contained within the circle of the sun disk, clearly demonstrating the ancient Egyptian focus on the spiritual realities at work behind the physical phenomenon of the sun's journey across the sky.

It is for this reason that the daily temple liturgy closely followed the course of the sun. The three main services were celebrated at sunrise, midday, and sunset, marking the three main phases of the sun's course through the day. The passage of time through the day was therefore ritualized; it was regarded as having an intrinsically sacred content. As Sauneron says: "Every important moment in the course of the sun called forth a special ceremony dedicated to the earthly embodiment of the divine radiance."[4]

Altogether, twelve metamorphoses of the sun during its passage across the sky were observed in ancient Egypt, and these formed a special subject for meditation.[5] In the Book of the Dead there are twelve chapters that one after another discuss the transformations accomplished by the solar principle, each one of which could be emulated by the human devotee of the sun god. Figure 4.6, from a late sarcophagus, shows these transformations in a schematic diagram. The sun god's journey begins on the right, as a young child. Passing through a series of extraordinary metamorphoses, the god finally takes the form of an old and bent ram-headed man on the left, who is ready to descend into the Underworld. The crucial point here is that in contemplating the changing qualities of the sun through the twelve hours of the day, one is able to form a relationship with the divine subject who eternally plays out these transformations in time.

Fig. 4.5. The morning and evening forms of the sun. Tomb of Merneptah, Valley of the Kings. Nineteenth Dynasty.

As with the day, so also with the night. But here the symbolism was more esoteric, for the sun's journey through the twelve hours of the night was a journey through a realm that cannot be seen; a realm, therefore, that lies beyond the manifest world, namely, the Dwat. In various New Kingdom mystical texts, the progress of the sun through the hours of the night, conceived as regions of the Dwat, is described in minute detail. The most important stage of this journey was the confrontation of Ra with the demonic serpent Apophis, who embodied the forces of darkness (fig. 4.7). Only after he had overcome Apophis was Ra then reborn again as Kheprer, the dawning sun. For the common people, little would have been known of the individual characteristics of the hours of the night. But the confrontation of Ra with Apophis in the depth of the night would have lived in the

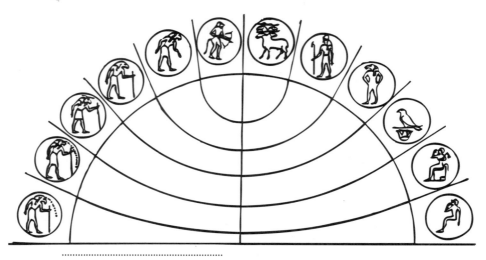

Fig. 4.6. The twelve metamorphoses of the solar principle through the day. From a sar-cophagus in the Cairo Musuem.

popular imagination as an image of midnight, counterbalancing that of Ra's majesty at midday.

In ancient Egypt, time, then, was experienced imaginatively. The passage of time each day and night was not related to by means of an abstract sequence of numbers, succeeding each other with monotonous regularity. It was rather a dramatic journey of transformations undergone by the sun, which was experienced not simply as a physical object but as a divine subject. At the higher levels of Egyptian spiritual life, this divine subject was experienced as dwelling deep within the human soul. One of the most exalted experiences available to the human being was to achieve union with Ra and thus to comprehend all life from the standpoint of Ra's paradigmatic journey. It is sufficient here, though, only to reiterate the fact that for the ancient Egyptians the sun was the outward form of a god. As such, its life and being belonged to the mythical domain: the domain of eternal, archetypal processes that lie essentially beyond time. In ancient Egypt, time existed in direct relationship to the eternal.

What has been described here of the sun's diurnal cycle in relation to the experience of time applies to all the natural cycles, for every natural cycle was felt to be an image of spiritual processes. The moon, for example, which governed the agricultural calendar and determined the timing of all the major festivals of the year, was not regarded simply as a physical

Fig. 4.7. The confrontation of Ra with the serpent Apophis at the midnight hour. The Book of What Is in the Underworld, division 7. Tomb of Ramesses VI. Twentieth Dynasty.

body. For the ancient consciousness, everything that existed outwardly was a manifestation of an inner reality. The outwardly visible cycles of the moon were the expression of inner spiritual processes influencing fertility, growth, and decay, and hence were ruled over by the god Osiris. The moon itself, however, was connected with a number of gods, the most important of which was Thoth, whose role in creation we have already considered.

Sirius

As with the sun and moon, so also with Sirius, whose heliacal rising in June (the term *heliacal* refers to the first appearance of a star, after a period of invisibility, shortly before sunrise or after sunset) heralded the inundation of the Nile. Sirius was not regarded simply as a far-off object in the sky, but as the manifestation of a divine being who, by virtue of being divine, was closely involved with the human and natural world. Modern cosmography staggers us with figures of the sizes of the stars, their distance from us, and the puny size of our own planet. But it is only in an age such as ours, which gives ontological priority to quantity, that this seems to assume significance. The ancients lived in a universe of gods; in such a world physical distance counts for nothing. For the ancients, space disclosed inward as well as outward realities; the divine beings that lived in the inner dimensions of space were not separated from the events that in the inner life of human beings were regarded as important or meaningful.

Accordingly, an inner relationship was felt to exist between the star Sirius

(Sopde) and earthly time cycles. This was experienced not only in the fact that the heliacal "going up of Sopde" heralded the Nile's flood; a far more subtle relationship was experienced between Sirius and the earth, which caused the Egyptians to establish their sacred calendar on the heliacal rising of Sirius. This event determined the date of the new year, as it occurred exactly every 365 1/4 days. It also formed part of the complex calendrical system in which the Sothic (or Sirius-based) calendar (of 365 1/4 days) was used in combination with a moving, civil calendar of 365 days (that is, 36 × 10 days—the Egyptian week being ten days long—plus 5 epagomenal or intercalary days). Because the civil calendar would each year fall short of the Sothic year by a quarter of a day, the coincidence of the Sothic new year and the civil new year occurred only once every 1,461 years. This period of time is a significant fraction of the much larger cosmic cycle caused by the precession of the equinoxes, in which the sun's position each spring slowly shifts against the background of constellations. After approximately 26,000 years, the vernal rising of the sun comes full circle.

According to R. A. Schwaller de Lubicz, this precessional period is, however, gradually diminishing.[6] He argues that in 3000 B.C. the observable precession would have corresponded almost exactly to eighteen Sothic cycles, whereas today it is somewhat less.[7] It must be remembered that, while it is possible that the Egyptians divided the sun's ecliptic into twelve zodiacal constellations, their main reference points were the thirty-six decans—the constellations in the southern sky. The precession of the sun in relation to the decans would have taken half as long as in relation to the Sothic cycles, namely, 730 years per decan. Such a period would correspond to a cosmic week, if we regard the length of time it takes for the sun to precess through a zodiacal sign as a cosmic month (remembering that for the Egyptians there were three weeks to a month, not four). Since each decan represented a divine principle, we can assume that the Egyptians would have regarded these "cosmic weeks" as each mediating different divine energies. Further significance of the decans is shown in the fact that a "cosmic day" would have corresponded to approximately seventy-three years, the life span of a human being, implying that each generation would have come under the influence primarily of one or two decans.

As for the star Sirius, there is no doubt that it held a position of cosmic centrality in ancient Egyptian cosmology. According to Schwaller de Lubicz, "for Pharaonic Egypt [Sirius] played the role of a central sun to our entire solar system."[8] This, of course, is to assume that although it formed no part of their exoteric cosmology, there was an esoteric knowledge of the heliocentric system within the temples. Certainly the complexity of the Egyptian calendrical system alone implies the existence of a far more sophisticated cosmology than that of the flat-earth scheme. The flat-earth scheme may best be understood as fulfilling the role of a meta-physical ontology in which the hierarchical nature of the universe is artic-ulated in symbolic images. Beyond that, however, the calendrical system aimed to align Egypt with subtle cosmic energies—an aim that lay beyond the more limited intention of the flat-earth scheme. Above all, the calen-drical system aimed to attune Egypt to the divine being who manifested herself in the star Sirius, and who was none other than Isis, the all-sustain-ing mother of the universe. In a late text, Isis says:

> *I am the one who rises in the Dog-star [Sirius].*
> *I am the one called goddess by women.*
> *. . . I separated the earth from the Heaven.*
> *I showed the paths of the stars.*
> *I regulated the course of the sun and the moon.*[9]

Isis can be seen in figure 4.8 in her manifestation as Sirius, "showing the path of the stars." She is followed here by three planets, possibly Saturn, Mercury, and Jupiter. Isis herself holds the *ankh* symbol of life, as well as a

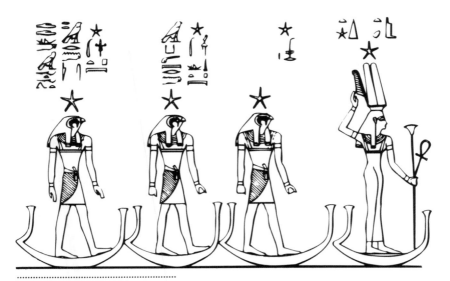

Fig. 4.8. Isis shows the path of the stars. Ceiling in the tomb of Seti I. Nineteenth Dynasty.

papyrus stem, symbolizing fecundity. The Egyptians referred to Isis-Sopde as "the Great Provider." That such an epithet could be used of a star so far from the earth is an indication of the fact that the ancient Egyptians perceived not only its outwardly visible aspect but also its inner qualities. From the time of the Pyramid Texts, Isis-Sopde was said to "prepare yearly sustenance" for the king and all Egypt, each New Year.[10]

The Nile

The temporal proximity of the heliacal rising of Sirius each year to the beginning of the Nile's flood was symbolically apt. For what was experienced outwardly as a proximity in time between two disparate natural phenomena was perceived to be the expression of a spiritual proximity in the relationship between two divine beings. The Nile was generally regarded as the physical form of the god Hapi. But the Nile in flood was no longer simply Hapi. A new spiritual force was perceived to infuse the Nile at the time of the inundation, for the swelling waters were filled with fertilizing power. The floodwaters carried the alluvial mud upon which the fertility of the land depended, and which was left as a deposit on the earth when the flood subsided. The Nile in flood then was no longer simply Hapi—it was Osiris, the god who ruled over the cycles of fertility and growth; Osiris, the husband of Isis.

When the Nile was at its lowest ebb in the months preceding the inundation, Osiris was effectively dead as a fertilizing power. In this condition, Isis mourns for her lost husband. According to Plutarch, Isis is the land, the parched earth, the soul of nature deprived of the waters of life.[11] In figure 4.9, Isis is shown with her husband, who lies with his face down upon

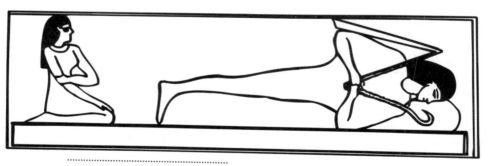

Fig. 4.9. Isis mourns Osiris. Temple of Hathor, Denderah.

the earth. In Isis, we have a depiction both of a cosmic deity and a deity who is deeply implicated in the fate of the land, and its fertility. For it is the same mother of the universe who brings forth life on earth as manifests herself in the mysterious brilliance of the star Sirius. The mourning of the land is a cosmic event, for the power of bringing forth life is one throughout the universe.

The tears of Isis in her cosmic aspect, as Isis-Sopde, cause the waters of the Nile to rise, for mythologically it is through the solicitude of Isis that Osiris is revivified and repotentized. Osiris is then able to inseminate her and father Horus. Thus, when the floodwaters retreat, the land passes under the protection of Horus.[12] In this way the season of Inundation (Akhet) is succeeded by the season of Emergence or Coming Forth (Proyet). In figure 4.10, the young Horus emerges from the folds of the wings of his mother Isis. This image can be read as an image of the transition of the seasons, accurately reflecting the change of energy that was taking place.

The rulership of Horus, however, is characterized by duality: Horus rules in opposi-

Fig. 4.10. Horus emerges from the protective wings of Isis. From a statue in the British Museum.

tion to Seth. Horus is the protector of life, the guarantor of order and harmony on earth. Seth is the destroyer of life, the instigator of disorder and chaos. During the season of Emergence, when the grain crops are growing, the contrast between these two universal forces is at its most vivid in the landscape. The Black Land, crisscrossed by a network of canals and ditches, diligently cultivated by the peasants, is the epitome of order bringing forth abundance; the desert wastes of the Red Land, of Seth, cannot conceal their essential impotence. But once the harvest is over at the end of the growing season, this desert impotence gains strength: the season of Deficiency (Shomu) is necessarily the time of the most intense conflict between Horus and Seth, between the universal forces of creation and destruction, order and disorder, acted out in the very landscape itself. In the heat of the months of Shomu, the fertilizing power goes out of the waters of the Nile; Osiris is slain, and Seth threatens to usurp Horus's legitimate right to the kingship. In this way, mythological realities were lived out on the material and temporal plane. The landscape and its seasonal transformations were the stage on which a mythological drama was enacted.

The realm of myth is the realm of spiritual forces apprehended in objective images—images, that is, that penetrate beyond the subjective life of human beings to universal realities. As Mircea Eliade put it: "Myth is bound up with ontology; it speaks only of *realities*. . . . Obviously these realities are sacred realities, for it is the *sacred* that is pre-eminently the *real*."[13]

Just because events occurring in time could be perceived as having a transcendent, mythological significance, the ancient Egyptian relationship to temporality involved the assimilation of the temporal into the transtemporal, the profane into the sacred, the world of appearances into the world of reality.

Festivals in the Marking of Time

The importance that the Egyptians placed on the celebration of festivals throughout the year clearly indicates this presiding characteristic of their relationship to time. For the nature of festivals in ancient Egypt was that they were always oriented toward the divine. The festivals were the principal means by which the people as a whole marked the passage of time, but their function was to transport those who participated in them into the nontemporal world of the gods. They were essentially means by which the general populace could let go of earthly ties and be taken up into the realm of myth. Through the festivals, time was marked by the regular experience of that which transcended time.

By all the accounts that have come to us, the festivals were occasions in which vast numbers of people gathered forming lively processions with chanting, singing, dancing and clapping. These processions along the banks of the Nile would accompany a cortege of sacred boats that bore a god or gods along the river. We must imagine an atmosphere of real celebration, with much color, with banners and flags waving above the jubilant (and often wine-intoxicated) crowds.[14] But the fervor that gripped the people was essentially religious fervor. All that was done was done in relation to the gods. It was done in their honor, in order to invoke or to acknowledge and celebrate their presence. Hence, at the center of all that took place were the priests, performing sacrifices and sacred rites.

The festivals were mass events in which whole communities—men, women, and children—took part. Herodotus gives astonishing figures of the amounts of people involved: seven hundred thousand regularly attended the festival of Bast at Bubastis in his time. Tens of thousands gathered to celebrate the festival of Isis at Busiris.[15] The festivals, however, were by no means simply mass events. There was also a very quiet aspect to them, alongside their loud and emotional outward celebration. Each major festival was also an occasion for the practice of esoteric rites within the temples. These rites were in many cases initiatory and were mostly performed within the context of the Osirian cult. So we should understand that, accompanying the clamor in the streets and along the banks of the Nile, intensive transformational experiences were undergone within the temples and their sanctuaries.

What follows will be a description of some of the main festivals specifically connected with the three seasons, as determined by the Nile. Many festivals were timed to coincide with the transition from one season to another, but we shall focus on those directly related to the mythological events which, on the material plane, were enacted in the Nile cycle.

INUNDATION

Around the time of the summer solstice, Sirius would reappear in the night sky. This "going up of Sopde," as it was called, was regarded as the true New Year's Day. It determined the starting point both of the Sothic and the lunar year, the latter beginning on the first day of invisibility of the moon (the day before the new moon) before sunrise and after "the going up of Sopde." The sacred festivals of Egypt were all timed to coincide with phases of the moon. The Egyptians in fact used three calendars: the "moving" civil calendar of 360 days plus 5 epagomenal days; the Sothic calendar of 365 1/4 days, and the lunar calendar that normally consists of only 354 days (12 lunar months). Because of this shortfall and the fluctuation of the lunar cycle in relation to the Sothic year, an intercalary month of about eleven days was inserted every two or three years, dedicated to Thoth.

Shortly after the ascent of Sirius, the Nile responded, and the inundation began. The flood was caused, mythologically, by the tears of Isis, and so the festival marking the beginning of the season of Inundation (Akhet) came to be known as "the Descent of the Drop." According to Heliodorus, writing in the fourth century A.D., this festival "was the most important of Egyptian rites. It was celebrated more or less at the summer solstice, at the beginning of the rising of the river; no other festival aroused in the Egyptians so much zeal."[16]

Fig. 4.11. Hapi, the Nile god, bearing gifts of water and flowers. Temple of Horus, Edfu.

At its most popular level, this festival was not Osirian. For the mass of the people, it was a festival in honor of the river god Hapi, who is portrayed in figure 4.11. Here he is typically hermaphrodite, wears a fisherman's girdle, and carries vases of water and flowers, which were his gifts to the people of Egypt. Because of the different degrees of understanding of the divine, ancient Egyptian seasonal festivals were not necessarily restricted to the cult of just one god. It was both possible and appropriate for Osiris to be implicated at one level, and Hapi at another.

Hapi had no formal temple cult, but was a god who really belonged to the stratum of folk religion. The famous Hymn to Hapi (which has come down to us in several versions) both expresses the intensity of feeling that was aroused at the beginning of the inundation and vividly describes the celebrations that took place:

> *Songs of the harp are made for you,*
> *people sing to you with clapping hands;*
> *the youths, your children, shout for joy over you,*

crowds adorn themselves for you;
you who come with riches, embellishing the land,
making everything flourish;
quickening the pregnant woman's heart,
oh you who love the increase in all creatures.

When you have risen to the royal residence,
the people feast on the gifts of the meadow,
wearing the perfumed lotus and fresh flowers.
Children's hands are filled with herbs,
they forget to eat.
Good things are strewn about the houses,
the whole land leaps for joy.

When you rise up, Hapi,
sacrifice is made for you;
oxen are slaughtered for you,
a great oblation is made for you.
Birds are fattened for you,
your generosity is repaid to you.

Offering is made to all the gods
of that which Hapi has provided,
choice incense, oxen, goats,
and roasted birds.

Oh joy when you come,
Oh joy when you come, Hapi,
Oh joy when you come!
You who feed the people and beasts
with your meadow gifts!
Oh joy when you come!
Oh joy when you come, Hapi!
Oh joy when you come![17]

To understand the elation of this hymn, we must remember that in ancient Egypt there was always the possibility of the Nile failing to flood sufficiently, and a recurrent anxiety that it might not flood at all: there are many references to famines in Egyptian history. There could be no real confidence that an adequate inundation would occur in any particular year, and the time of the inundation could also vary considerably from one year to another. It is not difficult to imagine the apprehension that would spread over the nation in years of a late flood. At the festival celebrated at Silseleh in Upper Egypt, the officiating priest (sometimes the king himself), having sacrificed a bull and geese, would then cast into the waters a sealed papyrus roll containing a written command to Hapi to flood to the right degree.[18] Thus the authority of Horus (in the king) was invoked in order to ensure that the river god acted in accordance with the universal principle of order.

But as we have seen, in addition to Hapi, another more powerful divine presence was felt to be within the swelling waters: Osiris. In the Pyramid Texts, we read:

> O Osiris . . . mount up to Horus,
> betake yourself to him,
> do not be far from him.
> Horus has come that he may recognize you;
> he has smitten Seth for you, and bound him,
> you are his [Seth's] fate. . . .
> Horus comes and recognizes his father in you,
> rejuvenated in your name of Young Water.[19]

The inundation is here described as the rejuvenation of Osiris. In the months of Shomu, when the Nile's power of fertility was reduced to nothing, Osiris was clearly impotent and his energy had gone out of the waters. Plutarch describes the ceremonies performed at the critical time of transition:

> Then the priests, amid other sad ceremonies, cover a gilded cow with a black linen garment and show it as a mark of mourning on the part of the goddess (for they consider the cow to be an image of Isis and of the earth) during four consecutive days from the seventeenth of the month. . . . On the night of the nineteenth day they go down to the water, and the stolists and priests take out the sacred box which was inside a golden casket. Into this they pour some drinking water which they have brought with them, and the people present shout: "Osiris has been found!" Then they mingle fertile earth with water and having mixed precious spices and incense with them, they fashion a crescent-shaped image, and this they clothe and adorn, indicating that they regard these gods [i.e., Isis and Osiris] as the principles of earth and water.[20]

Fig. 4.12. The raising of Osiris by Horus signifies the beginning of the flood. Temple of Hathor, Denderah.

These rituals were of very ancient origin. References to Isis and Nephthys, and sometimes Horus, "finding" Osiris on his side on the riverbank abound in the Pyramid Texts—an event generally located "on the banks of Nedit," near Abydos.[21] In figure 4.12, Osiris raises himself on one side in response to Horus, who has come to where Osiris was lying prone on his deathbed. As with the Fisher King in the Grail legend, the healing or revivification of Osiris in the mythological realm has consequences that directly affect the physical. As Osiris raises himself up, the life-giving waters of the Nile begin to flow again.

The "finding" of Osiris was probably one part of a much greater Osirian festival held at Abydos. Elsewhere, festivals celebrating the rising of the Nile would have taken different forms, but many would have been essentially Osirian in content, accentuating the transition of the god from a state of defeated impotence to one of life-giving power.

The rituals enacted at these festivals must have been performed with the sense of actually participating in the spiritual events that gave rise to the flood. For the ancient Egyptians, nothing occurred in the physical world that did not have its spiritual cause. The cause of the Nile's flood was the renewal of Osiris's divine potency, which streamed into the realm of life from the realm beyond life (the Dwat), where his resurrection took place. In ancient Egyptian times, the Nile's flood was both a spiritual and a physical occurrence. Insofar as it was spiritual, it belonged to the realm of myth, and was thus susceptible to ritual invocation and reenactment by human beings. As much as they celebrated its renewed presence, the rituals dramatically invoked the spiritual power that lay within the flood. The ritual acts performed by the priests and the people resounded in the spiritual realm, the realm of the gods and of primary causes. They should be regarded not simply as religious practices, but also as magical in their intention and effect.

In addition to, or perhaps as a further aspect of, the Osirian festival, Heliodorus indicates that a third and entirely esoteric celebration took place within the temple sanctuaries. Here the higher initiates had "the most clear revelations," which transcended the level of mythical imagery altogether.[22] But beyond the report of Heliodorus, it is not possible to say exactly what occurred in these secret initiatory rites.

COMING FORTH

In October/November, at the end of the season of Akhet (Inundation), as the great flood began to recede, revealing the mud-coated fields once again, the festival of Khoiak was celebrated. Recorded on the walls of the temple of Denderah as an eighteen-day festival, it took place during the second half of the month of Khoiak, that is, during the period of the waning moon, culminating in the death of the old moon and rebirth of the new moon. This was the equivalent of a north European spring festival, for it was at this time of the year that wheat and barley were sown, as well as many other crops requiring the milder weather of the Proyet months (the season of Coming Forth or Emergence).

The festival of Khoiak seems to have been overwhelmingly Osirian in tone. It reenacted the drama of the death and resurrection of Osiris. For the common people, Osiris was apprehended in the grain, as its power of growth. It was he who "made corn from the liquid that is in him to nourish the nobles and the common folk."[23]

At Philae, there is a relief that shows a cow-headed goddess (Isis-Hathor-Sopde) pouring water from a vase onto the black (= irrigated) land, from out of which springs grain. Above the grain, rising from it, is the soul-form of Osiris (fig. 4.13). The relief illustrates the belief that as a result of the floodwaters having poured over the earth, not only do the seeds then grow, but the sprouting of the vegetation is also the "rising up" of Osiris.[24] The implication is that the sowing of the seed was regarded as

Fig. 4.13. The soul of Osiris rises above the corn. Temple of Isis, Philae.

a burial or entombment of Osiris, prior to his "resurrection" in the living plants. Plutarch's report of the Egyptian peasant's attitude to seed sowing supports this view: "When they hack up the earth with their hands and cover it up again after having scattered the seeds, wondering whether these will grow and ripen, then they behave like those who bury and mourn."[25] This is not to say that Osiris was ever regarded simply as a vegetation god, or simply identified with the corn. His cult had too many other facets for this to have been the case, even for the peasantry. Rather, we should say that Osiris was apprehended as a power immanent in the seeds sown. Osiris was the power by means of which the life-potential of the seed became manifest in the outwardly visible physical form of the plant. Osiris governed the processes of manifestation whereby that which existed spiritually came to acquire outer, physical embodiment. When the influx of life-forces into the physical world was not taking place, Osiris was evidently "lost" or "dead." But when these processes were set in motion, this was due to the activity (or reactivation) of Osiris in the Beyond. The divine power of growth, wrapped up in the seed, is—to the extent that it is an unrealized potentiality—effectively dead. For the seed to grow and manifest its inner potentiality in outward form, the immanent divine power must become active, and insofar as it does so, the growth of the plant will reveal something of the divine presence.

For the ancient Egyptians, there was an intimate relationship between the mythical and the natural worlds. In the mythical world was apprehended the true reality, within which the natural world participates. The Osirian myth expresses in images the dovetailing of the two worlds, and through these images the relationship of the spiritual to the phenomenal levels of being can be experienced.

It is from this standpoint that we should approach the formal rituals that characterized the festival of Khoiak. The festival opened on the twelfth day of Khoiak with a ploughing and sowing ceremony, in which two black cows were yoked to a plough made of tamarisk; the ploughshare was made of black copper. A boy following behind scattered barley seed at one end of the field, flax in the middle, and spelt at the other end. A ritual chapter of "the sowing of the fields" was recited.[26] It is likely that this ceremony was a symbolic enactment of Osiris's death and entombment. In some places, the boy was followed by an ass, symbolic of Seth, who would tread the seeds into the ground. This, and other rituals of similar form, would have taken place throughout Egypt, to mark the commencement of ploughing and sowing by setting these activities in a mythological context. It is perhaps as a reference to this part of the festival that ploughing scenes are so often depicted in papyri of the New Kingdom Book of the Dead, as a standard part of representations of the sojourn of the deceased in the Dwat. Since the Dwat is the place of transformation and rebirth, such symbolic reenactments of the passion of Osiris would clearly have magical efficacy. Figure 4.14 shows the scribe Ani ploughing in a certain region of the Underworld, often referred to in earlier Middle Kingdom texts, which belonged to the White Hippopotamus. As we shall see in chapter 10, this hippopotamus was a possible allusion to the goddess Ipy, who concerned herself with the rebirth of the soul.[27]

Paralleling this, a second rite, which we know from Ptolemaic times, was performed within the temples.[28] It involved filling a hollow gold effigy of Osiris (in mummiform) with a mixture of barley and sand. This was done in the presence of the goddess Shenty, apparently represented by the image of a cow made of gilded sycamore wood. It was then laid in a shallow stone basin, and watered daily for nine days. On the ninth day, it was exposed to the sun just before sunset. The following day the effigy, with its germinating

Fig. 4.14. Ploughing with oxen, a symbolic as well as a practical task. Papyrus of Ani. Eighteenth Dynasty.

seeds, underwent a ceremonial voyage on the sacred lake of the temple—a voyage that may have lasted three days, after which it was buried in a chamber called "the House of Sokar" (an important Underworld god), from which the effigy of the previous year was removed.[29]

The performance of this rite was by no means restricted to the priests and temples, but was probably conducted (using simpler materials) by the common people throughout the land. Figure 4.15 is one of the many images of this rite that have come down to us. It is a bas-relief from the temple of Philae, and it shows the corn growing from Osiris's prostrate

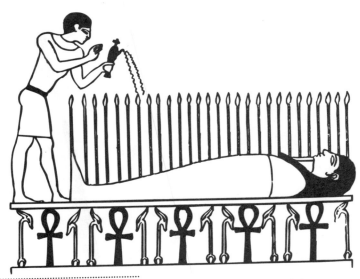

Fig. 4.15. The corn grows from the body of Osiris. Temple of Isis, Philae.

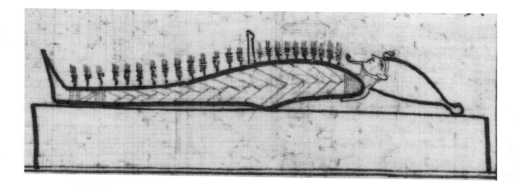

Fig. 4.16. The germination of the seed is due to the awakened sexual energy of Osiris. Jumilhac papyrus, Louvre, Paris.

body in response to its being watered. In figure 4.16, the germination of the seeds is linked to the sexual arousal of Osiris. Osiris's awakening involves the activation of the universal sexual energy from which all life arises. This sexual energy is mediated by Osiris in the Dwat, from whence it is chanelled by him into the world.

The burial of the effigy occurred on the day of "the interment of Osiris," the last day of the season of Inundation.[30] This meant that the sprouting of the seed from the body of Osiris would have occurred in the burial chamber. In the lunar calendar, the burial or interment corresponded to the last day of the waning moon. It is likely that since the first day of the month was the day during which the moon could not be seen, Osiris would on this day have been regarded as "lost."

The next event in this sequence of rituals would then have occurred on the following day, the day of the new moon.[31] This event was the raising of the *djed* column, symbolic of Osiris's resurrection, and the renewal of the powers of life. Key events of this ritual are portrayed in the temple of Seti I at Abydos. In figure 4.17, the *djed* is shown first on the left, being raised up by Seti with the assistance of Isis. Once erected, on the right, a cloth is tied around its middle, and offerings of linen are presented to it.

The symbolism of the *djed* is highly complex, and can only be touched on here. On one level it represented Osiris's backbone. Lying on the ground it expressed the inertness and lifelessness of the dead Osiris. Raised up, it signified his transformation into the Lord of Life, the source of life-giving forces flowing into this world from the Beyond. It is probable that

Fig. 4.17. Seti I raises the djed *column. Temple of Seti I, Abydos.*

the *djed* originally had ears of corn tied to it in tiers, and it has justifiably been described as "a symbol of power in which the energy of the grain was preserved."[32] A purely naturalistic interpretation of the *djed*, however, would be to distort its deeper significance as an emblem of Osiris, who was a god par excellence of the psychic domain: the raising up of the *djed* column also symbolized the rebirth of the soul.

The raising of the *djed* brought in the new season of Proyet, and "opened" the year. Hence, despite its occurring in the fifth month, it was regarded as another New Year's Day.[33] For the Egyptians, the flow of life-giving forces into the world of nature was dependent on the resurrection of Osiris "on the other side" in the spiritual realm of the Dwat. It is for this reason that the festival of Khoiak was considered the most propitious time for the coronation of the king, the accession of Horus being profoundly related to the "resurrection" of Osiris.

The temple rituals ended with the first day of the season of Proyet. On this day there was a general celebration of festivities throughout Egypt.[34] These would have been comparable to the north European May Day festivities. To what extent the temple rites were generally reflected in the celebrations of the populace is hard to ascertain. All festivities would have been celebrated with different degrees of spiritual involvement. While at the popular level the festival was Osirian, yet the understanding of the deeper mysteries concerning the presence of Osiris in the natural and spiritual worlds, and his relationship to the human soul, would have varied greatly. To judge from Plutarch, however, we may suppose that the mass of the people would have lived in the radically different moods of mourning followed by rejoicing, which accompanied the passion and resurrection of the god.

HARVEST

The third major festival of the year was the festival that marked the transition from the season of emergence and growth to the season of deficiency. The festival corresponded to harvest time, in March/April, and was celebrated twice: once in the eighth and once in the ninth months of the Egyptian calendar. Whereas the festival of Khoiak began with the full moon and culminated with the reappearance of the new moon, the harvest festival seems to have begun with the new moon in the month of Renenutet (eighth month). It was at the new moon that the first fruits were offered to the goddess after whom this month was named.[35] But the main celebrations in honor of Renenutet fell at the time of the full moon.[36]

Renenutet was a goddess of the people, and was worshiped in village shrines rather than temples. During the gathering of the corn and pressing of the grapes, offerings were made at her shrines, in which she was represented as a snake-headed goddess[37] (fig. 4.18).

Renenutet could equally well be represented as a snake with a woman's head. In figure 4.19, for example, the goddess is shown as a cobra with a woman's head, to whom the worshiper presents flowers, fruit, and cakes.

It is significant that she was sometimes portrayed carrying the still immature god Neper, the god of the grain, whom she nurses to maturity (fig. 4.20). In later times, Renenutet was assimilated to Isis, implying that inasmuch as she was mother to Neper she was also his wife, since Neper (from the perspective of the official religion) was an aspect of Osiris. The relationship of Isis to

Fig. 4.18. Worship of the snake-headed goddess, Renenutet. New Kingdom.

Fig. 4.19. Offerings are made to Renenutet in the form of a cobra with a woman's head. New Kingdom stele.

Min sometimes carried the same kind of ambiguity, as did her relationship to Horus.

At the beginning of the ninth month, at the time of the new moon, the divine presence presiding over the harvest shifted from Renenutet to Min. Normally represented as an ithyphallic god, Min was preeminently a god of fertility. By the Middle Kingdom, Min had been brought into association with Horus, and references are frequently made to the syncretized god Min-Horus, whose mother was Isis. However, Isis could also be Min's consort, and Horus their child. Either way, the pharaoh, as the living embodiment of Horus, had a special relationship to Min. At his coronation, there was a huge procession and feast in honor of Min, which both injected Min's regenerative energies into the kingship and reaffirmed the powers of fertility throughout the land. The procession and feast of Min was then repeated each year at the time of the harvest.

Fig. 4.20. Renenutet and Neper, the grain god. New Kingdom.

85

Fig. 4.21. The Festival of Min: the King appears. Temple of Ramesses III, Medinet Habu.

Min's festival began on the first day of the ninth month (the beginning of the season of Shomu) on the day before the new moon.[38] The sequence of the events of this festival are to be found carved on the second pylon of the Ramesseum (Nineteenth Dynasty) and in the second court of Ramesses III's temple at Medinet Habu (Twentieth Dynasty). Despite these representations belonging to the New Kingdom, there is reference to a "procession of Min" in a mastaba tomb at Giza (Fifth Dynasty) indicating that his feasts were also observed in the Old Kingdom.[39] Although we know the details of Min's festival from the Theban temples of Ramesses II and III, they were celebrated in similar fashion throughout Egypt at the time of the beginning of the grain harvest, in March/April. [40]

The festival opened with a splendid procession in which the king was carried in state to Min's sanctuary (fig. 4.21). There he burns incense and pours libations before the god. This opening ceremony concluded, a second, larger procession sets off from the temple sanctuary, in which the god is carried on poles on the shoulders of priests (fig. 4.22—only the heads and feet of the priests can be seen here). The procession was led by priests carrying ensigns of gods and images of royal ancestors. Behind them, the sacred white bull of Min was led by a rope. Behind the bull walked the

Fig. 4.22. *The Festival of Min: the god is carried in procession. Temple of Ramesses III, Medinet Habu.*

king, or where the king was not present his place was taken by the chief priest. The image of the god followed the king, borne aloft by shaven-headed priests; while behind the god further groups of priests carried bundles of lettuce (the long-leaved *Lactuca sativa*) sacred to the god, and regarded throughout the ancient world as having aphrodisiac qualities. The procession was accompanied by the chanting of hymns in honor of the god.

At the end of the journey (probably in the fields), Min was set down on his throne, called "the staircase," under a canopy. Sacrifices were made and offerings brought to the god (fig. 4.23). The chief act of this ceremony now took place: the king (elsewhere the chief priest) symbolically reaps the first ears of emmer wheat and then presents them to the god. According to Frankfort, it is possible that the king and queen had ritual sexual intercourse at this stage of the ceremony, with the king taking the role of Min himself.[41] The ceremony ended with the release of four sparrows to the four cardinal points of the compass, to carry news of Min's festival, and of the prosperity of the king, to all parts of Egypt.

Through the performance of these rituals, the god Min became a tangible presence. A fusion took place between the mythical and natural realms. Min is the archetypal principle of fertility and regeneration; the celebration of a festival in his honor would have had the purpose of invoking and

Fig. 4.23. Offering incense to Min. Temple of Ramesses III, Medinet Habu.

"bringing down to earth" the potency of the god. It is particularly significant, therefore, that the king should at a certain stage of the ceremony
become the living embodiment of the god. In his being, the merging of the
archetypal and the physical realms was accomplished. Since one of the
king's principle roles in Egypt was himself to ensure the fertility of the
land, his fusion with the god was not only symbolically appropriate, but
necessary. The timing of this fertility festival so that it coincided with the
harvest, however, requires further explanation. Fertility festivals are normally connected with the sowing of seed, rather than its harvest. In order
to understand the nature of the harvest festival, it is necessary to see it in
its Osirian context.

Since Osiris was regarded as the life-force within the grain, it would follow that the cutting of the grain symbolized his death. Diodorus Siculus
relates that farmers beat their breasts and lamented over the first sheaf of
corn cut, and at the same time called upon Isis.[42] In the Dramatic
Ramasseum Papyrus, Osiris appears as the barley that is beaten (i.e.,
threshed) by Seth in the form of an ass. This is described as "hacking the
god to pieces." A similar threshing ritual, probably dating back to the Fifth
Dynasty, involved the driving of calves over the grain in order to thresh it.
This was possibly to conceal the place of Osiris's burial from the forces of
Seth. But if the cutting and threshing of the grain symbolized Osiris's

death, then why was the harvest festival primarily a festival of fertility?

The key to understanding the festival must lie in the relationship of Osiris to Horus. It is significant that in the ritual depicted at Medinet Habu, the cult statues of the royal ancestors (collectively Osiris) are present as witnesses of what takes place. It is through Osiris's death that Horus ascends to the throne and is able to ensure the fertility and prosperity of the land. As we have seen, the god Min was, at least from the Middle Kingdom, associated with Horus rather than Osiris; Horus and Min were regarded as a single deity, sharing the same mother, Isis.[43] The festival, then, was one in which the establishment of Horus was emphasized rather than the death of Osiris. Hence in the chief ceremony, the king, the living embodiment of Horus, was hailed as "Min-Horus the Powerful."[44] Thus in each Min festival throughout the land, emphasis was placed on the regeneration of the life-principle.[45] But this was an affirmation made not in spite of the death of Osiris but *because* of it. For it was precisely through Osiris's death that Horus became the mediator of life-forces in the earthly sphere. And then, having assumed this role, Horus is able to bring about the resurrection of Osiris in the Otherworld.

The harvest festival was thus based on an awareness of the complex interrelationships obtaining between the Dwat and the sense-perceptible world of nature. At this time of the year, at the advent of the season of Deficiency (Shomu), the festival ensured that these interrelationships were correctly established. The festival presents a clear example of how rituals were intended to affect the dynamic between the physical and spiritual worlds. The rituals were essentially magical rites through the performance of which human beings caused a particular moment in time to be fused with the eternal divine order.

Other harvest rites may be viewed in the same way. It is likely that Osiris's resurrection was symbolized, and thus aided, by the winnowing of the grain, in which clouds of chaff rose heavenward.[46] Insofar as the old grain god Neper was assimilated to Osiris, the texts that assert his rebirth would apply equally to Osiris in this aspect. For example, we read in the Coffin Texts that "it is the grain god who lives after he has died."[47] In achieving revivification, Neper becomes Osirified. In figure 4.24, the grain is winnowed on the right, while on the left oxen thresh it by trampling over it. The threshing, gathering, and transporting of grain all carried symbolic value. For example, a Twelfth Dynasty coronation drama included rituals involving oxen treading on barley in order to thresh it. The oxen were driven round the threshing floor by Horus, who says, "I have smitten for thee, O Osiris, those that smote thee." The threshed grain was then gathered and

Fig. 4.24. Threshing and winnowing grain. New Kingdom.

taken away on the backs of donkeys, symbolizing "the ascent of Osiris to heaven supported by Seth and his confederates."[48]

In a culture in which the physical world was experienced as transparent to the divine, it was a natural human responsibility to ensure that the relationship between the physical and the divine order did not become opaque through neglect of sacred rituals. The seasonal festivals served to maintain this "transparency" between the physical and spiritual worlds. They may be understood as deliberate attempts to bring about periodic conjunctions of the natural and divine realms, so that the passage of time continued to reflect eternal realities.

5 THE MARRIAGE OF MYTH AND HISTORY

We have seen that in ancient Egypt time was experienced as inextricably bound up with the cosmic and natural cycles of the sun, moon, Sirius, and the Nile. Not only was time therefore experienced as essentially qualitative, it was also experienced in relation to the nontemporal dimension of divine agencies and beings who lay behind these phenomena. All the physical bodies, by whose movement or change the passage of time was marked, were regarded as the outward forms of gods. Since the gods are eternal, the marking of time in the regular celebration of sacred rites and festivals was a means by which the temporal world was periodically transcended. In ancient Egypt, time was regularly projected into, and assimilated with, the eternal order that lies beyond time.

In this chapter we shall explore further the ancient Egyptians' relationship to time by considering their attitude to history. But in order to do this, we shall first have to consider two concepts crucial to ancient Egyptian religious thought: the concepts of the First Time and *maat* or "truth." In addition to having a direct bearing on the ancient Egyptian attitude to history, both concepts were also directly related to the ancient Egyptian understanding of the function and purpose of the kingship, an office in which the fusion of the temporal and the eternal was institutionalized.

The First Time

As we have seen, the cyclical view of temporality as conceived in ancient Egypt meant that time periodically merged with the nontemporal or

91

transtemporal order. It is in this transtemporal dimension that the gods, and the myths that record the deeds of the gods, have their reality. But if there are transtemporal beings who exist and perform deeds, then in a certain sense there must also be a "time" in which the divine patterns of action are established. Neither the gods nor their deeds are subject to mundane temporality: there must be a supramundane temporality in which they exist and live, which transcends the historical flow of mundane time. It is this supramundane or nontemporal temporality that the Egyptians referred to as the First Time.

The concept of a "nontemporal" time makes as much, or as little, sense as the concept of a "nonspatial" space. The difficulty only arises if we stick rigidly to the presupposition that both space and time are the conditions of the externality of one object or event to another. But if we can accept the possibility of space and time opening to an interior dimension, then the contradiction is apparent rather than real. Just as the Dwat can be described as an interior space because of the inward mode of existence of the beings who dwell in it, so the First Time may be understood as an "interior time" because the events that occur in it are the spiritual archetypes of what may be unfolded in outer time. Indeed, events that occur in outer time only attain full reality to the extent to which they reenact outwardly the events of the First Time.

The First Time literally means "the first occasion" in Egyptian: *tep* is "first" and *zepi*, "occasion." The occasion referred to is that of the passage from nonexistence, symbolized by Nun, to existence, established when Atum-Ra first stirred in Nun's primordial sea. This moment initiates an era, or cosmic condition, in which the gods alone exist. The First Time refers, therefore, not only to the initial momentous event of divine emergence, but also to the whole ageless age of the gods that it inaugurated. All of Egyptian mythology from the awakening of Atum to the vindication of Horus and the redemption of Osiris belongs to the First Time.[1] All the deeds of the gods are, as it were, "First Time" deeds. "Before" the First Time, there is just the eventless and nonexistent state of Nun; "after" the First Time, there is history, when events must necessarily occur only once, uniquely and ephemerally, and are preceded and followed by quite different events. The occurrences of the First Time, by contrast, are in the words of Mircea Eliade "indefinitely recoverable, indefinitely repeatable."[2] The First Time is both an era so long ago that it existed before time as we know it came into being and a dimension of existence ontologically prior to that in which events occur in mundane time. The First Time is sacred time. As Eliade says, it "always remains equal to itself, it neither changes nor is exhausted."[3] It is the spiritual dimension in which all actions and events occurring in profane time must participate if they are to have real and effective existence.

The concept of the First Time is comparable to that of the realm of being in which the Platonic Ideas exist. In Egyptian thought, though, it is not abstract ideas that are to be found here, but living gods and the archetypal relationships that obtain among them. The First Time is the realm of metaphysical realities conceived in terms of symbolic images and myths. These are the patterns that are reflected in the mundane world and that need to be participated in if mundane events are to be filled with archetypal power. It is in the First Time that the Egyptians posited their notions of perfection: it is the golden age "before rage or clamour or strife had come about."[4] This is not to say that the mythical events of the First Time are all images of harmony and peace; antagonism and strife may also be depicted, only to be eternally resolved on the side of order, justice, and truth. The latter always prevail in the First Time, whereas in mundane time such resolution on the side of order, justice, and truth cannot be guaranteed.

Maat

Implicit in the concept of the First Time is the concept of *maat*. Variously translated as "right," "truth," or "justice," *maat* is the order that characterizes the mythological realm, the realm of divine forces and agencies. If the First Time is the era during which the gods come forth from the original primeval waters of Nun, then intrinsic to the divine emanation is *maat*; for the nature of the divine emanation is that it is ordered and ordering rather than chaotic. From one point of view, Nun may be seen as the archetype of chaos, which is then subsumed under the divine ordering powers of the universe. The unfolding of the divine world order is at the same time "the establishment of *maat* in the place of disorder."[5]

But *maat* is more than a concept or universal principle. Maat is a being, a goddess. She is the daughter of Atum-Ra, and is often depicted as a beautiful, winged figure, looking more like an angel than a goddess, as if no animal would suffice to convey her universal, and somewhat abstract, attributes. In figure 5.1, we see her with her wings outspread, and wearing an ostrich feather in her hair, an emblem she shares with Shu (fig. 5.2), suggesting that the two deities were originally closely linked.

In the Coffin Texts, it is related how in the very beginning, when Atum desired to differentiate himself from the waters of Nun and thereby

Fig. 5.1. The goddess Maat. Tomb of Queen Nefertari. Nineteenth Dynasty.

initiate the whole process of creation, Nun admonished Atum with the following words:

> *Kiss your daughter Maat,*
> *put her to your nose,*
> *that your heart may live,*
> *for she will not be far from you;*
> *Maat is your daughter*
> *and your son is Shu whose name lives.*
> *Eat of your daughter Maat;*
> *it is your son Shu who will raise you up.*[6]

In the text, Shu is given an active role ("raising up" Atum), while Maat, Shu's sister, seems to be more passive. It is suggested that Ra will "eat of his daughter." Here, as elsewhere, it is indicated that Ra actually feeds on her substance.[7] Maat, then, is a goddess whose existence would appear to consist of a perpetual giving of her substance in order that the divine powers can continue to function in an orderly and harmonious way. She is literally the bread by which Ra lives,[8] and so by implication she is the food of all the gods, who are but the limbs of Ra. What better substance than truth could there be for the gods to feed on?

Maat, as both concept and goddess, is the internal or spiritual order of the universe that pervades the First Time. The manifest cosmos on the whole reflects this inner order. Stars, planets and seasons, rivers, plants and animals are all ultimately in harmony with Maat. But whereas in the First Time, the forces of disorder are eternally and confidently subdued, in the temporal world there can be no such confidence. This is especially the case in human society, which is continuously threatened by enemies without and moral decay within. It is as if the eternal is broken into fragments in the temporal world. And the connecting links between this world and the First Time are ever fragile and uncertain. The temporal world is characterized by contingency, rather than the necessary truths pertaining to the realm of spiritual archetypes. Maat has therefore to be constantly established and reestablished in society.

In ancient Egypt, the task of establishing *maat* within the social order was specifically that of the king. We could almost say that the raison d'être of the office of kingship was to ensure that the conditions of the First Time were reflected in society. The theme of social dissolution and the restoration of *maat* by the king was a liter-

Fig. 5.2. The god Shu with the ostrich feather in his hair, a symbol he shares with Maat. Tomb of Ramesses III. Twentieth Dynasty.

ary commonplace from at least the First Intermediate Period, but probably has a much earlier origin in oral tradition.[9] According to the literary tradition, the inherent tendency of human society to fall out of *maat* results in periods of social disintegration usually referred to as "times of troubles," which are characterized by neglect of temples, civil strife, breakdown of communication systems, and the neglect of justice.[10] It then falls to the king to restore *maat* throughout the land. Thus, for example, after the years of the Akhenaton heresy during which Egypt's age-old religious traditions had been systematically attacked and destroyed,

> *Tutankhamon drove out disorder from the Two Lands,*
> *and firmly established* maat *in its place;*
> *he made lying an abomination,*
> *and the Land is as it was at the First Time.*[11]

Whether or not there had been a "time of troubles," it was always the avowed policy of the incoming king to "make Egypt flourish as in the First Time, in the condition of *maat*."[12] The central task of the kingship was to align the social with the cosmic order. It fell to the king because the king, being both human and god, lived as much in the eternal as in the temporal realm. He was able to bring about a fusion of the two by virtue of his intrinsic divinity, which extended toward the very highest levels of the divine hierarchy. Thus we read how "Amenemhet II drove out disorder by appearing as Atum himself."[13] Being divine, the king subsisted on *maat* along with the other gods. He could say: "I have made bright *maat* which Ra loves, I know that he lives by it; it is my bread too; I eat of its brightness."[14]

From all periods of Egyptian history, texts are to be found affirming the king's direct relationship to *maat*, and his fulfilling the sacred function of putting *maat* in the place of disorder.[15] Through the mediation of the king, therefore, it was possible for *maat* to be brought down into the human and natural spheres. Or, put another way, it was possible for these lower spheres of existence to be magically projected into the First Time and thus assimilated to *maat*. For this to happen, however, the antithesis of *maat—isfet* (generally translated as "disorder" or "falsehood")—had to be overcome and driven out of the land.

It is interesting that whereas Maat is a divine being, a goddess, her opposite is nothing more than a concept. Disorder and chaos may be attributes of gods (for example, cosmological disorder is an attribute of Nun; moral disorder an attribute of Seth), but there is no god Isfet, for it is in itself without positive ontological status.

Either side of the First Time, the world swings toward disorder, whether it be the primeval chaos of Nun, or the contingencies that accompany temporal existence. Maat is established only *at the creation*. She is, in a sense, the very substance of the First Time, and since the coming into being of temporality, Maat must constantly be renewed and reestablished in the face of the cosmological and moral tendencies toward disorder.

Maat does not simply belong to the metaphysical realm, she is also present in the moral dimension of human decisions and actions. It is the disordered human soul that does wrong. And, as Petosiris states: "No one reaches the salutary West unless their heart is righteous by doing *maat*."[16]

Ancient Egyptians were constantly exhorted to "do *maat*" and to "speak *maat*."[17] By so doing, they came closer to the divine, kingly principle in themselves, and thus transcended the merely human and contingent. In the Book of Gates, we find "the Just" in the first division of the Dwat (figure 5.3). They "spoke *maat*" on earth and now they "live on *maat*." Ra says

Fig. 5.3. The Just, who are in the Dwat. Book of Gates, division 1. Tomb of Ramesses VI.

to them: "Maat is yours that you may live. Your bread is destined for you, O Truthful [*maat*-ful] Ones." And the commentary pertinently states: "They are masters of their refreshment, which is fiery water to the sinful and the evil ones."[18] The divine substance, *maat*, is delightful only to those whose souls have become inwardly truthful and righteous. To those who are at variance with or opposed to Maat, she is experienced as a burning liquor.

It should be apparent by now how the concepts of the First Time and *maat* affected the whole way in which the ancient Egyptians regarded temporality. The temporal world is a world specifically "outside" the divine and eternal, which is by definition an "interior," spiritual realm. There is an inherent tendency toward arbitrariness and disorder in the world of time that must be constantly checked. The mundane world must continually be drawn back and realigned with the spiritual, reattuned to *maat*. For the ancient Egyptians, the historical process as such veers away from *maat*, and must be guided back toward the archetypal patterns that pertain to the First Time. Not only the social order, but also the moral lives of individual human beings have to be consciously brought into connection with *maat* if they are to become fully realized.

The Ordering of Time

Given the ancient Egyptians' predisposition to view time as inherently degenerative, the modern concept of progress would have been quite alien to them. Rather than looking forward to a more perfect future, they located their Golden Age in the far past in which time itself seemed to expand. It was imagined that earthly time was completely assimilated into cosmic epochs of unearthly duration, each one ruled over by a great god. Under the rulership of the gods and, following them, the demigods, these vast epochs proceeded in accordance with the rhythms of the stars, by far the most important of which was Sirius. Ancient Egyptian chronology based itself on time cycles related to Sirius—not only the well-known long Sothic cycle of 1,460 or 1,461 years, but also less well known smaller Sothic cycles, which we shall soon be considering. It was as if for the Egyptians Sirius was the heavenly mediator between the material and the spiritual planes. By arranging time periods to accord with Sothic cycles, mundane temporality came to reflect or participate in sacred temporality.

According to Manetho, who is the most important ancient chronologer of Egyptian history, before any mortal king reigned in Egypt there was a succession of nineteen gods and demigods who reigned for a total of 13,870 years. The figure at first strikes one as totally arbitrary, but when it is considered in the light of the long Sothic cycle, it shows itself to be highly significant. For it amounts to exactly nineteen semi-Sothic periods of 730 years, or nineteen "cosmic weeks."[19] On average, then, the nineteen gods and demigods reigned for precisely half a Sothic cycle each.

A similar tradition is recorded in the late Book of Sothis, in which the total period of the reign of the gods (this time including human god-kings) spanned 36,525 years. Again, this vast number seems at first glance completely to lack any meaning, and apparently bears no relationship to Manetho's figure. But it actually consists of twenty-five Sothic cycles of 1,461 years.[20] Evidently, these ancient chronologers of Egyptian prehistory and history were working with a cosmic formula.

According to these traditions, as the rulership passes from god to god, and from the gods to the demigods (or "followers of Horus" as the Turin Canon—another major source of ancient Egyptian chronology—describes them) there is a gradual diminution in the lengths of their reigns. Each reign lasts for respectively shorter and shorter periods of time. Thus, in the Book of Sothis, Ra is recorded as having reigned a full 30,000 years; the twelve gods that follow him reign for but 3,984 years altogether; and the eight demigods and 113 human god-kings together rule for only 2,541 years.[21] Other chronological schemes concur with the basic principle of a gradual diminution in the lengths of reigns, as the kingship passes from heavenly hands into the hands of gods incarnate in mortal flesh, namely, the pharaohs.[22] As the regnal epochs move closer to the present, the scale according to which they are measured becomes rather more human than cosmic.

And yet, given the Egyptians' attitude regarding time, they could not allow history to fall out of relationship to the divine cosmic cycles.

Although the regnal periods contract to human lengths, the more "realistic" time spans of the human god-kings nevertheless retain cosmic correspondences. The purpose of the chronological records kept by the ancient Egyptians was not simply historical (in the modern understanding of the word) but was also metaphysical and symbolic. Their purpose was to organize mundane time so that it corresponded to heavenly or sacred time.

Apart from the long Sothic cycle of 1,460/1 years, the Egyptians used a shorter cycle of 19 years. Throughout most of early pharaonic history, the heliacal rising of Sirius coincided almost exactly with our Julian year of 365¼ days. In a 19-year period (of 6,939 days), there would have been just one coincidence of the heliacal rising of Sirius with the new moon. Owing to a slight discrepancy, the true coincidence would have occurred exactly every 76 years (4 × 19), but the 19-year lunar-Sothic cycle was sufficiently exact for it to provide the basis of early pharaonic chronology.[23] Thus we find the New Kingdom Turin papyrus recording the reigns of five Second Dynasty kings (the only reigns of the archaic period whose lengths are preserved in the papyrus) oriented around this 19-year lunar-Sothic cycle:

Neferkasokar:	8 years	(8 + 11 = 19)
illegible:	11 years	
Bebti:	27 years	(= 19 + 8)
Nebka:	19 years	
Zoser:	19 years	

As O'Mara states, this series "is not a fortuitous listing of realistic years. The series is a rational construct built around astronomical phenomena."[24]

Precedence is given to the number nineteen throughout the Turin Canon and can also be discerned in Manetho's later king list. In both, kings are arranged in groups of nineteen. The Turin papyrus lists exactly 19 kings from Menes to Zoser (fig. 5.4). Manetho lists 19 kings each for the Ninth and Tenth Dynasties and 76 (4 × 19) for the Fourteenth Dynasty, while stating that the kings of the Seventeenth Dynasty reigned altogether for 151 years (symbolical 2 × 76) and those of the Thirteenth Dynasty for 453 years (3 × 151).[25]

The utilization of the number nineteen in the organization of both regnal years and dynastic groupings was deemed appropriate because of the connection that was felt to exist between the king and the star Sirius. Just as Sirius was the heavenly mediator between the material and spiritual planes, so the king was the earthly mediator, uniting in his person both divine and

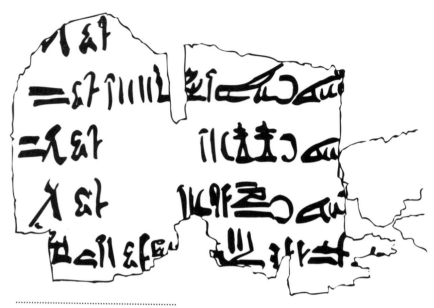

Fig. 5.4. A fragment of the Turin papyrus. Nineteenth Dynasty.

human attributes. The Pyramid Texts repeatedly affirm an intimate relationship between the king and Sirius. Sometimes the king is identified with Sirius, as in the following text: "O Merenre, you are the Great Star [Sirius], the companion of Rigel, he who crosses the sky with Rigel."[26] At other times, the king is said to be the "son of Sirius": "Sirius lives, for it is Unas who lives, the son of Sirius."[27]

In this case, Sirius would seem to be Isis. But then the union of the king's father with Isis, in order to beget his son, was a union that took place in the stars.[28] Whether the king is identified with Sirius, is the consort of Sirius, or the consort-to-be, it is clear that he was in some sense the human counterpart of the heavenly body. It is relevant that before the falcon became the royal sign, it was the star (the early dynastic King Scorpion was literally "Star King Scorpion"). Egyptian chronological records were so designed that this symbolic identification was maintained by making the lengths or number of kings' reigns incorporate the sacred and cosmologically significant number nineteen.

In addition to the nineteen-year cycle, both the relatively early king list of the Palermo Stone (Old Kingdom) and Manetho's king list employed a seventeen- or thirty-four-year cycle, linked to the simultaneous appearance of Sirius at its heliacal rising and the quarter phases of the moon. During a seventeen-year period, if the heliacal rising of Sirius occurs in conjunction with a new moon in year one, in year seventeen it will coincide with the moon's quarter phase and in year thirty-four with the full moon.[29] This is not to say that the king lists kept by the Egyptians were purely artificial: it is rather that the Egyptians thought it necessary to refer the reigns of their kings to cosmic cycles. As O'Mara says:

> The observation that "realistic" dates are not realistic in our sense of the word does not invalidate Egyptian chronological records. From the Fifth Dynasty on the canons contain broad layers of striking accuracy. But it means that true time was tailored to fit abstract number structures and that the years of the kings and of the dynasties become part of a huge geometrical construct. That chronological years formed an intelligible pattern was an essential criterion of their reliability in the Egyptian concept of time.[30]

A further cosmologically significant number utilized in Egyptian chronologies is the number 144. Instead of the modern preference for the century, the ancient Egyptians reckoned in terms of 144-year periods. Once again this number relates to a Sothic cycle: $144 = 4 \times 36$, that is, the 36 weeks of the year times the number of years in the smallest Sothic cycle, namely, the period during which Sirius continues to rise on the same day of the civil calendar. So, for example, the Old Kingdom Palermo Stone links Manetho's Third and Fourth Dynasties into a single era of 144 years, while the Turin Canon gives several dynastic totals that contain the standardized element of 144, or some fraction thereof:

> Sixth Dynasty: 181 years plus some months = symbolic 182
>   ($2 \times 19 + 144$)
> Eleventh Dynasty: 143 years plus some months =
>   symbolic 144
> Twelfth Dynasty: 213 years plus some months =
>   symbolic 214 ($144 + 70$)
> Fifteenth Dynasty (the Hyksos): symbolic 108 years ($3/4$ of 144)[31]

The Egyptians were undoubtedly painstaking chronologers. Classical writers attest to the fact that they faithfully kept annals from remote antiquity.[32] Herodotus, whom we tend to regard as the first true historian, had no hesitation in proclaiming the Egyptians "the best historians of any nation of which I have had experience."[33] And Redford's detailed study of pharaonic king lists, annals, and daybooks demonstrates the Egyptians' capacity for, and delight in, record keeping.[34] Nevertheless, such record keeping—especially in the pharaonic context—was universally subsumed under symbolic requirements. In the theocratic state, mythological accuracy took precedence over mundane correctness: if the kingship is mythologically conjoined with Sirius, then the chronological records must reflect this fact. Individual reigns and dynasties are assigned the cosmically appropriate numbers of suitable symbolic value. Profane time is thus made to fit sacred time.

The Cycles of History

We are so used to our dating system in which historical events are ordered in a linear sequence stretching from the centuries B.C. to the centuries A.D. that we are inclined to forget the presuppositions upon which it is based. Our computations of time turn on the event of the birth of Christ, the incarnation of God in human form. The significance of this event for world history we unconsciously acknowledge every time we cite a date. Whether or not our spiritual orientation is Christian, our historical orientation is unavoidably so. Despite attempts to replace B.C. and A.D. with B.C.E. (Before Common Era) and C.E. (Common Era), the fact remains that the era that is held in common is implicitly Christian.

The Egyptian view of history was, in this respect, not so different from our own. For they too dated events by reference to the incarnation of God in human flesh. The standard form of address to the king was, interestingly, not "Your Majesty" but literally "The Embodiment" or "The Incarnation."[35] Each king was an embodiment of the god Horus, and with the death of the king, Horus became excarnate. The coronation of the next king was the momentous occasion of the reincarnation of the god once more in a human being.

In the Christian view, the incarnation of Christ was an unrepeatable event that changed the very structure of history. As a result of the incarnation, we now live, until Judgment Day, "in the year of our Lord," Anno Domini. For the Egyptians, the incarnation of Horus was an event repeated over and over again. The coronation of the new king was the beginning of a new cycle of time that lasted for the duration of the reign of that particular Horus incarnation. Historical time was therefore reckoned in terms of the year of a particular king's reign, using the formula, "the year x of the reign of King N. . . ." In the New Kingdom, events were dated by the year of the king's reign, followed by month, season, and day. The computation recommenced with every reign, because with each new reign the previous cycle of time came to an end, and a new era was established.

It should be emphasized that this was not simply a convention; it arose out of a deeply felt religious view of the sacred office of the kingship. The king, as god incarnate, was the crucial link between the human and divine worlds, mediating beneficent energies from the latter to the former. The king was, ultimately, the source of the well-being of the whole country, not only causing human society to flourish but also causing natural processes such as the succession of seasons, the Nile's flood, the growth of crops, and so on to take place in an orderly and beneficial way.[36] In other words, the king ensured that the social and natural worlds were in tune with *maat*. On the death of the king, therefore, Egypt fell out of *maat*. The interregnum was a period during which the country was exposed to the forces of disorder and chaos. This period could last several months, for although the new king acceded to power immediately after the death of his predecessor, the coronation—itself a cosmic event—had to coincide with some natural process of cyclical renewal, such as the beginning of the flood, or its subsidence several months later. The dangers of the interregnum were not definitely overcome until the coronation had taken place, and it was only then that the new era could formally begin.[37]

The feeling of relief and joy with which the Egyptians greeted their new king is a clear indicator of the significance that the event of the coronation held for them. The following hymn celebrating the accession of Merneptah illustrates well the widespread effects that were felt to accompany the beginning of the new reign:

> *Rejoice, you entire land, the good time has come!*
> *A Lord is appointed in all countries. . . .*
> *O all of you who are righteous, come and see!*
> *Truth [Maat] has repressed falsehood.*
> *The transgressors have fallen on their faces.*
> *The covetous ones are turned back.*
>
> *Water is plentiful,*
> *and the Nile carries a high flood.*
> *The days are long, the nights have hours,*
> *and the months come in due order.*

The gods are content and their hearts are happy,
and life is spent in laughter and wonder.[38]

What is described here is little less than a reenactment of creation itself, for the interregnum represented literally the "end of time," the end of a divinely ordered epoch. It was as if the waters of Nun once more engulfed the country, and had once more to be subordinated to the divine organizing principle. Thus the installation (as distinct from the coronation) of the new king, immediately on the death of his predecessor, occurred at sunrise, in conjunction with Ra's daily defeat of the forces of disorder. Although the king was Horus incarnate, the kingly prototype was always Ra, the creator god. The king, as "son of Ra," was the successor of the creator god, occupying like him the same "throne of Atum" or "throne of Ra," and priding himself on achieving "what had not been done since the time of Ra" and restoring conditions "as they were at the beginning."[39]

In the Egyptian theocratic state, history was king-centered, just as the state religion was Ra-centered. The king, as the image of Ra upon earth, was the pivot about which history turned. That the king each morning ascended the stairs of the House of the Morning synchronously with the sunrise, and that he was described as "shining" like Ra whenever he appeared in public, serves to reinforce this picture of the fulcral position of the king.[40] In figure 5.5 Ramesses II "shines" from the special "window of appearance" at Abydos, while Queen Nefertari stands behind him. The relief records Ramesses' appointment of Nebwenef as high priest of Amon.

The pharaoh was as the sun not only in relation to his officials and society in general, but in relation to all events that might occur. We have already considered the relationship between the king and Sirius, and in chapter 4 we noted the view of Schwaller de Lubicz that for pharaonic Egypt, Sirius played the role of a central sun to our entire solar system. Just as the sun, Ra, was an image of Sirius on the scale of our solar system, so the king imaging Ra was the earthly counterpart of the same celestial sun. We find him addressed as "Thou rising sun, that illumines the Two Lands with its beauty! Thou sun of mankind that banishes darkness from Egypt!"[41]

Does it not follow that each king's reign was but another species of Sothic cycle? And if we can so regard it, then need we be surprised that just as the length of the reigns in the king lists must correspond to a higher cosmic reality, so events that occur on the earthly plane during the king's reign must be submitted to symbolic requirements dictated by the cosmic and divine status of the king? In other words, history must be submitted to the higher mythical order if it is to have any real validity.

Fig. 5.5. Ramesses II "shines" from a special "window of appearance." Queen Nefertari's head can be seen behind his shoulder. Nineteenth Dynasty.

The Mythologization of History

The regnal cycles into which historical time was fitted were cycles presided over by a heavenly being—the god Horus—who happened to be incarnate in a particular human king. The reality in which this heavenly being existed was so far beyond the contingencies of what we like to call "actual historical events" that the latter tended either to be ignored altogether by the ancient chronologers or else absorbed into a mythic archetypal pattern.

In the Old Kingdom, the tendency to leave out even important events from the official records has meant that there is a paucity of information on the activities and achievements of the Old Kingdom kings.[42] The Palermo

Stone, for example, records the deeds of various Old Kingdom kings, but these consist entirely of grants and benefactions to the gods, performed by the god-king Horus. There is no mention of battles fought, canals dug, buildings erected, or even feasts celebrated, all of which, in the Fifth Dynasty (to which the Palermo Stone belongs) were presumably deemed too transitory and ephemeral to be considered worthy of being recorded.[43] Insofar as one can speak of royal annals of the Old Kingdom, one has to admit that they are really religious memorials in which the human individuality of the king is absorbed into a mythical prototype.[44]

According to the mythical prototype, not only is the reigning king a god, born of a god, but the deceased kings also are gods: gods who have "gone to their *kas*," or who have united with Ra or with Osiris.[45] The royal ancestors, in whatever form, were not felt to be consigned to the past. They were, on the contrary, still "present," but present on a different plane—the heavenly plane. By virtue of the fact that this plane dovetailed into the earthly, they were also an active and powerful presence in the community of the living. In figure 5.6 it is the small figure standing in front of the king who is the living Horus. The large figure of the king actually represents his dead predecessor, Mentuhotep, to whom homage must be given in order for the reigning king (and thereby the whole country) to prosper. It was a central feature of Egyptian society as a whole that the dead were not only held in high regard, but were so revered because they were expected to intervene in the affairs of the living.[46] Death itself, which for the modern mentality is the most forceful demonstration of our vulnerability to time, was for the ancient Egyptians but a transition into an eternal present beyond historicity. In many respects the living and the dead formed a single community in ancient Egypt, as in other ancient cultures.

From a ritualistic standpoint, the Egyptian kingship was a formal fusion of the divine powers represented in the living Horus, his immediate predecessor, and all the royal ancestors, who were merged in the one divine being, Osiris. The kingship was a "dual kingship" involving both Horus and Osiris in necessary and reciprocal relationship.[47] It was thereby an office that to a large extent functioned on the mythical plane, beyond historical contingencies, and it is to this plane (or to the impact of this plane on the earthly plane) that most of the pharaonic records refer. The king lists that have survived were, with the possible exceptions of the Turin Canon and the Manethonic lists, compiled primarily for cultic purposes, namely, to represent the royal ancestors to whom offerings were made by the reigning Horus. What seems to us the "correct" chronological order

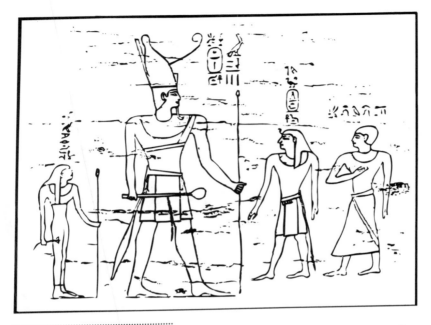

Fig. 5.6. King Mentuhotep I receives the homage of his successor, "the living Horus" Mentuhotep II. Eleventh Dynasty.

of the royal ancestors was not the most important requirement for Egyptian chronologers. It was, for instance, sometimes regarded as appropriate to list kings of certain dynasties in reverse order. In the Saqqara list of Tjuloy (or Tjuneroy), the names of over fifty kings are preserved, but only those of the Twelfth Dynasty are in correct order.[48] A portion of the Saqqara list is reproduced in figure 5.7, showing familiar cartouches of kings of the Fifth Dynasty in reverse order (top row).

Nor was completeness of a king list given priority: it was often felt necessary to leave out many kings who for some reason were less significant to the cultic purpose of the list.[49] Even the apparently more "objective" lists of the Turin Canon and Manetho were far from being the kind of records that we would describe as purely historical. This needs to be emphasized here because otherwise we may succumb to the temptation to overlook, or simply dismiss as crude propaganda, the far more blatant "distortions" of historical fact that we are now going to consider.

If in the king lists, historical facts are made to serve religious requirements, then the surviving pharaonic records of battles fought, enemies

Fig. 5.7. The Saqqara king list of Tjuloy. Nineteenth Dynasty.

conquered, and the heroic deeds of the victorious king were made primarily with regard to the requirements of myth. The intention was rarely, if ever, simply historical. How else are we to understand the following? In the Fifth Dynasty funerary temple of King Sahure a group of Libyan chieftains is depicted who have been taken prisoner alongside a number of cattle specified as having been taken as booty. But the identical scene is portrayed two hundred years later in the Sixth Dynasty temple adjoining the pyramid of Pepi II, where the Libyan chieftains bear exactly the same names. And again, almost two thousand years later, the same scene is to be found in a Nubian temple of the Ethiopian king Taharka (ca. 690 B.C.).[50] This is not an isolated example of the mythologization of history. Ramesses III made a list of all his conquests in Asia; but this list is a replica of a list made a hundred years earlier by Ramesses II, who had himself utilized a list of Thutmosis III three hundred years before his reign.[51] Such replication of historical details served the metaphysical purpose of dehistoricizing them: they were thereby elevated to the status of myth, which eternally repeats itself. No matter who the enemy are, they are always the same. Thus Ethiopians (to the south), Libyans (to the west), Asiatics (to the east) become symbols of the archetypal enemy whom the king of Egypt eternally defeats.

Mythologically, the enemy is Seth, for in whatever form the enemy comes, it comes threatening chaos and destruction. By the same token, we find the peoples who were the traditional enemies of Egypt described in a way that clearly indicates their Sethian qualities. Whenever referred to,

the Asiatics are always prefixed by the adjectives "miserable" or
"wretched":

> The miserable Aam [Asiatics of southern Palestine],
> it fares ill with the place wherein he is. . . .
> He has been fighting ever since the time of Horus,
> but he never conquers nor is he ever conquered.[52]

From roughly the same period (Middle Kingdom) comes a description of
the Ethiopian:

> When one rages against him he shows his back;
> when one retreats he starts to rage.
> They are not people worthy of respect;
> they are cowards, craven-hearted.[53]

By contrast, the king of Egypt is an invincible god who, from the First
Dynasty onward, was depicted single-handedly smashing the foreheads of
the mythic enemy. Figure 5.8 shows the legendary founder of Egypt,
King Narmer, dealing in this way with the luckless foe. Early portrayals
of kings in the "warrior pose" invariably show the king wearing the white
crown of Upper Egypt. He wields a mace with one hand and grabs the
hair of the submissive enemy with the other. Figure 5.9 is a second example, depicting King Sekhemkhet smiting the Bedouin of Sinai. Once
again the king is on his own, and overpowers the enemy with seeming
effortlessness. While such scenes doubtless commemorate actual historical events, these events are cast into the one archetypal form of the godlike figure of the king pulverizing the wretched opponent, who clearly
doesn't stand a chance.

Later reliefs from the New Kingdom are more realistic insofar as they
depict the Egyptian army "assisting" pharaoh. But they scarcely detract
from the mythic truth that the god-king is the one responsible for the
defeat of the enemy. In figure 5.10, which shows the defeat of the invading Sea Peoples, the Egyptian army is represented by a handful of bow-
men, who stand diminutively in front of the giant-sized figure of the king
(in this case Ramesses III) who, positioned on a heap of enemy corpses,
fires arrow after arrow into the confused mass of the invading army. The
latter seems almost to personify the forces of chaos, contrasting vividly
with the spatiousness and aura of calm self-confidence on the Egyptian
side.

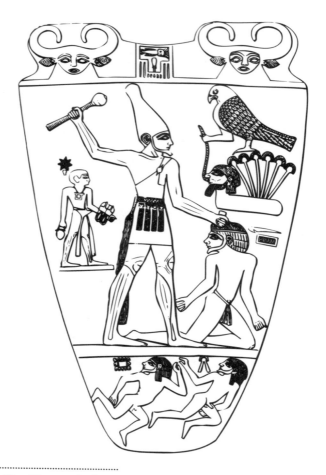

Fig. 5.8. King Narmer, the founder of the united Egyptian state, smites the enemy. Narmer Palette. Ca. 3100 B.C.

Mythologically, such scenes take us back to the order established in the First Time by Ra. The pharaoh is not only Horus confronting Seth; he is also the "Son of Ra," the image of Ra on earth, reenacting the deeds of creation. In the Megiddo Victory Hymn of Thutmosis, the king's victory is due to his being favored by Ra (or Amon-Ra), who enables him to overcome the powers of darkness in the Foreign Lands on the edge of the ordered world.[54] In defeating the enemy, the king of Egypt reestablishes *maat*. As Frankfort says: "Victory is not merely assertion of power; it is the reduction of chaos to order." He continues:

Fig. 5.9. King Sekhemket smites the enemy. Relief in the Wadi Maghara. Third Dynasty.

> Pharaoh does not act arbitrarily. He maintains an established order (of which justice is an essential element) against the onslaught of the powers of chaos. This function is independent of the accidents of history. It is an eternal truth and therefore the main subject of the artists at all times.[55]

The actions of the pharaoh are filled with mythic power; they are not, strictly speaking, historical actions. Their source, being mythological, is beyond the historical circumstances in which they come to expression.

The king is attuned to the mythic dimension whose stamp he imposes on the particular historical circumstances in which he finds himself. When we read of how Thutmosis III, while campaigning in Syria, killed seven lions and captured twelve wild cattle before breakfast, or of how Amenhotep II attacked a Syrian town single-handed, returning with sixteen captives, twenty severed hands, and sixty cattle (after which the startled town duly surrendered), we are reading myth.[56] Myth not in the sense of falsehood, but in the

Fig. 5.10. Ramesses III defeats the Sea Peoples. Temple of Ramesses III, Medinet Habu.

sense of historical possibility suddenly thrown open by the impact of the divine; what could not take place ordinarily here takes place because the ordinary is in collision with the extraordinary, and is lifted out of the plane of normality. The supernormal energy of the god-king, streaming from the mythic dimension, enables him to accomplish superhuman feats. It is futile to argue that such reports were mere propaganda to bolster the image of the king. For the point is that the human king was no mere human being but a god incarnate, for whom things were possible that are impossible for ordinary human beings. The Egyptian king lived in a different kind of reality from that of ordinary people; by bringing this reality into contact with "ordinary" reality, the laws pertaining to the latter could be transcended. The question of "historical fact" is not so much at issue here as the deeper question of our own metaphysical orientation.

The Battle of Kadesh

The most revealing example of how a penetration of ordinary historical reality by mythic or archetypal reality was effected through the person of the king is found in the account of the battle of Kadesh. The battle of Kadesh took place during the campaigns of Ramesses II in the Middle East against the Hittites. Commemorative reliefs and inscriptions recording this famous battle are preserved on the walls of the temples of Abydos, Luxor, Abu Simbel, and the Ramesseum. That the battle is commemorated on temple walls is enough to alert us to its transhistorical significance. While the account of the battle contains sufficient historical detail for the course of the events to be accurately reconstructed by modern scholars, a merely historical reconstruction falls short of what actually took place. For the Egyptians, nothing that the king did was enacted simply on the plane of mundane time and history: such historical events were simultaneously mythical.

The inscriptions record how Ramesses marched into Syria with an army of four divisions and, as he approached the city of Kadesh, was met by two spies from the Hittite army who, pretending to be deserters, gave the king false information about the position of the Hittite army. Ramesses, thinking the enemy was far away, went on ahead of the main body of his army and camped on a hill northwest of Kadesh, where he "took his seat on a throne of fine gold." Shortly, however, two enemy scouts were captured who revealed that a vast Hittite army, swollen with troops from many countries, was amassed northeast of Kadesh with infantry and chariotry "more numerous than the sands of the shores." The king hastily sent messengers to urge his army to hurry forward, but the marching army was already under attack, and the king soon found that his camp was encircled by Hittite chariots. At this moment of supreme danger, the king rose up like "his father" the warrior god Month; he seized his weapons, donned his armor, mounted his chariot, and charged into the midst of the enemy:

> No officer was with me, no charioteer,
> No soldier of the army, no shield-bearer;
> My infantry, my chariotry yielded before them.
> Not one of them stood firm to fight with them.[57]

Ramesses, alone and deserted by his troops, offers a long prayer to "Father Amon," asking for the aid of this great god. The prayer ends with these words:

> I call to you, my father Amon,
> I am among a host of strangers;
> All countries are arrayed against me!
> I am alone, there's none with me!

My numerous troops have deserted me,
Not one of my chariotry looks for me;
I keep on shouting for them,
But none of them heeds my call.
I know Amon helps me more than a million troops,
More than a hundred thousand charioteers,
More than ten thousand brothers and sons
Who are united as one heart.
The labors of many people are nothing.
Amon is more helpful than they. . . .[58]

Amon hears the prayer of his son Ramesses, and calls to him "as if nearby":

Forward, I am with you,
I, your father, my hand is with you,
I prevail over a hundred thousand men,
I am lord of victory, lover of valor.[59]

Whereupon the pharaoh is infused with supernatural strength. He becomes "like Seth," the god of violent destruction, slaughtering at will all who come near him. Noticing Ramesses fighting completely unaided, the chief of the Hittites gathers together a thousand chariots that he sends against the lone king. This proves to be a rash move:

Their total of a thousand chariots came straight into the fire.
I charged toward them, being like Month.
In a moment I gave them a taste of my hand.
I slaughtered among them, they were slain on the spot.
One called out to the other saying;
"No man is he who is among us,
It is Seth, great-of-strength, Baal in person;
These are not the deeds of a man,
They are of one who is unique,
Who fights a hundred thousand without soldiers and chariots,
Come quick, flee before him,
To seek life and breathe air. . . ."[60]

Ramesses single-handedly routs the enemy, causing the plain of Kadesh to be so filled with dead that "it could not be trodden because of their mass." He fells "hundreds of thousands" with his strong arm, while his own soldiers faintheartedly shirk battle. The poem describing the battle ends with the king marshalling his soldiers "at dawn," and once more plunging into the fray. And now, as the sun rises,

> *I was like Ra, when he rises at dawn.*
> *My rays, they burned the rebels' bodies,*
> *They called out to one another:*
> *"Beware, take care, don't approach him. . . .*
> *Anyone who goes to approach him,*
> *Fire's breath comes to burn his body."*
> *Thereupon they stood at a distance,*
> *Kissing the ground before me.*[61]

The symbolic import of the poem becomes clear when it is read with the reliefs that accompany it.[62] At Luxor, these are distributed over the pylon at the entrance to the temple. On the west wing of the pylon, Ramesses is shown seated on his "throne of fine gold," facing the west, the sunset (fig. 5.11). Gold, of course, is a metal symbolic of the sun. That Ramesses should take his seat on a golden throne at the beginning of the battle emphasizes his own status as human representative of the sun on earth.

To the right of this image is a second image of the king mounted on his chariot, charging into the night. And between the seated king and the figure of the charging king are six chariots rising diagonally toward the west, where they meet the enemy chariots at the top of the relief, immediately above the figure of Ramesses in his chariot. The Egyptian hours of the night began at 6 P.M., and it is as if the six diagonally rising chariots take us through the first six hours of the night to the hour of midnight. It would seem, then, that these chariots represent the initial stages of the battle, up until Ramesses learns from the captured enemy scouts that he is in fact in dire peril. Now, it was believed that each night the sun, having set in the west, must traverse the regions of the Underworld in order to rise again the next morning in the east. The hours of the night therefore can be understood as corresponding to stages in the Underworld journey. As the earthly representative of the solar principle, the king riding into the night is at the same time riding into the Underworld. The battle of Kadesh takes place as much in the mythical time zone of the Underworld as in ordinary time.

On the same wing of the pylon, the king is in fact depicted again, partly superimposed over the first seated figure. The complete picture is as given in figure 5.12. But notice that the second, superimposed figure is

East

West

Fig. 5.11. Ramesses faces the west and charges into the night. Luxor Temple, west wing of pylon.

almost twice the size of the first, and that he is now facing east. What does this second, superimposed image signify? To suggest that it is due to a mistake or a change of mind on the part of the sculptors would be an easy answer, but it would be an answer that would guarantee missing any symbolic import that the scene may harbor. For it is as if, having gone forth into the Underworld, the king—like the sun—must face the east in order to continue his journey through the hours of the night and reach the dawn. This "turning about" of the king indeed seems to correspond to the moment of his greatest danger, when, cut off from the main body of his army, he learns that he is surrounded by overwhelming enemy forces. Immediately underneath the king's feet, one can see the captured scouts being beaten into confessing the whereabouts of the Hittite army. It is at this moment that Ramesses must turn to Amon for aid.

In the Book of What Is in the Underworld, a mystical New Kingdom

East   West

Fig. 5.12. Ramesses turns to the east in his moment of greatest peril. Luxor Temple, west wing of pylon.

text relating the sun's journey through the Underworld, it is during the seventh hour, the hour of midnight, that Ra encounters the demonic serpent Apophis, who would prevent his further progress (see figure 4.7). This, it would seem, is the moment that Ramesses has now come to. And it is exactly at this point that the action shifts to the eastern wing of the pylon, for it is here that the prayer of the king to Amon is inscribed. Beyond it the king, mounted on his chariot, now charges from west to east (toward sunrise) wreaking havoc on those who oppose him (fig. 5.13). Just as at this hour Ra butchers Apophis, so Ramesses butchers the Hittites, the earthly counterparts of Apophis.

In Ra's Underworld journey, it is following this vital event of the defeat of Apophis that the tide of opposition is turned in support of Ra. And so at length, having filled the plain of Kadesh with enemy dead through a long "night" of slaughter, Ramesses marshals his forces at dawn while the enemy kiss the ground before him.

East

West

Fig. 5.13. Ramesses charges into the Hittites. Luxor Temple, east wing of pylon.

Symbolically, then, as Schwaller de Lubicz says, "all the action takes place in the darkness of the night, the sun being below the earth or within it."[63] No matter if "in fact" the battle was fought in the day. We do not understand the accounts of the battle of Kadesh unless we go beyond the factual, historical descriptions to the mythical episode that determines the events of the battle and guarantees its outcome. The symbolism of the poem is cosmic.

In the temple at Abu Simbel, the record of the battle ends with the king fifteen years later signing a peace treaty inscribed on a silver tablet by the enemy chief, whereupon Ramesses marries his enemy's daughter. She is presented to Ramesses by her father along with numerous gifts. The marriage stele at Abu Simbel, which Ramesses had carved as a memorial of this event, declares that his new wife received the name "She who sees the beauty of Ra"—the title of the last hour of the night in the Book of What Is in the Underworld. According to Schwaller de Lubicz, the new wife of the king symbolizes the moon, now waxed full after fifteen "years" since the battle was fought.[64] The marriage thus symbolizes not only the earthly reconciliation of opposing forces, but also a cosmic union of opposites, the union of the solar and lunar principles.

The account of the battle of Kadesh is a fine example of what may be termed mythic history. The modern instinct, however, is to carefully separate out the "historical facts" from the "mythical overlay." When Egyptian history is approached with unexamined modern assumptions about what is fact and what is fiction and what is real and what is bogus, the unity between the mythic and historical dimensions that existed in ancient Egypt is destroyed.

Let me quote Eliade again: "Myth is bound up with ontology; it speaks only of *realities*."[65] For the ancient Egyptians, the mythical spoke not only of the real, but of the highest realities. The realm referred to in myth is the spiritual realm from which all things and events on the natural plane originate. History divorced from myth is history severed from its source. Now this may well describe the way in which we experience history today, but it would seem that the ancient Egyptian experience was different from our own. Hence, in ancient Egyptian times care was taken to place historical events in their appropriate mythical setting. And this was not something done after the event, but was absolutely intrinsic to determining the outcome of the event. In other words, the course of history was steered by its being projected into a mythical context. The course of the battle of Kadesh and its triumphant outcome was predetermined because of the king's mythical status as representative of Ra on earth.

What really happened at Kadesh? This cannot be adequately answered by sifting the "facts" from the mytho-historical account. Rather, we should first examine our own presuppositions about "reality," and the epistemological standpoint that the modern cult of the fact is based upon. Since the seventeenth century, the mainstream European view of the world has equated the real with the sense-perceptible. The modern fact is a statement that can be supported by the evidence of the senses. But from the point of view of the ancient Egyptians, the modern severance of facts from myth could only be the result of a distorted perception of reality, for it leaves out the most important components of any event: gods and myths. When trying to determine what "really happened" in history, the presupposition that only the sense-perceptible has ontological status inevitably results in a falsification of Egyptian history as the Egyptians experienced it.

For the ancient Egyptians, myth was not fiction. Nor were the archetypal deeds, or the dramatic interventions, of the gods mere fictions. On the contrary, these were regarded by them as far more real than our much loved facts. What really happened at Kadesh was a conjunction of the mythical and the historical planes. Such conjunctions were by no means infrequent in ancient Egypt. Neither, when they did occur, were they simply fortuitous, but were often deliberately brought about. Indeed, they formed the basis of that art or science of which the Egyptians were renowned practitioners, and that we call magic. It is to this subject of magic that we must now turn.

6 THE THEOLOGY OF MAGIC

Religion Versus Magic

There are some formidable obstacles to approaching magic as it was practiced in ancient Egypt. Most obviously there is the heritage of European religious thought that, conditioned by the theology of the Christian Church, has created a spiritual atmosphere in which magic is viewed with fear and mistrust. The attitude of the Church to magic has been, and remains, hostile and condemnatory. At the beginning of the century, the *Catholic Encyclopaedia* defined magic as "the art of performing actions beyond the power of man and with the aid of powers other than the Divine," and condemned it and any attempt at practicing it as "a grievous sin against the virtue of religion, because all magical performances, if undertaken seriously, are based on the expectation of interference by demons or lost souls."[1] The Church here speaks for the whole of society, and at the end of the twentieth century there is little to suggest that its attitude toward magic has changed.

For centuries in the Christian West any relationship to the spiritual world other than that sanctioned by formal religion has been discouraged. And so magic—and along with it "occultism" in general—has been widely regarded as a dangerous deviation from the norms of belief and worship established and promulgated by the Church. What applies to Christianity here applies also to the other "religions of the Book." The very word *religion* has become almost inseparable from what is practiced in church, mosque, or synagogue. The security vouchsafed by these institutions of the various monotheistic orthodoxies contrasts with the widespread sense of insecurity when it comes to magic. It is felt that with magic the forces of darkness and light, evil and good, are at best not clearly distinguished; at worst, as we have seen from the definition above, magic involves the conjuring of demons.

This division between religion on the one hand and magic on the other is a product of a changed relationship to the spiritual world from that which existed in ancient times. It has characterized the last two thousand years, but we should always bear in mind that it is only during this unique period of Western history—during this unique historical and cultural phase—that the rift between occultism and exoteric religion has taken place. Before the Greco-Roman era, and in fact well into the Greco-Roman period (though with signs of growing decadence), religious life was not divided off from practices in which occult powers were contacted and initiatic experiences undergone. Religion and magic were not separated: religion was magical.

In our own era, the gradual separation can be followed as a historically traceable process: from the decline of the Mysteries and oracles lamented in the first century A.D. by Plutarch, through the establishment of Christianity as the state religion of the Roman Empire and the missionary campaigns of the Church during the Dark Ages against the remnants of the old paganism, to the crushing of heresies in the Middle Ages and the murderous witch-hunts of the Renaissance period. Occultism was forced underground, and was tolerated only in the veiled forms that it assumed, for instance, in alchemy or Rosicrucianism. While it went underground, however, it never died. The resurgence of the occult sciences in the Renaissance, despite the dangers of persecution by the Church, may be seen as a resurfacing of teachings and practices having pre-Greek roots. The *Corpus Hermeticum*, translated by Ficino during the latter part of the fifteenth century, transmitted magical teachings purportedly of ancient Persian and Egyptian origin.[2] In the Renaissance, one finds more mystically inclined thinkers striving to heal the schism between formal religion and magic. It is notable that both Pico della Mirandola and Giordano Bruno appealed to the pope to reunite orthodoxy with the magical and Hermetic tradition.[3] Jacob Boehme stated bluntly: "Magic is the best theology, for in it true faith is both grounded and found. And he is a fool that reviles it, for he knows it not, and blasphemes against both God and himself, and is more a juggler than a theologian of understanding."[4] In more recent times, the extraordinary proliferation of occult teachings points toward the possibility that a gradual reconciliation between religion and magic might now be taking place.

Magic Defined

The word *magic* derives from the Greek *magos*, which was the term used by the Greeks to refer to the priests and itinerant seers who came from the region of Mesopotamia and Persia. The "magi" referred to in the Gospel of Matthew (in Greek *magoi*)[5] were representatives of a spiritual outlook that was at variance with both Greek and Judeo-Christian spirituality. The Greeks feared these *magoi* because they were still in contact with powers that they had themselves for the most part lost touch with. It is a fear that we have inherited and accompanies our use of the term *magic*. The Greek word *magos* in fact derives from Old Persian roots: *mog*, *megh*, and *magh*, which signify "priest," "wise," and "excellent." It is from these words that the Chaldean term *maghdim* originated. Maghdim means "sacred philosophy" or "supreme wisdom."[6] The much later definition of Paracelsus perfectly corresponds to this original sense: "Magic is the greatest wisdom and the knowledge of supernatural powers . . . acquired by obtaining more spirituality and making oneself capable to feel and to see the things of the spirit."[7] From the perspective of the ancient, pre-Greek world order, of which the Egyptians were, of course, a major representative, the philosophy founded by the Greeks was but a shadow of the sacred philosophy or *maghdim* that preceded it. As Plato himself records, the Egyptians regarded the Greeks as mere children when it came to spiritual understanding.[8]

Whereas magic (in the sense of knowledge of the supernatural) died a more or less natural death in Greece, it had to be fought against and driven out of the religion of the Israelites. And again, throughout the Christian era, magic has had to be battled against, not readily acquiescing to the prohibitions made against it. And yet, at the same time, the appearance of the "magi" at the birth of Christ can be viewed as a symbolic acknowledgment by them that their own time had to give way to a period in which the magical consciousness was eclipsed. What was an appropriate mode of relating to the spiritual world in one epoch would be inappropriate in another. The last two thousand years of European history have entailed the development of the specifically nonmagical faculties of scientific observation and abstract logical reasoning necessary for the development of a consciousness that could function independently of the gods. As this period draws to a close, however, a reexamination and exploration of the magical mode of consciousness appears increasingly relevant.

Significantly, in ancient Egypt there was no word for "religion." The nearest thing to it was in fact the word commonly translated as "magic"—*heka*. As A. H. Gardiner writes: "From the Egyptian point of view we may say that there was no such thing as 'religion'; there was only *heka*, the nearest English equivalent of which is 'magical power.'"[9] Like *maat*, *heka* is a principle personified as a divine being. It is typical of the Egyptians to regard magic as a being rather than as a science: one must enter into living relationship with *heka* in order to know it.

In the Coffin Texts, the god Heka states that he exists within the primeval creative utterance of Atum, by means of which the gods came into being.[10] He describes himself as the divine energy that safeguards everything that has been ordained by the Godhead. And it is in this role, as the creative power contained in the divine Word, that Heka gives life to the gods, and thus claims priority over them:

> *I am he who gives life to the companies of the gods,*
> *I am he who did whatever he wishes,*
> *the father of the gods. . . .*
> *All things were mine*
> *before you came into being, O gods!*
> *You only came afterwards,*
> *for I am Heka!*[11]

The divine being Heka is not simply "father of the gods," he is father of all that becomes manifest. For Heka is the all-pervasive power that underpins everything that exists, whether spiritually or materially. The god Heka can be seen in figure 6.1, from a New Kingdom papyrus. He is shown holding in his clenched fists two snakes, which cross his body diagonally. Upon his head is the hieroglyph of the hindquarters of a lion on the top of a standard. From the Twentieth Dynasty onward, this hieroglyph commonly replaces the phonetic spelling of the god's name. Its own phonetic value is *pe* or *pehety*, and, as we have seen (chapter 3), it can mean "creative word." More commonly, its meaning carries the connotations of "power" or "strength"—an attribute that definitively belongs to Heka.

In chapter 3, we considered an illustration that shows Heka in the place of Shu holding Nut aloft (fig. 3.13). The inscription reads, "Heka, Great God, Master of the Sky."[12] It is through this deed of parting heaven and earth that what is essentially spiritual is enabled to become physically manifest.[13] In company with Shu and Thoth, but with a singleness of purpose that they lack, Heka is the power by which the spiritual becomes manifest, for he is the connecting link between the Godhead, Atum, and all that comes forth from Atum.

In order to understand Heka, therefore, we have to think of these two related aspects: Heka as the divine creative power that underpins and pervades all that exists in the spiritual and material world; and Heka as the means by which the different spiritual and material levels connect with each other and can flow into each other. In his study of Egyptian magic, the French scholar Christian Jacq writes:

> This magic can perhaps be defined as the essential energy which circulates in the universe of the gods as well as in that of humans. . . . Spirit and matter are woven out of the same substance. The important thing in the practice of magic is to identify the thread which links everything and unites all creatures in a chain of cosmic union.[14]

Fig. 6.1. The god Heka. Detail from the papyrus of Khonsu-Renep. New Kingdom.

To understand, to harmonize with, and then to activate *heka* in given situations is the sacred science and practice of magic.

It follows, therefore, that a path of inner development is the prerequisite for the ability to wield magical power. For the personality or the ego cannot command gods: only Heka itself can. So the magician is one who has made him- or herself a clear channel for transmitting Heka. Thus King Pepi says: "It is not I who says this to you, you gods; it is Heka who says this to you, you gods!"[15] The king, in other words, has himself "become" Heka; only thus does he command the gods. An image expressing the thorough integration of magic into the person is that of swallowing it and digesting it, so that it resides in a person's belly. In the so-called Cannibal Hymn, the magician-king eats the *heka* of the gods and "enjoys himself when their magic is in his belly."[16] Only thereby can he make his way through the spiritual world. This is a theme reiterated elsewhere in the Pyramid Texts, as for instance in the following passage: "I will ascend and rise up to heaven. My magic is in my belly. I will ascend and rise up to heaven."[17]

In the Book of the Dead we find again and again that the possession of magic and of magical "words of power" is essential if one is to overcome the many obstacles encountered in the journey through the Dwat. In chapter 24, the Underworld traveller gathers magic with the aid of the following spell:

> I gather magic from every place
> and from everyone who has it,
> swift as a greyhound, quick as light. . . .
> Form-creating magic,
> which comes from the womb of the Mother;
> God-conjuring magic,
> which comes from out of the silence;
> God-warming magic,
> which comes from the Mother.
> Now this magic is given me from every place
> and from everyone who has it,
> swift as a greyhound, quick as light.

It is by means of magic, especially in the sense of esoteric knowledge, that the Underworld traveller is able to pass through the gates of the Dwat, and to overcome the many monsters and demonic forces that are to be met there. In order to gather magic, it is necessary to have a net in which *heka* can be harnessed and then projected forth. It is in this manner that the opposing serpent Apophis is subdued in the ninth division of the Book of Gates (fig. 6.2).

The accent of the Book of the Dead is somewhat different from that of the earlier Pyramid Texts, insofar as magic in the Book of the Dead has the role more of being the key to the process of inner transformation than (as in the Pyramid Texts) a power that is acquired only after such transformation has been effected. The opposing forces encountered in the Dwat are essentially of a psychic nature, and the overcoming or mastery of these forces is an event prior to entering the heavenly world as such, and this is the main focus of the Book of the Dead. By contrast, the Pyramid Texts place far less emphasis on the journey toward union with the divine. This is often described in a single dramatic image of ascension, rather than, as in the Book of the Dead and other New Kingdom texts, in terms of a lengthy progress through gates and pylons, and so on. The kings of the Pyramid Texts, already in the Upperworld, use magic to make themselves masters in the realm of the gods. This is a subtle but significant difference

Fig. 6.2. Catching and projecting magic with nets. Book of Gates, division 9. Tomb of Ramesses VI.

of emphasis, for it points to the fact that, by the New Kingdom, magic had become a necessary condition for the work of inner transmutation.

Heka is the aboriginal divine creative power, wielded at the deepest level by Atum-Kheprer. Through Heka, one is able to fill oneself with the creative power of Atum-Kheprer, beyond which there is nothing stronger.[18] Magic, then, is a mysterious divine force through which the spiritual and physical universe becomes manifest, and hence a force permeating and linking all levels of reality from the highest to the most material. But it is also—and this is an especially important aspect of the way the ancient Egyptians understood magic—the means by which the human being, and ultimately all creation, returns to the supreme Godhead, the unmanifest source of all that exists. In both respects, Heka is intimately connected with Maat, the "right order" of the universe established at the beginning of time, to which it was considered vital to attune political, social, and moral life. Heka and Maat can be seen together, on either side of the sun god, in figure 6.3. They seem as brother and sister here, performing the same essential gesture in relation to the solar principle.

For the ancient Egyptians, any alignment of the physical with the spiritual, of earthly with heavenly forces, required the activation of Heka and resulted in Maat. For Heka is the all-sustaining spiritual power that underlies creation. Since illness was regarded as arising through disharmony between the spiritual and physical in the human being, it is hardly surprising that magic was a central component of healing, as we shall shortly see.

The Activation of Magic

Broadly speaking, four factors were necessary in order to activate magic:

- the magician
- sacred images
- sacred words
- ritual actions

We shall look at each of these factors in turn, and then in the next chapter go on to consider the practice of magic in ancient Egypt.

THE MAGICIAN

Although essentially secret, magic carried immense prestige in ancient Egyptian society and its practitioners were highly respected. Most (though not all) magicians were priests connected with a temple and belonging to an orthodox hierarchy. Magicians were "establishment figures," influential in practically every area of life—in religion, diplomacy, statecraft, war, architecture, agriculture, and medicine. Generally speaking, it was necessary to be a magician in order to hold high office of state. The reason for this is that the purpose of all state activities was to ensure that Egyptian society was attuned to *maat*; that is, to ensure that there was a harmonious flow of energy between the different levels of being so that what was carried out in, say, the social or the agricultural spheres was informed by, and in attunement with, benevolent spiritual forces. To be a minister of state, one had to have some relationship with, and understanding of, *heka*: for it was through *heka* that such harmonization was achieved.

Magicians were trained in colleges of sacred science that were attached to all the main temples, somewhat as the schools of the Middle Ages were

Fig. 6.3. Heka and Maat on either side of Ra-Harakhti. Papyrus of Khensumosi. New Kingdom.

attached to cathedrals. These colleges were called "Houses of Life," and in them the temple libraries were kept. A symbolic representation of the House of Life is given in figure 6.4, which is from a papyrus containing a ritual for the protection of the House of Life (Papyrus Salt 825). In the center is the figure of Osiris, standing within a mummy case, and looking toward the *ankh* hieroglyph in the top right-hand corner of the inner rectangle. The House of Life was literally *per* (house) *ankh* (life), and in a sense Osiris is the key to the meaning of what this institution really was. Surrounding the inner enclosure are hieroglyphs denoting the names of various gods: Thoth, Isis, Nephthys, and so on. Around the outside of the square the four cardinal points are shown.

The word we translate from ancient Egyptian as "magician" is literally "scribe of the House of Life." Despite the large collections of books known to have been kept in the Houses of Life, the training offered by them was by no means simply book learning. For the study of the sacred texts was

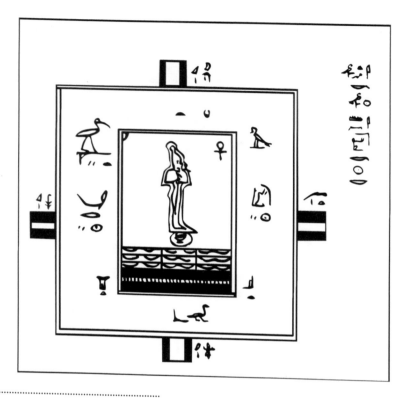

Fig. 6.4. A symbolic diagram of the House of Life. Papyrus Salt 825. Nineteenth Dynasty.

pursued in order to acquaint the student not with abstract concepts but with those nonphysical energies and forces that were under the guardianship of the *neters* or gods. Thus Ramesses IV states that he studied the written texts of the House of Life in order to discover the secrets of the gods.[19] These secrets cannot be known merely intellectually. We should assume that the training undergone in the House of Life was primarily experiential.

Some idea of this training may be arrived at by considering the fact that magicians were required to be able to bring spiritual energies to bear on the physical level. In order to do this, they had to become familiar with the subtle planes of existence—both the confusing world of psychic energies, and the levels beyond this, both above and below. According to Gardiner, the Books of the Dead—which are really manuals concerning the world of psychic energies and their transmutation—"were characteristic products of the House of Life," which is what we should expect. It was also in the House of Life "that medical and religious books were written."[20] For the Egyptians, medicine was a subject that could not be divorced from religion, since both illness and health were due to the influence of spiritual forces on a person's soul and body. It might, for instance, be necessary to drive off demonic influences in the event of sickness; in which case, the magician would have to be able not only to identify the demonic power that he sought to confront, but also to summon the aid of a god or gods so as to defeat this power. This presupposes a high degree of inner clarity: the magician had to learn to see accurately into the spiritual spheres. In order to do this, it is necessary to learn to recognize the less-than-spiritual forces that encumber the human psyche, which can derange the mind and attack the body—forces that, when fully known, can assume the aspect of demons.

The training in the House of Life was an esoteric training, a training that gave knowledge of the invisible realm through and by means of a path of inner development. It was only by actually journeying into the Underworld that the student could come to know what was there; and it was only by experiencing the world of the gods that the student could understand their nature. The Houses of Life were therefore initiatory centers in which various degrees of symbolic death and rebirth were undergone. This is why in the diagram of the House of Life Osiris is in the center. For without having died to the physical and been reborn in the spiritual, it would not have been possible for the magician to function effectively in the world of the *neters*, and to bring the energies under their guardianship into a benevolent relationship to the physical realm. It seems highly likely that the texts that are known today as "funerary texts" designed for the use of the dead—texts like the Book of the Dead and the Book of What Is in the Underworld—were also meant to be used by those whose vocation required a thorough knowledge of the Underworld. Thus we find certain spells in the Book of the Dead indicated as being of help to those still "on earth," a phrase repeated in the Book of What Is in the Underworld, where it is explicitly stated that the knowledge set forth will be "useful for one who is on earth."[21]

Given the nature of the Houses of Life and the type of learning pursued in them, and given the fundamentally theocentric intention of the Egyptian social order, we may understand how leading figures of the establishment could claim an advanced degree of spiritual adeptship. The titles of various high-ranking officials clearly indicate that they were no mere bureaucrats or politicians in our sense of the word. We find, for instance, that the Old

Kingdom minister Ti, the overseer of the pyramids and sun temples at Abu Sir and superintendent of works, was also "Master of Secrets."[22] Most guidebooks fail to mention this fact, which as John Anthony West says "is normally taken as a vain boast that the deceased enjoyed the confidence of the king." West's suggestion that the title, on the contrary, "refers to some very high level of initiation" seems closer to the mark.[23] The Middle Kingdom vizier to Sesostris I, Oukhotep, in addition to being treasurer and unique confidant to the king, was also "Unique of all his kind and without rival, who masters the secrets that only one knows."[24] And again, the New Kingdom vizier to both Thutmosis III and Amenhotep II during the height of the empire—Rekhmire—was described in these terms: "There is nothing on earth, in heaven or in any part of the Beyond of which he does not have knowledge."[25] These are not examples of mere empty bragging. They are formal statements of the level of accomplishment achieved by each of the individuals concerned, each statement claiming for that person a high degree of esoteric knowledge.

Magicians, then, while being a class apart from the rest of society because they lived in direct contact with the gods, nevertheless occupied the most important positions within the political and social order. Egyptian society was theocentric: it depended on the magicians to keep it in harmony with the gods. In addition to the establishment magicians, there were also magicians who apparently lived and practiced their art on the fringes of society, and may perhaps better be described as sorcerers or shamans. We hear of one such figure in the Papyrus Westcar, whose powers extended to being able to restore magically the severed head of an animal to its body, to tame lions, and to know the future.[26] It may also be assumed that every village would have had its resident medicine man or local shaman, not attached to any institution.[27]

SACRED IMAGES

In order to begin to appreciate the role of sacred images in ancient Egyptian religious life, it is necessary to realize the extent to which modern Western consciousness is still in thrall to the second commandment of the god of the Israelites: "You shall not make yourself a carved image or any likeness of anything in heaven or on earth; you shall not bow down to them or serve them. For I, Yahweh your God, am a jealous God."[28] This injunction still exercises power over our minds and even our moral sense. But idolatry only became an issue at a certain stage in the evolution of consciousness. It became an issue at that profound moment in the history of the human psyche, recorded in Exodus, when the god of the Israelites, having "brought them out of the land of Egypt," pronounced his Ten Commandments. The deeply symbolic event of bringing the Chosen People out of Egypt entailed forging an entirely new relationship not only to the divine but also to the natural world.[29] The "jealous God" of the Israelites was a god whose nature could not be represented. For the Egyptians, on the other hand, physical representations of the gods were capable of becoming suffused with divine content. The Egyptians themselves did not experience any gulf separating the spiritual from the physical realm. There was little in nature that could not effectively communicate a divine power. The stars, sun, moon, wind, and earth—all were gods or expressions of gods to them. Animals, plants, trees, serpents—all were capable of mediating a divine presence. For the Egyptians the natural world was full of gods. And the world of physical objects could equally become filled with divine powers. Certain forms and certain substances (of which the forms were made) could provide effective mediums for spiritual powers to become manifest on the physical plane. The Israelites—and hence the Judeo-Christian tradition as a whole—having crossed the Red Sea, came to experience the physical world as opaque, no longer capable of mediating a divine content. In time the sense of there being a continuum between the physical and the spiritual such as would allow a flow of energy between the two worlds was lost. Physical objects came to be experienced simply as physical; they no longer opened onto an interior dimension. They became simply "idols."

The Egyptians never worshiped idols and idolatry was never an issue for them. Why not? Because an idol is a physical object and nothing more than a physical object. There were no such things as idols in ancient Egypt, because the ancient Egyptian mentality could not conceive of any such notion. The concept of an idol was introduced by the Israelites. Defined in the words of the Psalmist, idols are

> products of human skill,
> have mouths but never speak,
> eyes, but never see,
> ears, but never hear,
> noses, but never smell,
> hands, but never touch,
> feet, but never walk,
> and not a sound from their throats.[30]

Fig. 6.5. Amenophis I gives an oracle. Tomb of Amenmose. New Kingdom.

As Owen Barfield explains, the idols as apprehended by the Israelites were "not filled with anything. They were mere hollow pretences of life. They had no 'within.'"[31] Idols such as this simply did not exist for the Egyptians. No representation was merely a representation: all physical images could become vehicles of an indwelling divine presence. They all potentially had a "within," and therefore had the capacity to see, hear, smell, and indeed could also speak—as did the colossus of Memnon at Thebes well into Roman times;[32] only the Israelites could no longer hear them.

In figure 6.5 we can see an example of "a speaking idol" recorded in a relief from the tomb of a New Kingdom priest named Amenmose. It shows an image of the dead pharaoh Amenophis I, who—formally deified—was the modern equivalent of a saint. He is being carried in procession on his festival day. Two disputants (not shown here) appear before the statue as it is carried out of the temple, and beg that the god Amenophis settle their dispute for them. Amenmose puts their request to the statue, who responds with an unequivocal judgment in favor of one of the disputants. The "voice" of the god was felt by the bearers of the statue in a thrusting movement forward or backward, which they themselves could not control. Forward meant yes, backward meant no. In this way the god expressed his judgment through the statue.

Mere trickery, we might say. But it is important that we remember that the world of the ancient Egyptians was—unlike our own—an *animated* world from the beginning. They started from a different place. This is not to say that the Egyptians "projected" the subjective contents of the psyche into the world. For they were aware of objective spiritual forces that, though apprehended "inwardly," dwell in an interior dimension that is essentially prior to the psychic. The argument pursued by C. G. Jung in *Psychology and Religion* and other works that the development of consciousness required "the withdrawal of projections" and the "return to the psyche" of everything of a divine and demonic character fails to take into account the profound metaphysical basis of the ancient "projections."[33] The historical process, rather than consisting in a withdrawal of projections, has been, on the contrary, a process of *introjecting* into the psyche spiritual powers that, for the ancients, had an ontological status that was independent of, and prior to, the psyche. The ancients did not project their gods into nature: they apprehended them there. A veil had not yet been drawn across the interiority of the world by a psyche ever more absorbed in its own subjectivity.

Fig. 6.6. *Diorite statue of Sekhmet from the court of the temple of Mut, Karnak. Eighteenth Dynasty.*

For the ancient Egyptians, therefore, it was possible for a coalescence to occur between the physical image and the spiritual power that it represented. The statue of the goddess Sekhmet in figure 6.6, for example, was not simply a physical representation of the goddess. Such statues were created with careful attention both to the material (hard diorite) and to the formal features carved into the stone. Important rites were performed upon the statue that had the effect of "opening" it toward the specific spiritual forces that the goddess mediated. Through a combination of skilled craftsmanship and the performance of certain specific sacred rites, the statue

135

could become the physical vehicle through which the goddess manifested as a tangible presence on the material plane. This is not idolatry: it is the invocation—and apprehension—of the divine in and through a material form, which is no longer simply a material form, but has acquired a "within"—a spirit.

With the exception of the Israelites and then, in their wake, the early Christians, this attitude prevailed throughout the ancient world. In the *Corpus Hermeticum*, for example, there is a discussion concerning the nature of the gods in which there appears to be total confusion between the gods themselves and their manifestation in "statues living and conscious, filled with the breath of life, and doing many mighty works."[34] We glimpse here a completely different consciousness of the physical world from our own. The gods could not be distinguished from their statues or images, and to have done so would have been as false to the ancients as it would be questionable for us moderns to distinguish between a person and his or her body. While that person is alive and well, such distinctions are not necessary, which shows that we too are animists, only we suffer from such a reduced animism that we are in danger of losing sight of the soul altogether.

We may feel tempted to dismiss the ancient animism, and the magical worldview that accompanied it, as a childish superstition that we have since outgrown. But perhaps this is because as the compass of our animism has diminished, so also has our perception of the more subtle planes of existence. We think we know more, but from the point of view of the ancients we know far less. Plotinus, writing toward the end of the age of polytheism, refers to "those ancient sages, who sought to secure the presence of divine beings by the erection of shrines and statues." These sages, he says, "showed insight into the nature of the All." He continues,

> they perceived that, though this Soul [the Soul of the World] is everywhere tractable, its presence will be secured all the more readily when an appropriate receptacle is elaborated, a place especially capable of receiving some portion or phase of it, something reproducing it and serving like a mirror to catch an image of it.[35]

Not only could a physical image (whether two- or three-dimensional) provide the "body" for an already existent spiritual entity, but images could also become the physical base of "thought forms" that were called into existence through their being represented on the physical plane. In this case the images carved on funerary stelae, painted on tomb walls or in

Fig. 6.7. Food offerings carved in relief and enjoyed for eternity. Stele of Amten. Old Kingdom.

papyrus texts, had the effect of activating in a higher dimension their spiritual counterparts. The food offerings portrayed in front of Amten in figure 6.7, for instance, called into activity the latent spiritual forms that the relief carving represented. The images (bread, meat, poultry, and so on) were thereby transubstantiated between two different dimensions of existence. The image, by invoking the essence of the substance imaged, was itself magically transformed from being mere image to being an image infused with the spiritual substance it portrayed. At the same time, it became absorbed into this spiritual substance on a spiritual level, and thereby gave access to it.

The experience of the possibility of a coalescence between physical representations and spiritual entities lies behind the practice throughout the ancient world of making offerings to gods and goddesses. In figure 6.8, King Seti I offers two vases of milk to the goddess Sekhmet. An offering of food like this could be made to a spiritual being only because the food offered was perceived to have a spiritual as well as a physical substance. Everything in nature was but an image of its spiritual archetype; the difference between actual physical food and a painting of food is, according to this mentality, of little significance when regarded from the perspective of

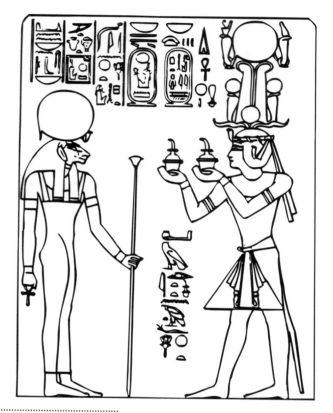

Fig. 6.8. Offering milk to Sekhmet. Temple of Seti I, Abydos.

their shared spiritual essence. For the point is precisely that true reality is located on the spiritual plane, and it is to this plane that the magical consciousness primarily refers.

A further, well-known example of this way of thinking is in the widespread utilization of servant statues (*ushabti* figures) in the funerary equipment of deceased persons from the Middle Kingdom on. The statues were supposed to "come to life" in the other world and perform tasks for the tomb owner. It is quite evident that they were not expected, nor required, to come to life on the physical level but rather to "answer" (*ushabti* means "answerer") for the deceased in the spirit world, if the person was called upon to do unpleasant chores. Hence they were often equipped with farm implements, and were usually inscribed with a spell such as the following:

O Ushabti, if I am called upon,
or if I am required to do any of the work
which is done in the Underworld,
you shall volunteer instead of me always
to cultivate the fields, to fill the canals with water
and to carry the sand of the east to the west.
You shall say "Here I am!"[36]

A drawing of a typical *ushabti* is given in figure 6.9. It is surely clear that we are dealing here, both in the magic figure and the spell written on it, with the physical bases of spiritual forms or essences. The *ushabti* figures facilitated the magical conjuring of forms on the spiritual plane, even though they—to our eyes—existed on the physical plane alone. The reason why they could be effective was that for the Egyptians what existed on the physical level drew to itself the specific spiritual energies of which that physical form was a type. For the magical consciousness, every ritual action done on the physical level, every form created, every word spoken or written, acted as the magnet to which its spiritual counterpart was irresistably pulled.

SACRED WORDS

To understand the ancient Egyptian attitude toward words, it is necessary to overcome some deeply entrenched modern presuppositions about the nature of language. These presuppositions took hold of the European mind in the Middle Ages, during which time there was a long and bitter dispute in the schools and universities concerning the metaphysical status of words. The protagonists in this dispute are known as the Realists and the Nominalists. Briefly, the Realists argued that the word we use to denote a thing expresses the very essence of that thing, and this essence has a spiritual, as opposed to a physical, reality. For the Realists, the essence of a physical object is laid hold of by the human mind in the concept it forms of that object. The concept formed in the mind is thus rooted in the spiritual world, to which the essence of the object belongs. This concept is then expressed in the name given to the thing. Opposing the Realists, the Nominalists argued against any such "reality of ideas." Words are merely empty sounds without any

Fig. 6.9. Ushabti figure.
New Kingdom.

intrinsic reference to things, let alone spiritual things like essences, and hence are without any intrinsic meaning. Words are applied to things simply for the convenience of the human beings who use them. Rather than our concepts laying hold of some spiritual essence of an object, the Nominalists argued that they are applied arbitrarily to objects. The meanings of the words that express concepts are agreed upon solely on the basis of human convention, and they express nothing of the inner nature of things in themselves.

Needless to say, it was the Nominalist view that won the day, and it has, in the centuries since that time, become deeply embedded in the Western mind. But the seriousness, and indeed ferocity, of the dispute between the Nominalists and the Realists in the Middle Ages should make us pause to consider both the historical and the epistemological relativity of our modern view. We can get a flavor of the premedieval perspective on this question if we turn to one of Plato's dialogues. In his *Cratylus*, the question of the metaphysical status of words is raised only to be summarily resolved on the side of the Realists, whereupon the rest of the dialogue concerns itself with elucidating the relationship of words to spiritual essences. In the dialogue, it is argued that the phonetic components of words—vowels, consonants, and mutes—express universal principles or energies that are also made manifest in the natural world. The whole of nature can be regarded as sound materialized, each creature visibly embodying a spiritual concordance of sounds, that human beings are then able to reexpress in language. A direct relationship thus exists between the sounds we utter and the things to which our utterances refer.[37] This, of course, is to imply that language is originally sacred, the sound elements of which it is composed reexpressing the divine creative power sounded forth in the Beginning. Throughout the dialogue, we are given the impression that the whole subject is sacred: reflection on the correctness of names involves contemplating superhuman powers.[38]

Plato is both closer in time and closer in spirit to the ancient Egyptian attitude toward words. The Egyptians had absolute faith in the divine origin of sound and in its creative power. As we have seen (chap. 3), the world of beings and objects comes into existence through the utterance of primordial sound. In the Memphite theology, the primordial sound is pronounced by the Ennead of gods, whose role in creation is defined in terms of their being "the teeth and lips in that great mouth which gave all things their names."[39] For the Egyptians, the world is sound made substantial. This was no abstract dogma—it was a truth lived out in the practice of magic.

Uttered ritualistically and with the appropriate intonation, every noun, verb, and adjective assumes substantiality and life. In the sacred language of ancient Egypt there is, or was, the possibility of a complete harmony between the verbal form and the spiritual content that it expressed, so that the latter could be brought into manifestation by the former. We no longer know how ancient Egyptian was pronounced: the vowel sounds in particular are not known to us. But according to Iamblichus, who was not alone in this view, the language of the Egyptians was "adapted to sacred concerns" for it arose through "having mingled the names of the gods with their own tongue." Iamblichus regarded ancient Egyptian as a language closer to the original "divine language" than his own much less ancient mother tongue of Greek.[40] Considering these opinions of Iamblichus, one becomes aware of how different was the feeling for language in ancient times from our own. If the language of the ancient Egyptians was "suspended from the very nature of things," as Iamblichus says it was, then it provided the basis—the experiential basis—of the magical spell that, when recited by one who was "true of voice," could bring into manifestation something that previously existed on a spiritual plane.[41]

There are many stories that have come down to us that relate the extraordinary feats of magicians in this respect. What lies behind these often apparently fantastical stories is not, however, pure fantasy. Rather it is a buried metaphysical teaching concerning the formative power of sound. An arduous training in the House of Life was the prerequisite for a magician to become "true of voice," for such skill could not be attained without intimate knowledge of divine powers. The magician had to learn the true names of things, the names given to them by the gods, in order to be able effectively to activate magic. In other words, the magician had to penetrate to the inner divine core of language, to the mysterious potency of sound.

It is no coincidence that Thoth, the Lord of Speech, who in the Beginning uttered the primordial sounds that thickened into tangible substances and thus brought into existence the world, was also the originator of writing. For in the hieroglyphic writing of the Egyptians the link between sounds and images is crucial; what the phonogram does is retain the link between a perceptible form and a sound value. Hence hieroglyphic writing is literally "sacred" (hieros) "carving" (glypho). To become master of the hieroglyphic script was to be initiated into the mystery of the relationship between sound and form. It also meant becoming initiated into the iconography displayed in the ideograms. According to Schwaller de Lubicz, "hieroglyphic writing is the ultimate esoteric symbolic writing, in the figuration of its signs as well as their color and placement."[42]

Figure 6.10 is an example of the hieroglyphic script as it appeared,

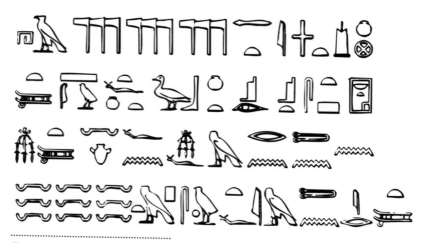

....

Fig. 6.10. The outward form of the hieroglyphic script, inseparably wedded to its inner content. Pyramid Text. Sixth Dynasty.

carved on the inner walls of the pyramids of the Sixth Dynasty. The text is addressed to the Ennead of Heliopolis, and can be translated as follows:

> *O you great Ennead which is in Heliopolis,*
> *Atum, Shu, Tefnut, Geb, Nut, Osiris, Isis, Seth and Nephthys,*
> *whom Atum, in giving birth to himself,*
> *brought into the world through the projection of his heart,*
> *in your name of Nine Bows.*
> *None of you is separate from Atum.*[43]

Looking at the hieroglyphs, and then looking at the translation, we may feel that through the translation we gain some access to the meaning of the text. But we cannot avoid also feeling that something is irretrievably lost when the hieroglyphs are converted into our alphabetic script. Does not our script seem dead by comparison? No matter how poetic the language we use in our attempt to convey the resonance of the hieroglyphs, it nevertheless falls short of their living content. Our script is the product of a different mentality. Its outward form displays no symbols, it harbors no secrets, it demands from its practitioners no reverence.

The reverential attitude of the ancient Egyptians toward their script is evidenced in the following words of Amenophis, son of Hapu, who lived during the Eighteenth Dynasty: "I was educated in the god's book and I

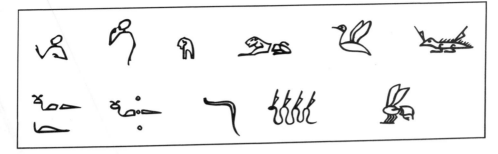

Fig. 6.11. Examples of hieroglyphs rendered harmless by mutilation.

looked on the tools of Thoth [hieroglyphic script]; I was prepared in their secrets and I delved into all their difficult passages." Or again, in the claim of Amenemhet Surer (also Eighteenth Dynasty) that he was "master of the secrets of the divine words [i.e., hieroglyphics]."[44]

Like the spoken word, the written word could draw into existence, or gain power over, the beings that it named. Like the carved or painted image, the written word could become imbued with the life of the thing or creature it represented. The practice of mutilating hieroglyphs arose out of an experience of the written word as potentially alive. In figure 6.11, the hieroglyphs representing dangerous animals have been knifed, cut in half, or decapitated in order to render them harmless. For the ancient Egyptians, words literally gave life to the realities to which they referred. All representations were capable of becoming the thing represented.

It was for this reason that, in the case of sacred manuscripts, simply to come into posession of the manuscript was considered sufficient to possess the power that the written words articulated. To eat it was even better.

RITUAL ACTS

In addition to sacred words and images, the activation of magic requires sacred actions. What makes an action sacred is its becoming filled with spiritual content. As with the hieroglyph, the spoken word, or the symbolic image, so also can the human gesture act as the mediator of a spiritual power. The gesture becomes spiritually potent, swelling up with an otherwise imperceptible content, as a sponge swells with water.

The sacred action is the action performed ritually. What is it that makes an action ritual? What is it that makes it into a rite? At the heart of the ritual action is the fact that it is no longer personal. The ritual gesture is not the gesture of this particular person, the individual who makes it. Likewise the sequence of ritual postures and deeds is not performed by a personality as such, but by a human being who has become the vehicle of *heka* in order that through this person *heka* may be activated. The priest-magician makes him- or herself into a kind of hieroglyph or sequence of hieroglyphs embodying and conducting powers that transcend the level of mundane reality. This is the overwhelming impression of so much Egyptian art that portrays human beings: what is being portrayed are potent ritual gestures and postures that do not express anything of the character of the individuals concerned, but seem rather to make the individual into an icon bearing a wealth of symbolic meanings (fig. 6.12).

It is fitting, therefore, that the master magician of all Egypt, the king, should have lived a life whose every detail was ritualized. According to Diodorus, every hour of the day and night was planned out in accordance with the ritual requirements of his office. This extended beyond his administrative duties to his personal life, which was so thoroughly regulated that his freedom to take a walk, to bathe, and even to sleep with his wife were all subject to control.[45] While it is true that by Diodorus's time, these things had gone to an extreme, they nevertheless reveal a basic attitude toward ritual that the Egyptians always held. An action that is not ritualized is merely human: through ritualized action, the human being becomes a mediator of the divine.

Ritual action is invocatory; by means of it the magician invokes spiritual powers. The ritual act thus takes place as much in the spiritual dimension as in the physical. Rituals occur in the realm of the gods; the gods are necessarily witnesses of and participants in the sacred rites—for this is precisely what makes them sacred. For this reason the ancient Egyptians, and other peoples throughout the ancient world (as well as those traditional cultures that survive today such as the Coggi of northern Colombia) maintained that their rituals were performed not only for the benefit of their specific human community, but for the benefit of the world as a whole. It is evident that the coronation ritual, for example, held a cosmic significance for the Egyptians. In the words of the hymn composed for the coronation of Merneptah, the results of this human-divine event are that

> *Water is plentiful,*
> *and the Nile carries a high flood.*
> *The days are long, the nights have hours.*
> *and the months come in due order.*
> *The gods are content and their hearts are happy,*
> *and life is spent in laughter and wonder.*[46]

Fig. 6.12. A selection of ritual gestures, each of which bears a distinctive meaning and evokes an archetypal mood. Top, left to right: submission, rejoicing, offering. Bottom, left to right: salutation, praise, offering. Various Old and New Kingdom sources.

As Frankfort has said, rituals such as this, and others included in the major festivals—like, for instance, the raising of the *djed* column—"are not merely symbolical: they are part and parcel of the cosmic events; they are man's share in these events."[47]

It is this conviction that underlies the apparently megalomaniacal "threats" made by magicians against the gods, should they fail to comply with the magicians' demands. The ancient Egyptian magician was deeply aware of the interdependence between the divine world and the human world. In this chapter we have seen how in those times these two spheres were not experienced as separate from each other in the way that they have come to be experienced today. It was the role of the magician, especially, to live in relationship to, and act as a conduit for, heavenly forces. The cosmos of which the magician was aware was primarily spiritual and only secondarily and, as it were, by derivation, material. Magicians aimed to bring their actions to life in the spiritual dimension toward which their consciousness was directed. The magical ritual was the bridge thrown between physical and spiritual reality, momentarily bringing them into conjunction.

7 THE PRACTICE OF MAGIC

A variety of techniques through which magic was applied can be found in ancient Egyptian texts. We shall consider five of the most important and, in so doing, it will become apparent how the various factors already discussed come into play in the utilization of these techniques.

Invoking the First Time

Central to all magical techniques was the invocation of the First Time.[1] By the First Time, the Egyptians meant the nontemporal realm in which archetypal events enacted by the gods take place. The First Time is the realm of myth, and hence of spiritual realities more powerful than anything merely physical. By identifying a given terrestial event with an archetypal First Time event, the former could become charged with a supramundane content. This was achieved through an act of invocation in which the supramundane or archetypal reality was brought down into the mundane, suffusing the latter with spiritual power. The technique could equally well be described as a projection of the mundane into the archetypal, causing a fusion of the temporal event with a spiritual paradigm. However we describe it, we are dealing with essentially one and the same magical act: the linking together of heavenly and earthly realities.

We come across examples of this technique applied as a matter of course in the functioning of the kingship. As the god incarnate in human form, the king of Egypt lived in two worlds, the heavenly and the earthly. His royal duties consisted largely of ensuring that his actions were an expression of the inner union of these two worlds in the office of kingship. As we have seen (chap. 5), the appearance of the pharaoh on ceremonial occasions was described as a "shining forth"—the verb being the same as that used to describe the first appearance of Ra on the Primordial Hill.[2] The king's appearance was thereby symbolically fused with the theophany of Ra in the First Time. In figure 7.1, the radiant king (in this case Tutankhamon) gives audience to the governor of Ethiopia, Huy, who stands before him with eyes lowered, holding a fan. Like the disk of the sun, the king's forehead is protected by the divine, fire-spitting cobra (*uraeus*). Like any god, he holds in his right hand the *ankh* sign of life. His canopy above is adorned with cobras; beneath his seat are lapwings, symbolizing the people of Egypt giving praise. Beside the king are written his names, "The King of Upper and Lower Egypt," "The god Ra for all beings," "the Son of Ra." The king here is portrayed as the image of Ra on earth.

In the New Kingdom Papyrus Anastasi, a model for a letter to the king is recorded that throughout emphasizes his solar nature: "Turn your face to me, O rising sun that illumines the Two Lands with its beauty! O sun of mankind, who banishes darkness from Egypt . . ."[3] This is not flattery; it is protocol that serves a specific magical function. In numerous texts, the ideas of creation, sunrise, and kingly rule are constantly merged. Thereby, the king is linked to the primordial realm of the gods, specifically the sun god on whom the life and prosperity of Egypt depended.

Serving the same purpose, the king's day commenced with a ritual known as the "toilet ceremony," which began before dawn, and in which the king was washed, censed, and given balls of natron to chew. Each of these ritual acts was magical. They corresponded to the cosmic and mythical event of the sun god's rebirth from the waters of Nun (washing), becoming Horus-of-the-Horizon (censing), and being reborn into the Upperworld (chewing natron). The king then ascended the stairs of the Temple of the Morning at exactly the same moment as his heavenly father Ra rose above the horizon. Just as the sun was purified and reborn each morning in the Temple Beneath the Horizon, then ascended into the sky, so the king underwent the same daily ritual. In this way the toilet ceremony projected him into the First Time in a repeated fusion of temporal and eternal realities, through which his identity as image of Ra on earth was daily reestablished.[4] Countless other rituals in which the king enacted a cosmic or heavenly event on earth were regularly performed. It was from their performance that the kingship derived its extraordinary power. This type of magic, then, in which human actions were aligned with supra-

Fig. 7.1. The king as image of Ra gives audience. Tomb of Huy. Eighteenth Dynasty.

human mythical events, was crucial to the successful functioning of the kingship.

This, of course, is state magic: magic practiced as part and parcel of the successful running of the Egyptian state. Magic held a central place in statecraft, which was never a merely secular business. A particularly vivid example of the practice of magic by the state involves a further elaboration of the mystical identification of the king and Ra. In time of war, the priesthood would engage in a variety of magic rites, one of which consisted in

149

identifying the enemy with Apophis, the archdemon of the Underworld and chief opponent of Ra. It would be unlikely that such rites were not performed by the magician-priests accompanying the forces of Ramesses II at Kadesh (chap. 5). As representative of the forces of destruction and chaos, Apophis is eternally vanquished by Ra in the Underworld. This is a mythical event, an eternal truth enacted in the First Time. By magically identifying the enemies of Egypt with the serpent Apophis, the Apophis archetype was made to adhere to the enemy in such a way that their defeat at the hands of Pharaoh, the son of Ra, was inevitable.

In the inscriptions recording the various accounts of the battle of Kadesh, there is no mention of the performance of magic rites. But in order to accomplish the adhesion of an archetypal pattern of events to a temporal situation, such as is described in the various Kadesh inscriptions, a complex of rituals would almost certainly have been necessary. Normally, a model of Apophis had to be made and indissolubly united to the enemy. Then the model was struck, pierced with knives, spat upon, and burnt,[5] while priests chanted a spell for "repulsing the serpent," such as follows:

> Back rebel, for his light is piercing.
> Ra has overthrown your words.
> Your face has been turned upside down by the gods;
> your heart has been torn out by the panther.
> You have been bound by the scorpion;
> your pain has been caused by Maat. . . .
> Fall, turn aside Apophis, enemy of Ra.[6]

In figure 7.2, the archetype of this ritual is shown, in which Apophis is caught and bound by Selkit (the scorpion goddess) in the Underworld. She is assisted by another god who lassoes his tail. Selkit knifes Apophis in six places, thereby destroying his power.

Beyond statecraft, invocation of the First Time was a common magical practice. We see it utilized, for instance, as a medical technique. In myth, Horus is badly wounded by Seth but is restored by his mother Isis. This archetypal pattern could be applied to a patient in a similarly dangerous condition to that of Horus. As the patient's bandages were taken off, the patient identified inwardly with Horus. In the text that follows, the patient first invokes the First Time event,

> Unbound he was, unbound he was by Isis.
> Unbound was Horus by Isis,

from all the evil done to him by his brother Seth,
when Seth killed his father Osiris.

Then the patient prays to Isis,

Oh Isis, great magician, unbind me;
deliver me from all evil, harmful and red things;
from a god's illness and from a goddess's illness;
from male death and from female death;
from male enemies and female enemies
who will come against me.[7]

The prayer is uttered as if the patient were Horus addressing his mother. In this way, the aid of the goddess is enlisted.

A second example also involves an incident in the life of the god Horus. As an infant, the young god is in serious danger when fire breaks out. His mother Isis, finding no water to hand, extinguishes the flames with milk from her own breasts. It was thus that the milk of a woman who had given birth to a boy was an essential ingredient in a mixture of substances used for the treatment of burns.[8] The glazed terracotta vase reproduced in figure 7.3 is shaped in the form of a woman with a child feeding from one breast, while she proffers the other breast with her other hand. Several vases like this have survived, and they were intended to hold human milk, for medicinal use.

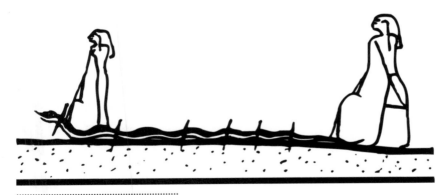

Fig. 7.2. Knifing and binding Apophis. Book of What Is in the Underworld, division 7. Tomb of Ramesses VI.

Fig. 7.3. Vase for holding human milk, used medicinally. Louvre, Paris.

Many further examples could be given to illustrate this fundamental magical technique of bringing about a conjunction of a temporal situation with a mythical event of the First Time. The effectiveness of this practice lay in the apprehension of the mythical as the truly real, as the spiritual repository and source of patterns of events that can occur on the mundane level. By conjoining the latter with a mythical paradigm, the mundane undergoes radical transformation, becoming injected with spiritual content.

Identifying With Gods

A second technique closely related to, and often forming an intrinsic part of, the invocation of a First Time event was the practice of identifying with a First Time entity, namely, a god. As we have seen, the defeat of the enemies of Egypt required the affirmation both that Apophis was manifesting in the guise of the enemy and that Ra was manifesting in the guise of the king. If these identifications were not properly established, the invocation of the First Time event of Apophis's eternal defeat by Ra would have been of little use. Beyond the realm of state magic, identification with gods was necessary if

Fig. 7.4. Anubis leans over a mummy. Papyrus of Nekhtu-Amen. New Kingdom.

one wished to attune oneself wholly to the energy of a particular god or divine principle. (The word *neter* is inadequately translated by our word "god," as it has connotations that are much more subtle than the simple personality type that we tend to associate, for instance, with Greek or Roman gods. "Divine principle" probably comes closer to the Egyptian understanding of *neter*).

In figure 7.4 Anubis, the god of embalming, leans over a mummy. This is a common enough image in Egyptian art, especially of the New Kingdom, and it is readily passed over without our remarking any more than "Ah, that is Anubis, god of embalming, leaning over a mummy." On reflection, however, we recall the fact that embalmment was actually carried out not by a god but by human beings. Or was it? At certain stages of the rites of embalming the body, the priests of Anubis responsible for the process wore masks in the form of a jackal's head over their faces. One such mask has been found dating from the Twenty-sixth Dynasty, but we know that this practice goes back to the earliest historical period.[9] In figure 7.5, a priest wearing a jackal mask is guiding a second priest. The wearing of the jackal mask was evidently intended to precipitate a mystical identification of the person wearing the mask with the god.

When we look at illustrations of ancient Egyptian funerary rites, we should remember therefore that, when Anubis is represented, we are in all likelihood seeing a priest who is enacting the role of the god. In figure 7.6 the figure supporting the upright mummy case may be viewed as

Fig. 7.5. A priest guides another priest who wears the jackal mask of Anubis. Late Period.

an incarnation of the god in human form. The priest has undergone a magical transformation in which he has *become* the god. Perhaps, after all, it makes little difference if we say: "Ah, now there is a priest wearing a jackal mask!" or if we return to our original statement; "There is Anubis."

This example must make us wonder to what extent in ancient Egyptian art representations of gods in human or semihuman form were in fact often human beings who had magically "become" the god in question. This is not to say that they were all human beings wearing masks. For while it is known that masks were used for purposes of ritual identification, mask wearing was just one, and by no means the only, way of effecting union with the energy of a particular deity or *neter*. As we saw in chapter 6 the ancient Egyptians regarded their language as the medium of divine powers, whose essential vitality could come to expression in the sounds and symbolic images of the hieroglyphs. Hence by assuming the name of a god, or magically endowing another person with that name, it was possible for a person to resonate with the energy of that god. We know, for instance, that the ritual Songs of Isis and Nephthys that were sung at the temple of Amon-Ra at Thebes were performed by two virgins "with the hair of their bodies removed, their heads adorned with wigs, tambourines in their hands, and the names 'Isis' and 'Nephthys' inscribed on their shoulders."[10] For the purposes of the rite, the two virgins were identified with the goddesses not simply through role playing, but through the power of the name.

In the Book of the Dead there exist a series of "Chapters of Transformation" in which the Underworld traveller is provided with spells to metamorphose into a variety of animals sacred to different *neters*—the swallow (sacred to Hathor), the hawk (sacred to Horus), the crocodile (sacred to Sobek), the heron (sacred to Osiris), and so on.[11] Each chapter is supplied with an image of the creature along with a complex and highly metaphysical sequence of thoughts with elaborate mythical allusions. It is as if, by a combination of visualizing the sacred animal and sinking oneself into the metaphysical and mythical content of the text, one has the possibility of becoming attuned to the specific energy of the *neter* with whom one wishes to merge.

Fig. 7.6. A priest as Anubis or Anubis as a priest. Papyrus of Hunefer. Eighteenth Dynasty.

Figure 7.7 belongs to one of these chapters (chapter 86). It shows a swallow perching on top of a mound. The chapter, which is for transforming oneself into a swallow—the divine manifestation of Hathor—begins: "I am a swallow, I am a swallow. I am the scorpion, the daughter of Ra."

The reference to the scorpion is to the goddess Selkit, whom we have already met lassoing and knifing Apophis. The text goes on to describe how the Underworld traveller longs to be "in the Island of Flame," in other words, the First Land that is the original manifestation of Ra in the primordial ocean of Nun. To reach the blissful state of consciousness that the island symbolizes, it is necessary to pass through the doors (and doorkeepers) that bar the way. To achieve this aim, the text offers many potent affirmations to be repeated by the Underworld traveller. It stresses, for example, the inner purity of the traveller, as well as a high degree of esoteric knowledge. All this is intrinsic to what it means to "become a swallow," and thereby to become attuned (as the swallow is) to the sacred energy of Hathor.

In a very different but nevertheless comparable way, the king could, in

Fig. 7.7. The vignette accompanying chapter 86 of the Book of the Dead, "for transforming into a swallow"—the sacred bird of Hathor. Papyrus of Ani. Eighteenth Dynasty.

various situations, draw on—or be drawn into—the supernatural energy of a god such as Seth, becoming infused with that deity's abundant destructive potential. In the battle of Kadesh inscriptions, Ramesses describes himself as being "like Month," and as appearing to the enemy as "Seth great-of-strength" and "Baal in person." The enemy are made to say, "No deeds of man are these his doings!"[12] Similarly, Thutmosis III, another warrior king, could be described as going into battle with "the strength of Seth pervading his limbs."[13]

Depending on the circumstances, one might seek to identify now with one god, now with another. In practice what this meant was that the psyche became imbued with or possessed by a spiritual force, and thus underwent a momentary, or perhaps even a lasting, transmutation. Today, we are only beginning to emerge from a kind of collective amnesia concerning these spiritual forces with which the Egyptians were so familiar. No doubt a long period of forgetfulness and ignorance has been necessary in order to develop a type of self-possessed consciousness that was not experienced by the ancient Egyptians. By "self-possessed" is to be understood a consciousness whose moods, emotions, thoughts, and impulses are regarded as belonging to oneself rather than as deriving from gods acting upon—or taking possession of—the soul. The modern belief that the contents of consciousness are subjective in the sense of "belonging to" the subject who experiences them is the outcome of a historical process that has taken place since ancient Egyptian times. One result of this process is that the idea of freedom can be applied to the inner life. The notion that we are free to choose how we act and must therefore take responsibility for our actions is a distinctively post-Egyptian idea, first formulated in the fourth century B.C. by Aristotle.[14] It is for this reason that the techniques of Egyptian magic cannot simply be appropriated by us today. On the other hand, because our modern consciousness is unfamiliar with the spiritual world of which the Egyptians were so evidently aware, it is important that we guard against the modern tendency to dismiss it as merely idle superstition or fantasy. Rather, the task is to develop the faculties that would enable us, from the ground of our modern "self-possessed" consciousness, to approach the gods once more.

In addition to identifying wholly with an individual god or goddess in order to accomplish superhuman things, it was also a common practice to identify oneself part by part with a number of different deities: the head, for example, with Horus; the limbs with the children of Horus; other members with Shu and Tefnut, and so on.[15] In the Book of the Dead, we find the following beautiful spell that systematically works down the body, identifying each part of the body with a god—literally imbuing it with the energy of that god:

> *My hair is Nun;*
> *my face is Ra;*
> *my eyes are Hathor;*
> *my ears are Upuat;*
> *my lips are Anubis;*
> *my molars are Selkit;*
> *my incisors are Isis the goddess;*
> *my arms are the ram, Lord of Mendes;*
> *my breast is Neith, Lady of Sais;*
> *my back is Seth;*
> *my phallus is Osiris;*
> *my muscles are the lords of Kheraha;*
> *my chest is He Who is Greatly Majestic;*
> *my belly and my spine are Sekhmet;*
> *my buttocks are the Eye of Horus;*
> *my thighs and my calves are Nut;*
> *my feet are Ptah;*
> *my toes are living falcons;*
> *there is no member of mine devoid of a god,*
> *and Thoth is the protection of all my flesh.*[16]

The first seven deities are shown in figure 7.8, which belongs to this text. They are, from left to right: Nun, Ra, Hathor, Upuat, Anubis, Selkit, and Isis. It is not hard to imagine how in sickness, or in health, this invocatory sequence of identifications would have had an empowering effect on the individual concerned.

Fig. 7.8. The gods into whom the body is transformed. Papyrus of Ani. Eighteenth Dynasty.

Confronting Demons and Invoking the Aid of Gods

The psychic openness of the ancient Egyptians to the spiritual influences that pervaded their world meant not only that a person could become possessed by a god, or absorb the specific qualities of perhaps several gods, but that there was also the possibility of becoming possessed by hostile spirits. If a demon entered into a person, then sickness was the usual consequence. In such cases the most effective way of treating the sickness was to address its spiritual cause. The ancient Egyptians would not have understood the peculiarly modern attitude toward illness that views it simply as a result of physical causes such as viruses. For them, everything physical was the effect or outward expression of a spiritual agency. If a person became ill, the illness was a sign that a spiritual event had taken place. Indeed, the illness itself was often regarded as a hostile spirit, or the manifestation of a demon that had entered into the person. In this case, the only viable treatment of the illness was to confront the demon directly, and drive it out.

The effectiveness of a doctor therefore lay less in his remedies than in his ability to tackle demons. This is not to say that the remedies were dispensable: they too were necessary for the healing of body and soul. But crucial to their efficacy was the spiritual power that they carried. Weidemann writes:

> the medicines administered . . . owed much of their virtue to spells repeated during their preparation. The cure was not due to the medicines, but to the conquest by spells and powerful magic symbols of

the demon who had entered into the man and caused his suffering. With the departure of the demon the sickness ended.[17]

The main action of the doctor took place on the spiritual level. First of all, the doctor, called to the bedside of the patient, had to identify the demon that was causing the illness. He then concocted a suitable remedy, instilling it with magic potency through reciting certain incantations. The purpose of the remedy was to make the body of the patient a particularly difficult and unpleasant habitation for the demon, while at the same time building up the strength of the patient.[18]

Before administering the remedy, it was necessary for the doctor first of all to engage the demon. If we imagine the patient has a serious cold, the doctor talks to the cold, quietly at first. He tells it that it has no place in the patient's body, it feels ill at ease there, it would far rather be somewhere else. He tells it that it has no power over the patient, it is weak, it is feeble, it has no power at all. The doctor lulls the cold demon into a state of inertia, leading it into a condition of impotence and defenselessness. Suddenly, when the demon is least prepared for it, he shouts out:

> *Begone Cold, son of Cold!*
> *You who breaks bones,*
> *Who shatters the skull,*
> *Who digs into the brain,*
> *so that sickness overtakes the seven openings of the head*
> *which are the servants of Ra, and the praise-singers of Thoth,*
> *See, I have brought the remedy against you!*[19]

The doctor then repeats this whole process several times before administering the remedy, first quietly draining away the demon's self-confidence, then haranguing it aggressively. One could imagine that this relentless psychic bombardment would be enough to make the fiercest demon feel decidedly uncomfortable. It is then that the doctor gives the remedy to the patient, who is required to say words of welcome to the remedy as he or she receives it. Words such as:

> *Welcome remedy, welcome,*
> *you who destroys the trouble in my heart*
> *and in these my limbs.*
> *This magic of Horus*
> *is victorious in the remedy.*[20]

In and through the remedy, the god Horus engages in battle with the demon. Thus the sickness was, in effect, projected as an aspect of Seth into the First Time, where its defeat was inevitable.

Horus in particular was the god with special power over the venomous bites of snakes and the stings of scorpions, as well as the bites of other dangerous animals. In the Late Period, Horus is often shown standing on top of one or more crocodiles, while he holds in his hands poisonous snakes, scorpions, and ferocious wild animals. These are all reduced to a state of utter helplessness by his superior magic. In figure 7.9, he appears in typical pose, standing on a submissive crocodile and grasping in his hands scorpions and snakes, a gazelle, and a lion. Above his head is the mask of the god Bes, a god whose role at this time was protector of the family. To the left stands Ra-Horakhti on a serpent, and to the right is a lotus surmounted by two plumes symbolizing triumph over the forces of death.

In the treatment of snakebite, a similar procedure to the one described above for driving out the cold demon was followed. But in this case the doctor invokes the god Horus by first making an image of the god out of wood—a little painted wooden hawk with two feathers stuck on its head. By reciting certain words of power, using an "opening of the mouth" formula, the doctor was able to bring the god into the statuette. The wooden image became filled with the presence of the god, with what one might call "Horus energy." The statue of Horus then underwent all the ritual procedures that normally applied to the images of gods. It was censed, symbolically anointed, offered bread and beer, and so on. All this secured the benevolent presence of the deity. The image was then carefully placed on the face of the person suffering from the snakebite, or over the area where he or she was bitten. Then the doctor said loudly:

> *Flow out, poison!*
> *Scatter yourself on the ground!*
> *Horus curses you, he wipes you out!*
> *He grinds you underfoot!*
>
> *You are weak and not strong,*
> *You do not fight,*
> *You are blind and do not see,*
> *Your head hangs,*
> *And you do not lift your face.*
> *You are turned back,*
> *And you cannot find your way.*

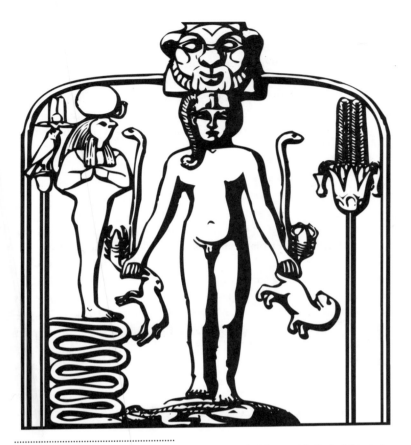

Fig. 7.9. Horus, the victor over dangerous animals. Metternich Stele. Thirtieth Dynasty.

> *You mourn and do not rejoice.*
> *You creep away,*
> *And are not seen again.*
> *So speaks Horus the Great Magician![21]*

The direct confrontation of demon spirits was of course by no means restricted to the treatment of illnesses. In the Book of the Dead, there are many examples of "psychic situations" in which the Underworld traveller might have to identify and name an opposing spirit (not an easy task), and then have recourse to pronouncing words of power against it.[22] This is really the opposite process to invoking a god or goddess although, as we have seen, it might involve the latter. Rather than seeking to become imbued with a specific spiritual energy, one was seeking to free oneself from it. It was necessary, therefore, to objectify it, to distinguish it from oneself, and then to drive this particular influence out of one's psychic environment. Or, put another way, one had oneself to pass out of *its* psychic influence. Normally, in order to do this, one needed to summon the help of a benevolent spiritual agency with sufficient power to overcome the negative influence.

Threatening the Gods

Magicians, however, did not always have a supplicatory approach to the gods. By definition, a master magician was totally familiar with, and expert at handling, divine energies. *Heka* was prior to the gods (as we saw in chap. 6) and so a magician at one with *heka* was capable of exercising control over the gods. Jacq goes so far as to define the meaning of *heka* as "to control the powers."[23] In the Pyramid Texts the king, in his role of master magician, was purported to have had extraordinary authority in the spirit world. In the so-called Cannibal Hymn, the magician-king is depicted as a terrifying ogre:

> *The sky is overcast,*
> *the stars rain down,*
> *constellations shake,*
> *the very bones of the earth-god tremble . . .*
> *when they see him appear as a living god*
> *who lives on his fathers and feeds on his mothers.*
>
> *He is the one who eats men and lives on gods.*
> *He is the one who eats their magic*
> *and devours their glory.*
> *The biggest of them are for his breakfast,*
> *the middle-sized are for his dinner,*
> *and the smallest of them are for his supper.*[24]

The imagery of eating was often used in the context of magic to express the notion of the complete integration of magical powers within a person. The master magician was capable of placing himself, as it were, at the hub of the universe of the gods (the *neters*), assimilating their power into himself. From such a position, the energies of the gods were at his command.

Uttering threats at the gods may seem an outrageous way to proceed, but it can be understood if we accept that *heka* itself was a force upon which the gods depended, and that the magician was able to act with or through *heka*. An example of how this might work is to be found in the text of the Metternich Stele.[25] Here Isis, who with Thoth was traditionally the deity through whom the ability to manipulate *heka* was gained, is described as being distraught because her son Horus has been stung by a scorpion. Letting forth a great cry to heaven, she causes the oarsmen of the sun boat to cease from rowing. The sun thus comes to a standstill in the sky, and Isis threatens not to allow the sun boat to continue its journey until Horus is healed. Incapable of proceeding on his journey, Ra sends to Isis the god Thoth, endowed with the requisite healing power, who says to her:

> *O Isis, goddess, glorious one,*
> *who has knowledge of how to use your mouth,*
> *no evil shall come upon the child Horus,*
> *for his protection comes from the boat of Ra.*[26]

Thoth then speaks the words of power that restore Horus to life.

It can be seen from this example that a magician needs only to have sufficient *heka* necessary to cause a major disruption in the cosmic order to force the required events to take place. Isis utilizes her "knowledge of how to use her mouth" to force Ra to send Thoth to heal her son Horus. This illustrates the way in which *heka* could be employed to control the gods. As the story features relationships between Isis, Ra, Thoth, and Horus, it is a First Time prototype, and hence was capable of being reactivated by a magician-healer, taking the role of Isis.

In order to understand the use of threats against the gods it is essential to realize that in the ancient Egyptian world there was a basic continuum between nature and the supernatural, and furthermore, a sense of self-location firmly within the divine-natural world order. The ancient Egyptians did not see themselves and the natural-supernatural world as functioning independently. Their experience of themselves in the world was primarily participatory. In all the temples of the land, what took place was by no means simply "worship" of the gods. It was rather the performance of rites that ensured the maintenance of the world order. The rising of the sun each day, the cycle of the seasons, the inundation of the Nile—all were dependent upon the sacred rituals enacted in the temples and upon festival occasions. As Henri Frankfort has said, "We must remember again that such rituals are not merely symbolical; they are part and parcel of the cosmic events; they are man's share in these events."[27] It is thus that we must understand the religion of ancient Egypt as magical. Magic implies a consciousness that is participatory: hence withdrawal of human participation in cosmic and natural cycles would be catastrophic for both nature and the gods.

The following example shows clearly how important the performance of temple rites for the gods was thought to be by the Egyptians. It again involves the use of threats to force the gods to intervene benevolently in a healing situation. A person is in mortal danger as a result of being poisoned. The magician says:

> If the poison spreads through the body,
> if it ventures into any part of the body,
> there will be no offerings laid upon the offering tables in the temples,
> no water will be poured over the altars,
> no fire will be lit in a room of the temple,
> no cattle will be led to the table of sacrifice,
> no piece of meat will be taken to the temple.
> But if the poison falls to earth,
> all the temples will be overjoyed,
> the gods will be happy in their sanctuaries.[28]

Now we might think that the only beings to be adversely affected by such a threat would be human beings, because they would lose the goodwill of the gods. But for the Egyptians, human actions had cosmic results, especially the sacred actions performed in temple rites. The gods were to a large extent in a relationship of dependency upon human beings whose religious activity involved the mobilization of *heka*.

It is from the perspective of this wider religious sensibility that we have to understand the use of threats in the practice of magic. If a doctor threatens that the sky will fall and the light disappear unless his patient is cured,[29] this is possible only because human beings in general experienced themselves to be inserted right into the heart of the cosmos. They were not "outsiders" looking upon a world in which they felt they did not belong. They were, on the contrary, so completely a part of the universe that they could potentially exercise extraordinary, supernatural influence within it.

Reordering Nature

In this final section we shall consider a certain type of magical practice that gave rise to phenomena that would seem to us to contravene the laws of nature. In considering this type of magic, we should remember that the idea of incontrovertible laws of nature did not exist before the scientific revolution. The concept of natural law—that there are certain rules that nature must obey—is a modern idea, and it is symptomatic of our modern relationship to nature. We can talk about laws of nature only because we experience nature as wholly externalized from us and also from itself. The nature that exists for the modern scientific consciousness is a nature that has no interior; it has no soul. Hence, all that occurs in nature has to be explained in terms of blind "obedience" to laws, originally conceived in the seventeenth century as commands imposed by God upon the natural world. Paradoxically, the lifelessness of the nature that obeys these commands is contradicted by the terms of the analogy. For the analogy of natural law is clearly based on the relationship of living citizens to their rulers. The reason why this analogy came to be regarded as appropriate, however, is that people's experience of God had become separated from their experience of nature. The spiritual was not beheld within the world of sense experience, but was felt to occupy a separate sphere. Therefore, the connection between the divine and natural realms could only be conceived in terms of the most remote and impersonal kind of relationship; it could be nothing more intimate than "law."

In ancient Egypt, the experience of the relationship between nature and deity was otherwise. The sun did not go round the earth in obedience to law, but as an expression of the life of the sun deity who passed through the different spiritual phases of Kheprer, Ra, and Atum, which were imaged in the sun's daily cycle. The sun was the countenance of the divine. It transmitted into the natural sphere an interior spiritual life, much as people's faces transmit something of what goes on in their souls. As for the sun, so for all of nature as the Egyptians experienced it: nothing in nature was simply an "it"—all was animated and alive. In such a nature there can be no question of "laws," because human experience of nature is essentially an experience of spiritual entities active within the physical domain. The relationship of sun god to sun could not be that of a lawgiver any more than could that of human soul to bodily gesture; the one manifests through the other. The spiritual does not impose laws on the physical, but expresses itself in and through the physical.

The winds, for example, blowing from the four directions, were essentially spirits, and were represented as such. In figure 7.10, we see the north wind pictured with four rams' heads, the south wind with the head of a lion, the west wind serpent-headed, the east wind ram-headed again. Each wind spirit is visualized with four wings. Now, in just the same way as the demon of a sickness could be confronted on the spirit plane, so also could the wind spirits. Precisely because the winds were animated, they could be addressed directly by those who were conversant with the spirit world. Christians are familiar with the story of Christ's stilling the storm on the Sea of Galilee. In the Gospel of Matthew, we read how Christ "rose and

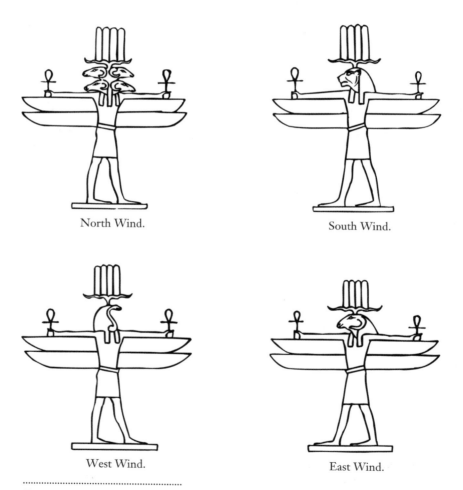

North Wind.

South Wind.

West Wind.

East Wind.

Fig. 7.10. The spirits of the four winds.

rebuked the winds and the sea; and there was a great calm."[30] The event is not described—and could not be described—in terms of Christ overturning "natural law"; rather, he "rebukes" the winds and the sea as if they were living entities. And so, of course, they were. It is only our modern consciousness that finds nature so hard to communicate with in personal terms.[31]

The event on the Sea of Galilee was, in fact, not so out of the ordinary even in Roman times. During the campaigns of Marcus Aurelius, an Egyptian holy man named Harnuphis saved the Roman army from disaster by causing a miraculous storm; and under the reign of Constantine a certain Sopater was executed on the charge of binding the winds by magic because the corn ships of Egypt and Syria were prevented by unfavorable winds from reaching Constantinople.[32] Throughout the ancient world, as in Egypt itself, the control of the elements through magical command of elemental spirits was an essential part of the practice of magic. As with the elemental spirits, so also with other important nature deities such as river gods, the lines of communication were direct. In Egypt, it was the king's special responsibility to ensure that the Nile rose at the right time and to the right degree, as both texts and rituals demonstrate. The pharaoh Merneptah, for instance, was given the credit for the high inundation that accompanied his accession, while the earlier king Amenemhet I could state in wonderfully animistic terms: "The Nile respected me at every defile."[33] We know of important rituals that were performed during the Twentieth Dynasty to promote such "respect" from the river. Offerings (usually a bull and geese) were sacrificed to the river at Silsileh in the name of the king in a special ceremony that also included throwing in a royal edict commanding the Nile to rise.[34] The title of the edict was "The Book Which Makes the Nile Come Forth from Its Source." In figure 7.11, the Nile god can be seen in his shrine at the source, within the protective coils of a cobra. In our age of big dams, and a purely technological attitude toward river control, this portrayal of the spirit of the river Nile, kneeling in his netherworld cavern, and needing to be coaxed forth with sacrifices and royal edicts, can still touch us. The Western mind seems so readily, and so ignorantly, to have acquiesced in the process by which the gentle spirits of nature have been bulldozed away that we may be prompted to ask ourselves, in all shame: What have we done? What have we become?

Control over the elements of wind and water is documented in the Bible in the well-known account recording the flight of the Israelites from Egypt. In Exodus 14, we read how Moses was able, by raising his staff and stretching his hand over the Red Sea (in Hebrew, *yam suph*, meaning the Sea of

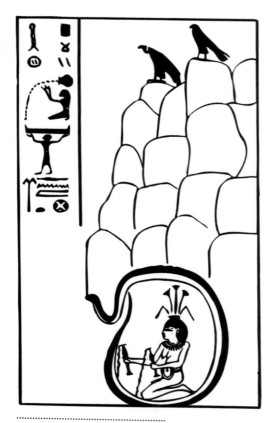

Fig. 7.11. The Nile god kneels in his netherworld shrine. Temple of Isis, Philae.

Reeds or Marshes, probably papyrus marshes in the Delta region) to part the waters. The text reads: "Moses stretched out his hand over the sea. Yahweh drove back the sea with a strong easterly wind all night, and he made dry land of the sea. The waters parted and the sons of Israel went on dry ground right into the sea, walls of water to right and left of them."[35]

Such spectacular feats of magical control over the elements were, as we have seen, by no means simply the prerogative of Moses and the god of the Israelites. It is not without significance that Moses was brought up within the Egyptian royal family, for it is likely that some training in magic would have been part of his education.

Division of waters was certainly a skill known to have been practiced by Egyptian magicians as far back as the Old Kingdom. The Papyrus Westcar relates how the Fourth Dynasty king Snefru (the predecessor of the better known Khufu or Cheops) was one afternoon enjoying a diversion from the cares of state by being rowed on his royal lake by twenty beautiful young women from his palace. Now it happened that one of these girls dropped her pendant in the water, and in her distress ceased rowing. Because she was the leader who set the stroke for all the girls on that side of the boat, they all stopped rowing. The result, we may imagine, is that the royal barge was soon going round in circles. King Snefru, finding himself unable to console the girl with promises of another pendant to replace the one she had lost, called for his chief magician, Zazamankh. Zazamankh hastened to reassure the king that all would be well. Then, stepping forward to the front of the boat, he proceeded to pronounce "words of power" over the waters. He then rolled back one side of the lake, piling it upon the other, so that a cliff of water was formed. The papyrus states: "Now, as for the water, it was twelve cubits deep in the middle, and it reached twenty-four cubits after it was turned back." As a consequence, the pendant could soon be discovered lying upon the exposed bed of the lake. The girl having retrieved it, Zazamankh once more pronounced words of power over the waters and returned the half of the lake that he had displaced to its original position.[36]

To the modern psyche, conditioned into viewing water as an inanimate substance obedient only to unchanging laws of nature, such a story must be dismissed as sheer fantasy. For the Egyptians, however, the story could have credence because they experienced everything in nature as ensouled and therefore as open to influence, persuasion, or even coercion. The type of possible interaction between human beings and the natural world extended beyond the range of what is generally accepted as possible today. The ancient Egyptian magician entered into relationship with the soul or spirit of an object, and working from this basis—a direct engagement on the soul or spiritual level—was able to induce changes in its physical behavior. Whether the episode recounted in the Westcar papyrus "really happened" is less the issue here than whether it is an event that can be understood within the context of the ancient Egyptian worldview. Whereas such events are incomprehensible in modern scientific terms and must therefore be dismissed by the adherents of the scientific view of the world, they are quite compatible with the animistic outlook of the ancient Egyptians. If a certain type of phenomenon is inexplicable within a certain set of presuppositions, but explicable within another, then perhaps we should question the adequacy of those presuppositions that fail to provide the groundwork for understanding the phenomenon, rather than question the reality of the phenomenon itself.

Let us consider a further example from the story of the conflict of the Israelites and the Egyptians, as related in Exodus. We read in Exodus 7 that Yahweh tells Moses: "If Pharaoh says to you 'Produce some marvel' you must say to Aaron: 'Take your staff and throw it down in front of Pharaoh, and let it turn into a serpent.'" Pharaoh duly asks Moses and Aaron to perform some marvel, and Aaron obliges by casting down his stick, which does indeed turn into a serpent (fig. 7.12). Exodus continues: "Then Pharaoh in his turn called for the sages and the sorcerers, and with their witchcraft the magicians of Egypt did the same. Each threw his staff down and these turned into serpents." Evidently, the feat of turning a stick into a snake was well within the powers of the magicians of Egypt. The point of the story, as it is told in the Bible, lies less in the performance of this act of transmu-

Fig. 7.12. Aaron turns his staff into a snake in front of an unmoved pharaoh. This was a feat easily matched by the magicians in Pharaoh's court.

tation than in the fact that Aaron's serpent swallowed up the serpents of Pharaoh's magicians, thus proving the superiority of Aaron's god.[37]

It is known from a range of Egyptian sources that the transmutation of something ostensibly inanimate into something animate was fundamental to the practice of Egyptian magic. It was part of the stock-in-trade of the magician-priest and practiced on a daily basis. In temples, for instance, the image of the pharaoh on the wall of the temple regularly became animated in and through the officiating priest. We have already considered (chap. 6) the metaphysical presuppositions that underlay the magical animation of images; but we need to go further now. For in the case of sticks becoming serpents, we are dealing with something more than the animation of images. And the questions raised are as much epistemological as metaphysical.

There is a story related by Lucian, in Roman times, of a Greek traveller called Eucrates who went to Egypt to study with priests and scribes. Eucrates travelled as far south as Thebes on his mystical journey, and was fortunate enough to receive some oracular verses from one of the statues of Memnon there. On his way back he met a magician who had spent twenty-three years in underground sanctuaries learning magic from Isis. This extraordinary man was able to ride on the backs of crocodiles without coming to harm, and seems to have developed exceptional powers over the water element. When the magician invited Eucrates back to his house, Eucrates gladly accepted, but was surprised to find no servants whatsoever in the magician's home. His surprise turned to wonder when in due course the magician took a broom and, covering it with some linen cloth, began to recite words of power over it. Whereupon the broom "came to life" and, at the magician's command, did all the work he required: cooking, sweeping, washing up. On recitation of more words of power, the broom returned to being a broom again. The magician also performed the same act of transmutation with a door bolt and a pestle.

We all know what follows, for the story is familiar to us as "The Sorcerer's Apprentice." Eucrates, in his eagerness to acquire magical skills, listens carefully when the magician recites the words of power over the pestle, and himself repeats the formula after the magician has gone out, and lo! the pestle comes to life. "Go fetch me some water so I can wash!" says Eucrates. The pestle fetches some water. But Eucrates did not learn how to stop the pestle from fetching water. More and more is brought, and Eucrates becomes increasingly distraught as the magician's house begins to flood. In desperation, he hacks the pestle in half. But to his dismay, now both halves bring water, inundating the house twice as fast. Disaster is averted only by the timely return of the magician.

Now Lucian was a satirical writer, but his stories were rarely pure invention. There is usually a basis of truth, or true report, in them. This story may of course be wholly fanciful. But we cannot help noticing that it falls into the same category as the Biblical account of the sticks being turned into serpents. Should we regard that account merely as a story told to entertain? It certainly reads as a description of a magical contest engaged in deadly earnest. Given the broadly animistic context of the ancient Egyptian worldview, it seems to me that we should pause before consigning this type of magic to the too easy category of fantasy.

Let us suppose—for the sake of argument—that the people who were present at Pharaoh's court genuinely experienced Aaron's staff turn into a snake. Should we, then, understand that it literally became a living creature, a snake? If we are prepared to accept that some such interview between Aaron, Moses, and the Pharaoh did take place, then why is it that this part of the interview has become problematic for us? The reason is that we have become accustomed to an experience of nature that precludes such events from occurring. Our deanimated nature can only behave in certain restricted ways, defined by the so-called laws of nature. The concept of natural law, however, has arisen only in relatively recent times as an expression of the specifically modern experience of nature. This modern experience of nature as something "out there," radically different from what we experience as "inner" or pertaining to our own, individual soul-life, is the precondition of the idea of nature obeying impersonal, objective laws. It is equally the precondition of an experience of ourselves as self-possessed, self-conscious egos, able to discriminate between what belongs to our own subjectivity and what occurs independently of our psyche. Hence we come to know things and events happening "outside" us as occurring in a different sphere from the thoughts, feelings, desires, and intuitions that apparently occur within us.

But this modern differentiation between the subjective inner world and the outer world of objective facts is something that has arisen historically. It has become the presupposition of a type of experience of nature that did not exist in ancient times. Human consciousness has not always been as we experience it today. And one of the clearest indicators of this is the fact that nature used to be experienced animistically, that is, as having an interior dimension, a soul-life. In order for such an experience to be possible, the boundaries of human consciousness must have been differently defined; perhaps we should say, less clearly defined. Interiority was not an exclusive attribute of the human soul, but was a quality equally attributed to river, wind, and sun.

Animism alone, however, is not sufficient to explain the magic we are at present considering. It must, though, be the foundation of the explanation we are attempting to find. For if we can accept that nature and the human psyche functioned much more closely together, and that nature was experienced as existing not just on the physical level but on the psychic level too, then we have the epistemological conditions that could lead to an understanding of the performance of such "miracles." For to say that nature was experienced as much on the psychic plane as on the physical is to imply that the two planes were intermingled. Thus—and this is the critical point—psychic events could be experienced equally with the same degree of veridical force as physical events. As we have seen, demons were directly addressed, gods could speak from statues, the spirit world was a reality that was less an object of belief than one of repeated experience.

The expertise of the magician lay in bringing together the spiritual and material levels in a deliberately engendered and powerful coalescence. Magic did not function exclusively on the physical or the psychic or the spiritual planes but on all three together. The transmutation of sticks into serpents was as much a psychic and spiritual (that is, involving the gods, the *neters*) as a physical event. It occurred through a fusion of these spheres of being, in a series of events in which it was impossible to distinguish between their different ontological levels precisely because they were, in those magical actions, fused. We might be tempted to describe what occurred as an essentially psychic, or hallucinatory, phenomenon. But that would be to interpret from a modern standpoint events that occurred within a completely different epistemological milieu from that which prevails today. Yes, those things "really happened," but if we, with our modern consciousness, were there as witnesses, no doubt we would not have had the same experience.

Theodore Roszak once pointed to a modern example of magical transmutation that emphasizes the dilemma we face in attempting to understand the epistemological basis of ancient Egyptian magical transmutations. At a shamanic séance attended by the anthropologist attached to the Canadian Arctic Expedition of 1913–18, every member of the Copper Eskimo tribe saw the shaman Higilak turn into a polar bear as part of the rite. Under the anthropologist's questioning, they insisted on this as an "incontestable fact." The anthropologist saw no such thing, and interpreted the event as a collective hallucination. Roszak comments wryly: "Since the empirical consensus was wholly against him—and since Eskimos are surely better authorities on what is and what is not a polar bear—I gather we must conclude that his interpretation is wrong."[38] What we experience is dependent upon our mode of consciousness. Our modern judgment of what is "real" and what is "not real" is conditioned by our consciousness. Call it what we may—the "scientific" consciousness, "objective" consciousness, the "observer" consciousness—it is characterized by a clear awareness of, and need to distinguish between, what is "within" us and what is "outside" us. The modern psyche defines itself by an act of differentiating what is inner from what is outer, what is "subjective" from what is "objective." In this way we feel we know where we begin and end, we have a definite sense of "I" as opposed to "not-I."

In ancient Egyptian times, this mode of consciousness did not exist. It had not yet come into being. This means that the experience of what was "real" and what was "not real" was different from our experience. The outer and the inner world were not so strictly partitioned and, as a result, the experience of the physical was much richer—it was infused with inner, spiritual qualities that today we would prefer to regard as subjective projections. At the same time, the experience of the spiritual was much more concrete, much more "objective," by which term we should understand "shared." For us, spiritual events are very private. In ancient Egyptian times, they were more collective. There was what one might call a "public imagination"—a public inner life that enabled experiences of a certain order to occur completely objectively.

The anthropologist was unable to experience the shaman turning into a polar bear, and no doubt we would be in a similar position were we transported back to Pharaoh's court, and observed with our own modern consciousness the magical contest between Moses, Aaron, and the pharaoh's magicians. Could it be that were we present at the parting of the Red Sea, we might not have experienced anything out of the ordinary happening at all? For the structures of reality are inseparable from the consciousness that experiences them. It is as well, therefore, that we now turn without further delay to consider the constitution of the ancient Egyptian psyche.

8 THE SOUL INCARNATE

The Gods and the Psyche

In order to comprehend the way in which the consciousness of the ancient Egyptians functioned, it is necessary to relinquish many of our modern presuppositions concerning both the nature of human consciousness and the relationship of an individual's consciousness to the objective or "public" world. Events that the modern mind would classify as occurring purely "inwardly," in the subjectivity of a given individual or number of individuals, for the ancient consciousness had the possibility of acquiring a veridical force equivalent to that which we experience through sense perception. Not only did outer or sense-perceptible events have an "inner" aspect, but inner events that we would regard as taking place within the psyche could be experienced much as we today experience "outer" events. This means that our modern sense of what is "inner" and what is "outer" had not hardened in ancient Egyptian times into the either/or dichotomy of today. There existed a "public imagination" in ancient Egypt that acted as the mediatrix for a certain type of experience that no longer has credibility for the modern psyche. In the public imagination people could experience things in common that were not confined to the private world of an individual's psyche, and yet neither were these experiences sense-perceptible. Thus, contrary to our modern orientation, non-sense-perceptible events were not necessarily confined within the subjectivity of any given individual, but had, or at least had the possibility of acquiring, objective and public status.

Furthermore, in various magical situations a person might identify with a transpersonal energy, or god, to such an extent that their psyche became wholly absorbed into this transpersonal power. They were no longer "themselves" but experienced themselves *as* a god, and were—or could be—so experienced by others. Through identification with a god, a person could expect to be able to achieve things that were normally beyond the range of human possibility. The ability to experience such supernatural identification was a prerogative of those with magical knowledge, or at least required the facilitation of a magician.

Apart from specifically magical contexts, it would also seem that relationship to the gods was an integral part of daily life for the mass of people. In chapter 1, we saw that nature was experienced as permeated with divine energies. The gods were not remote but formed the background of people's daily experience of nature. The gods, however, were not simply confined to nature. A god such as Seth may have been vividly experienced as manifesting himself in the characteristic qualities of desert and storm, but he could equally well manifest in human violence, savagery, quarrelsomeness, drunkenness, and sexual license. None of these qualities were necessarily always regarded as evil. Likewise Thoth may have been most directly experienced in nature as the divine presence behind or within the moon, but Thoth was equally experienced in the human psyche in such qualities as the ability to learn and to think and act wisely. As with Seth and Thoth, so also with other deities—most of them were experienced as psychic, not simply natural, forces. Even if a deliberate invocation of a god—or a deliberate attempt to project oneself into the energy field of a specific deity—were not made, there would nevertheless have been a widely prevalent sense of the gods as forces operating within the human psyche, and becoming more or less present to different individuals at different times.

The degree of awareness and the accuracy of knowledge of these divine energies may not have been very developed in the mass of the population, but the gods were nevertheless constantly at large for the ancient Egyptian psyche. If we grant that it was the specific task of the magicians to develop a deeper and more accurate awareness of the gods within the framework of the occult knowledge and spiritual training that formed the "curriculum" of the Houses of Life, we should not forget the extent to which the ancient Egyptian psyche in general was permeated by the gods. Most people, in their experience of psychic processes, must have felt that they were sometimes, or even often, engaged by a god. Seth and Thoth are two examples. But the Egyptian pantheon was extremely large. We may ask the question: how many psychic functions that we today attribute to "our own" faculties were experienced in ancient times as involving the mobilization of a divine energy? It is not an easy question to answer. For one thing, it would be a mistake to attempt some facile correspondence of specific psychic functions and gods (on the lines, for instance, of violent emotions = Seth; acquisition of knowledge = Thoth). A person might have a particularly close relationship to a certain deity who might inspire a range of thoughts, feelings, and desires. And again, depending on the context, different people might come under the sway of a certain emotion that, precisely because of the different spiritual contexts, could carry the energy of a range of deities. We should therefore be circumspect when attempting to characterize the psychological qualities with which certain deities were associated. It is more valuable to try to get a feeling for each god or goddess as an energy field, in and out of which the ancient psyche moved. This can be done by contemplating the images, texts, and rituals relating to each of the deities—a task that lies beyond the scope of this book. The point is that it is incumbent upon us, if we wish to understand the consciousness of the ancient Egyptians, not only to consider the fact that the gods were felt to be active within the psyche, but also to try ourselves to develop a sensitivity toward how this might have been experienced by them. The following example may be helpful.

We know that Hathor, who is commonly referred to as the Egyptian goddess of love, was celebrated in her festivals with music, dancing, and the consumption of large quantities of wine. In figure 8.1 we see a procession of Hathor devotees: on the left, a man plays a double reed flute; in front of him a woman bends over and, having hitched up her skirt, slaps her buttock in time to the music; in front of her another woman wearing a long dress carries a pair of clappers and dances sensuously; in front of her is a man playing a lyre. They all have lotus flowers on their heads—the flower that symbolizes spiritual regeneration. The procession moves toward a shrine of the goddess (off this picture) in a mood of joyful self-abandonment.

Now this mood of joyful self-abandonment is preeminently the mood of the goddess. It is a mood that is experienced in just those activities through which the goddess was celebrated: in music making, dancing, eroticism, and drunkenness. This is not to say that the energy of Hathor is always present in these activities. When drunkenness, for instance, becomes ugly and destructive then one would feel rather the presence of the god Seth than that of Hathor. But where there is a lightness of spirit, a benevolent intoxication, then the ancient Egyptian would sense the closeness of Hathor. The celebrations of Hathor were thus at the same time *invocations* of her presence. The celebrants became imbued with her spirit, and we may surmise that the individual personality of the celebrant was lifted into

Fig. 8.1. Procession of Hathor devotees. Soapstone bowl from Coptos. Sixth century B.C.

a state of consciousness in which he or she felt possessed by the trans-personal energy of the goddess.

While other deities (and indeed Hathor herself) were not necessarily experienced with such an obvious relinquishment of self-control, every ancient deity must have had a powerful impact on the psyche. Precisely because they were transpersonal forces, the encounter with a deity must have taken a person to a psychic level in which his or her own sense of individual selfhood was dwarfed. It would seem, then, that the ancient Egyptians lived more deeply than we do. Their collective consciousness was open to archetypal depths (and heights) that in modern times we would tend to locate in our collective *un*-conscious. In consequence, their sense of ego must have been considerably less strong than ours—just because their collective consciousness was so much more open and responsive to the transpersonal energies that we are ordinarily much less aware of.[1]

It follows that an eclipse of the collective awareness of the gods was a condition—even a necessary condition—of the development of the modern ego. It also follows that if we examine ancient Egyptian texts and illustrations in which reference is made to various aspects of the psyche, we should expect to discover not a Freudian or Jungian psychological map such as we are familiar with, but something rather different.

Body and Soul

It is a striking feature of ancient Egyptian literature—both religious and nonreligious—that qualities of soul were very often located in parts of the body. Limbs, sense organs, internal organs, even teeth and bones, all seem to have been invested with psychic attributes. They each carried relatively specific soul qualities. This means that when the Egyptians wanted to express a quality of desire, thought, or intention, they would often do so as if the quality were an attribute less of a unified self, as we would understand it, and more as an attribute of a particular part of the body.

Qualities of will, for instance, were often referred to as belonging to limbs: powerful legs or strong arms indicated strength of will and the capacity to carry out one's wishes. There is a chapter in the Book of the Dead for "gaining power in the legs," an expression that must, given its context, refer to the strengthening of the qualities of soul normally associated with the lower limbs. In it the Underworld traveller says: "My strides are made long, my thighs are lifted up; I have passed along the great path, and my limbs are strong."[2] The Underworld context makes it most unlikely that such an affirmation was meant in the purely literal sense. And indeed, vignettes illustrating this chapter usually feature the *ba*, or soul, of the traveller in the form of a bird flying forth from the tomb, using wings rather than legs as its means of locomotion. Figure 8.2, from the papyrus of Khare, is typical.

Just as "having power in the legs" should be understood as referring to a person's psychological state, so also must statements concerning "having two arms." For instance, King Sesostris I mentions the importance of "having two arms": "Skill and alertness belong to him who is free of slackness. All works belong to the instructed. He who has two arms is effective."[3] To "have two arms" would appear to mean to apply oneself diligently to a task. As with legs and arms, so also with feet and hands. The feet, like the legs, were bearers of the will; while the hands

Fig. 8.2. The ba *(or soul) with "power in its legs" flies forth. Papyrus of Khare. Eighteenth Dynasty.*

179

mediated a person's relationship to others. To trust someone, for instance, was literally "to give them your hands."[4] Similarly, we read in the Book of the Dead how a person's hands could become "filled with rectitude."[5]

Now we could regard this manner of expression as simply a literary convention arising directly out of the visual concreteness of the hieroglyphic script. We could even argue that the ancient Egyptians were positively constrained by their hieroglyphic system of writing to express abstract qualities in a crudely physical way. Against such an interpretation, it is important to bear in mind that language is not simply the vehicle of expression of a given mentality, it actually *is* that mentality giving expression to itself. The very structures of language are the articulation of the mentality. We should be wary of thinking that the ancient Egyptian mind was "really" like ours, but was constrained by the hieroglyphic script. Rather, the hieroglyphic script was the medium most appropriate for the articulation of the ancient Egyptian mentality. Far from being crude, it reflected richly symbolic modes of conceiving and relating to both the physical and the psychic spheres of existence. It has already become apparent that these two spheres were not experienced as separated from each other—as we today tend to experience them. It is now necessary to go further, and seriously consider the idea that psychic attributes were indeed experienced as "situated" in various parts of the body. The pictorial character of the hieroglyphic form of writing made possible a quite effortless translation of this experience into the written word. For the hieroglyphic script, because it was pictorial, had not yet created a division between concrete and abstract, between "outer" and "inner." And it had not done so just because the ancient Egyptian mentality had not done so.

We are constantly presented with modes of expression that point to the fact that the ancient Egyptian sense of self was "distributed" in different parts of the body. Sense organs, limbs, internal organs, and so on, seem to take on a life of their own, to such an extent that we have the impression that they functioned virtually autonomously. It is the nose, for instance, that breathes, the mouth that speaks, the ear that hears. In the "Hymn of Merikare," we read that god made air in order that "our nostrils may live,"[6] and it was common to describe—and indeed to portray in ritual gesture— a god giving life to the nose, as if it were acting on behalf of the whole person (fig. 8.3).

In the stele of Sehetep, we read how "noses turn cold" when the king is in a rage.[7] It is a curiously vivid turn of phrase, evoking the image of people petrified by fear. As the mediator of life-giving air, the nose has an obvious and important function in the psychophysical organism. To bow down

Fig. 8.3. The gods give life to Thutmosis IV's nose. Tomb of Thutmosis IV, Valley of the Kings.

before a god or powerful person so that one's nose touched the ground was a way of acknowledging that one's own life was dependent on theirs.[8]

In a similar way to the nose, we find that it is the mouth that speaks or does not speak.[9] And furthermore, because it is the mouth that speaks, the moral quality of what was said was regarded as pertaining to the mouth. A common phrase used to describe an honest person was to say that he or she had "straight lips." The mouth was also regarded as the entry and exit point of life. The ceremonies concerned with animating a statue concentrated on the mouth—they were literally ceremonies for "opening the mouth." Likewise, the rites for the release of the *ba* (or soul) from the body at death required that the mouth be opened. An episode within this long and complicated rite is shown in figure 8.4, which depicts Nebseni having his mouth opened by the Guardian of the Balance, who gestures towards Nebseni's mouth with his hand.

A further phase in the rites involved the use of the sacred adze, which was made of iron and lifted to the mouth of the person who had died by the priest, who says: "I have opened your mouth with the instrument of Anubis.

Fig. 8.4. *Nebseni's mouth is opened by the Guardian of the Balance. Papyrus of Nebseni. Eighteenth Dynasty.*

I have opened your mouth with the instrument of Anubis, with the iron tool with which the mouths of the gods were opened."[10] The raising of the adze to the mouth is shown in figure 8.5. While other parts of the body were also included in these rituals, the mouth was by far the most important, and several chapters in the Book of the Dead are devoted specifically to opening the mouth or "giving" a mouth to a person so that he or she would be able to "speak with it" in the Underworld.[11] The mouth, then, was endowed with important attributes in its own right. It was singled out as the symbolic representative of the interface between the physical and psychic realms, the mediator between life and death and between death and renewed life.

Along with the mouth, the eye was included in the opening-of-the-mouth rite. During this rite the eyes, too, were opened, the eye being the psychic center of a person's health, well-being, and power.[12] In the Pyramid Texts there is the remarkable verse:

> *Unas' shelter is in his eye;*
> *Unas' protection is in his eye;*
> *Unas' victorious strength is in his eye;*
> *Unas' power is in his eye.*[13]

The eye, as source of vision, was also source of inner strength. It was here that a person's courage, or lack of it, resided. Thus in the Pyramid Texts we read how the king puts "terror into the eyes of all the spirits who look at him and of everyone who hears his name."[14] In the Middle Kingdom "Story of Sinuhe," it is said of the king: "The eye which looks at you shall not be afraid."[15] The nuance of meaning is not quite the same as a modern description of someone having (or not having) fearful eyes. For the ancient Egyptians, the eye had both psychic and magical properties, which meant that reference to the eye was reference to specific attributes that the eye intrinsically possessed. The fact that human beings have eyes meant that the properties attributed to the eye could then be utilized by human beings. But the eye was regarded as an entity in its own right, existing virtually as an independent spiritual archetype. As such, it was personified as the sacred *wedjat* eye, a potent symbol of divine creative and destructive power that was often employed in a protective

Fig. 8.5. Opening the mouth with the sacred adze. Tomb of Pe-ta-Amen-Apet. New Kingdom.

capacity in ancient Egyptian religious art.[16] It is sometimes depicted winged or, as in figure 8.6, with an arm so as to emphasize its independent status. In figure 8.6, which is from a New Kingdom tomb, the eye presents incense with its arm to Osiris. Below it the tomb owner, Pashedu, raises his arms in adoration. It is an extraordinary image, and it drives home the point that the eye must have been experienced by the Egyptians as imbued with intrinsic psychic qualities, for otherwise this symbol of the *wedjat* would have lacked real vitality.

It is interesting that the ear did not achieve an independent symbolic status similar to that of the eye. For the Egyptians the spiritual prototype of the eye was essentially cosmic—the sun and moon were regarded as the divine eyes of the ancient sky god Horus. The *wedjat* personified these cosmic eyes. But the ear had no such cosmic reference. Nevertheless, the human ear was, like the human eye, regarded as endowed with certain psychic attributes. In particular, the ear was the organ through which the mental faculty of attention was directed to the world, especially to its spiritual order. Hence the act of hearing carried a much wider meaning than it does for us today. One's mind, really one's wisdom, was where one's ear was. So it was possible for the Old Kingdom vizier Ptahotep to pray for "hearing" as we might pray for wisdom and to pronounce that "He who hears is beloved of God, but he whom God hates, does not hear."[17]

For the Egyptians, the gift of hearing was the basis of the perception of spiritual truth. Since the world came into being through the original divine utterance, the ear rather than the eye was the organ that opened the mind to the deepest levels of reality. As one might expect, the god Ptah, who created the world through articulating aboriginal sound with his tongue, was also a god "great of hearing." Other gods were also described as having "hearing ears" (for example Thoth, Isis, and Horus)—a phrase that meant both that the gods were very wise and that they were compassionate, for they listened to human needs as well as divine harmonies. For this reason many stelae exist with images of ears carved on their surface, in order to persuade the god to attend to the prayer or supplication. Figure 8.7 is one example.

Fig. 8.6. The wedjat *eye makes an offering. Tomb of Pashedu, Deir el Medina.*

Along with limbs and sense organs, internal organs also had an important psychological status as centers of psychic functioning. In the "Maxims of Ptahotep," the belly is characterized as the seat of impulsive desires, appetites, and feelings. The belly could be "hot" or "cold" depending on the degree to which its impulses had been integrated within the wider social and moral context. Slander is described as the "spouting of the hot-bellied person," whereas the amiable man is "cool-bellied."[18] In the Old Kingdom "Instructions to Kagemni," the belly is described in terms that indicate that it was felt virtually as a semi-autonomous psychic center: "Vile is he whose belly covets when mealtime has passed, / He forgets those in whose house his belly roams." And in a similar vein, Ptahotep comments: "The trusted man . . . does not vent his belly's speech."[19]

At the same time, the belly was regarded positively as the power center of a person. We have already seen how magicians integrated magic by lodging it in their bellies: "I will ascend and rise up to heaven," says the magician-king, "my magic is in my belly."[20] Powerful men could be portrayed as having big bellies. The standard way of depicting an important man was with one foot forward, a staff in the left hand, and a scepter in the right. In the statue in figure 8.8, from the Old Kingdom, the scepter is missing but the statue is obviously of "a man of substance," and we note his large belly.

What is lodged in the belly has become habitual or instinctive; once in the belly it endures forever. Thus Ptahotep, in seeking to express enduring affection, naturally places it in the belly: "Love of you endures in the belly of those who love you."[21] This way of viewing the belly as the place of fully

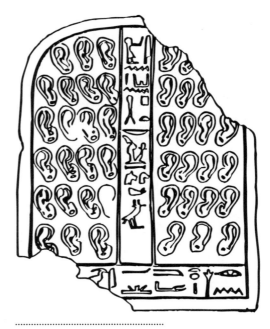

Fig. 8.7. Prayer stele addressed to Ptah. New Kingdom.

integrated capacities, feelings, and thoughts we meet again in the New Kingdom "Instructions of Amenemope," where the reader is admonished to let Amenemope's sayings "rest in the casket of your belly."[22]

When conceived negatively, the belly is often contrasted to the heart:

> He whose heart obeys his belly
> puts contempt of himself in place of love;
> his heart is bald, his body unanointed.
> Greatness of heart is god-given,
> but he who obeys his belly has acquired an enemy."[23]

That the heart could be "misled by the belly"[24] meant that there was always a degree of ambivalence concerning the belly, which we do not meet in relation to the heart. Physically higher than the belly, the heart was also psychologically higher. It was regarded as the spiritual center of a person, the place where a person would come closest to his or her *ka* (or vital spirit), which was associated with the heart: "Follow the heart as long as you live. . . .

185

Fig. 8.8. A big-bellied man. Fourth Dynasty.

Don't lessen the time of following the heart, for this offends the *ka*."[25] In figure 8.9, Ani stands with his arms lifted in adoration before a vase that hieroglyphically symbolizes the heart. It is raised up on a standard placed in front of four gods who are seated on a pedestal that, appropriately, has the form of the symbol of *maat*.

In the Book of the Dead, Ani says of his heart: "You are my *ka* within my body which forms and strengthens my limbs."[26]

The *ka* was the source of a person's vital energy, and it is interesting to find the expression "to wash the heart" having the connotation of a person becoming energized. The hunter exulting in the joy of the kill was said to "wash his heart"; while outbursts of anger could literally be described (and thus presumably felt) as a "washing of the heart."[27] The washed heart was a heart that had become charged with energy by giving expression to a strong emotion, and thus connecting with the *ka*.

But the heart was also a place of reflection, of contemplation. According to Ptahotep, "it is the heart which educates its owner in hearing or not hearing."[28] It was a "listening place" where one might come to a deeper level of understanding of, and harmony with, life. It was in the heart that a person opened him- or herself to *maat*: "I am a listener who listens to *maat*, who ponders it in the heart."[29] The heart was also the seat of memory and, it would seem, of intention. The heart that "is not opposed" was in our terms the wish or desire that is not frustrated.[30] But the true wishes of the heart are mediated by reflection and attuned to *maat*, unlike the impulses stemming from the belly. For, as the organ in the body most associated with the spiritual self, the heart was essentially pure. It was therefore considered necessary to protect the heart from corrupting influences or tendencies. We thus find admonitions to "conceal" or to "seal" the heart.[31]

This idea of the essential purity of the heart is linked to that of the heart as the source of a person's being. In chapter 30b of the Book of the Dead, the Underworld traveller addresses the heart as mother:

Fig. 8.9. Ani adores his heart. Papyrus of Ani. Eighteenth Dynasty.

> *My heart, my mother,*
> *My heart, my mother,*
> *My heart whereby I came into being . . .*[32]

The address is followed by a petition to the heart not to stand against the person as a witness at the judgment, as if the heart were another person within the person. Elsewhere in New Kingdom writings, the heart is referred to virtually as an indwelling god that a person helps to "enter its shrine" when he or she cultivates wisdom.[33] The heart, then, was a part of oneself that ultimately could not be identified with any of the desires, decisions, or actions that were out of tune with *maat*. The heart was the incorruptible core of a person, and thus detached enough from all that was mundane in them to stand as witness against them.

> *"May my heart be with me" pleads the Underworld traveller,*
> *"May it be with me,*
> *May it be at peace within me."*[34]

This plea from the Book of the Dead is accompanied in the papyrus of Nebseni by a vignette that shows the god Anubis giving to Nebseni his heart. The heart is being handed over to Nebseni as if it were a great treasure, and is received by him with reverent awe (fig. 8.10).

Of all the parts of the body, it was the head that seems to have corresponded most to the whole person as an individualized being. Hieroglyphically the head shown on its own could represent the whole person (or equally the whole god or animal). The legend that the head of Osiris was

Fig. 8.10. Anubis presents Nebseni with his heart. Papyrus of Nebseni. Eighteenth Dynasty.

buried at Abydos was one and the same with the claim of Abydos to be the burial place of the whole god. Since the head bears our individual facial features, it most naturally symbolized the whole person and was—of all parts of the body—least prone to being invested with the kind of psychic autonomy that we find attributed to other members or organs. It is significant that the ancient Egyptians represented the *ba* (the soul of a person freed from the body) as a bird with a human head. The head would have the individualized features of the person to whom the *ba* belongs. In figure 8.11 Nebseni's *ba* is portrayed in this typical fashion. It was imperative, therefore, that a person travelling through the Underworld in the *ba* condition should retain their head. Thus Ani chants:

> *The head of Osiris was not carried from him,*
> *the head of Osiris Ani shall not be carried away from me.*
> *I have bound up my limbs,*
> *I have made myself whole and sound,*
> *I have become young,*
> *I am Osiris, Lord of eternity.*[35]

A tentative connection can thus be made between the *ka* and the heart, and the *ba* and the head. As we shall see shortly, however, these associations must not be pressed too far.

When we come to consider the body as a whole rather than its individual physical components, it is difficult to resist the impression that when the Egyptians referred to it, they conceived of something virtually inert. For them, it was the *parts* of the body that were animated—literally ensouled—and bore specific vital and psychic attributes. But the body taken as a whole lacked this ensoulment. One of the most common terms used to refer to the body was *khat*. Concerning this term, Budge says:

The physical body of man considered as a whole was called *khat*, a word which seems to be connected with the idea of something which is liable to decay. The word is also applied to the mummified body in the tomb, as we know from the words "My body (*khat*) is buried."[36]

As the "mummified body," *khat* is translatable as "corpse." Another word for body was *sha* or *shat*, often written with the determinative for a piece of flesh or meat. Once again the word evokes decay rather than life. In the Pyramid Texts we read: "Soul [*ba*] to heaven, body [*shat*] to earth."[37] Such a saying would not have been applied to the arms, legs, or internal organs, least of all the heart. The animated parts of the body were not destined for the earth. Contradictory as it may seem to us, only the body as a whole was thought to return to the earth because the different parts of the body were infused with psychic or spiritual qualities, and these continued to function as if still conjoined with the organs or limbs that were their physical vehicles during life. These psychospiritual qualities were not felt to belong to the body as a totality but only to the various members that together constituted the body and infused it with

Fig. 8.11. The ba *of Nebseni, a bird with a human head. Papyrus of Nebseni.*

life. Considered as an entity in its own right, the body as such was the recipient rather than the bestower of life-forces. For this reason the *shat*, like the *khat*, could equally well be translated as "corpse."[38]

Transcending the Distributed Psyche

All these considerations point us toward the idea that, for the Egyptians, there was not the same kind of relationship to the body as exists for us. The different components of the body were experienced as in some sense existentially prior to the body as a whole. We constantly read about animated hands, arms, thighs, lungs, bellies, and hearts, but when we meet the body as a whole, it is always lacking in animation. In this respect there is an exact parallel between the ancient Egyptian view of the living body as a plurality of organs and limbs and what is found in early Greek literature. In Homer the word *soma*—which subsequently came to mean "body"—is never used with reference to the living person, only to the corpse. The living body was always referred to in the plural by words such as *guia* and *melea*, both of which denote limbs.[39] Thus, the early Greeks had no way of describing psychic functions independent of the physical organs such as the heart, lungs, and diaphragm with which the various psychic functions were experienced as indissolubly connected.[40] The same can also be said of the ancient Mesopotamians, for whom liver, heart, and head were each important psychic centers. In Mesopotamian literature we read, for instance, of livers "rejoicing" or being "pacified," of hearts "becoming strong" or "relenting," and of dreams occurring specifically in relation to the head.[41] There is a meaning in all this, and it is not that the ancient psyche was afflicted by a curious form of schizophrenia.[42] We must assume a de facto unity of consciousness, but with the life of the soul clearly not experienced in the same way that it is today. In ancient times, the soul-life was experienced much more physically than it is for us because the modern division between soul and body, "inner" and "outer," had not yet arisen. In normal waking life, limbs and organs and senses were all experienced as psychically charged, as the bearers of specific psychic functions. No part of the physical body was simply physical, just as no part of nature was simply material.

The soul of the ancient Egyptian may be described as a unity that had a diversity of semi-autonomous psychic functions distributed among different parts of the physical organism. It is for this reason that the living body was referred to in the plural (*shru* = "members"), while the body considered only in the singular was precisely a dead, deanimated body. For each member of the living body was the bearer of an attribute of soul. It was only through initiation or after physical death that a more unified self-consciousness such as we experience today could arise, as a counterpart to which the body was experienced "from the outside" as a unity; but precisely as such it was deanimated. The modern, post-Cartesian, dualistic experience of a unified inner self-consciousness as opposed to the "outer" physical body was attainable in ancient Egyptian times only in what we should describe as an out-of-body state. That is, the ancient Egyptian would have had to have gone through a radical and traumatic separation from the normal psychophysical consciousness in order to attain an intensified experience of self such as we take for granted today. The attainment of this experience was one of the purposes of the ancient Egyptian initiation rites, and it is largely in an initiatory context that the psychospiritual terminology of *ka*, *ba*, and *akh* should be understood. The *ba*, for example, is often translated as "soul," and while it may be thought of as an individualized psychic center comparable to our modern experience of soul, for the Egyptians the *ba* was always a disembodied soul, experienced only in a disembodied state, as we shall see in chapter 9.

A further consideration arises from our description of the ancient Egyptian psyche as distributed among a diversity of semi-autonomous psychophysical functions. This also has a bearing on a fundamental initiatory experience. We must assume that for the Egyptians there was not the same sense of psychic centricity in their normal waking consciousness as we experience today. Where we might conceive of the soul as a psychic center that embraces within itself a variety of functions such as thinking, feeling, desiring, and intending, in ancient times there was no such concept of a monocentric soul. Not only were these various functions attributed to semi-autonomous, psychically charged bodily organs or limbs, but in many cases thoughts, feelings, desires, and intentions were all experienced as emanating not from the human being at all but from the gods acting upon the human being.

Viewed in this light, the many surviving prayers for the deification of the members of a person's body that were referred to previously ("My hair is the hair of Nun. My face is the face of Ra. My eyes are the eyes of Hathor. My ears are the ears of Upuat . . ." and so on down through the body to the feet, and ending with the affirmation "There is no member of my body which is not the member of some god") can be seen as means of preserving the integrity of the psyche, distributed as it was among these members. Each semi-autonomous member had to be brought into the sphere of the deity appropriate to its specific area of psychic operation. Just as the gods were present in the landscape—in desert, river, plant, and animal—so they could become present in the members of the human psychophysical organism, in hair, face, eyes, and hands. By drawing the gods in, in this way, a greater sense of self-integration was achieved.

The degree to which people could claim their inner experiences as their own was necessarily compromised, and this meant that the overall experience of unitary self-consciousness was far more attenuated and fragile than it is today. In the process of initiation it was broken down altogether in order to rebuild it more strongly. The important initiatory idea of physical dismemberment becomes comprehensible when it is seen as the only way of describing the experience of catastrophic psychic fragmentation. To a consciousness for which the parts of the body were all psychically charged, the mutilation of the body undergone by Osiris was the prototype of psychic fragmentation that must have been experienced by the initiate in a psychophysical way. This psychic fragmentation was precipitated as a prelude to the initiates reidentifying with a new psychic center that transcended the "distributed psyche." The reintegration of the body must have involved coming to a new relationship with one's "members," a relationship in which "possession" of the parts by the person was frequently emphasized:

> You have your heart, O Osiris;
> You have your legs, O Osiris;
> You have your arms, O Osiris;
> So too my heart is my own;
> My legs are my own;
> My arms are my own.
> A stairway to the sky is set up for me
> That I may ascend on it to the sky;
> I ascend on the smoke of the great censing.[43]

The relationship of "possession" seems to indicate a new level of integration of the members under a strengthened psychic center, not located physically: "'My limbs which were in concealment are reunited' . . . says Unas, 'I go forth today in the true form of a living spirit.'"[44] The form of self-consciousness referred to ("living spirit") clearly presupposes the reuniting of Unas's members. The implication is that Unas's initiatory ordeal of dismemberment leads to an experience of a higher degree of psychophysical integration and, at the same time, an intensified consciousness of himself as an autonomous "living spirit." Thus the initiatory ordeal inaugurated a type of unitary self-consciousness that was otherwise inaccessible to the normally "distributed" self-consciousness of the ancient Egyptian member-based psyche. Varying degrees of unitary self-consciousness were distinguished, which were experienced as a result of the pursuit of an initiatory path of development. It is to this spiritual psychology that we must now turn.

9

THE SOUL DISCARNATE

We are now in a position to approach the spiritual psychology that permeates ancient Egyptian religious literature. This literature describes states of awareness that in ancient Egyptian times were not usually attained in normal waking consciousness, but were experienced on a path of spiritual development toward self-integration and enlightenment. It should be borne in mind that this spiritual path was, in the Old Kingdom, reserved for royalty and a small spiritual elite. It was not until the New Kingdom that it became more widely accessible, and even then it was still open only to a small minority of the population. So what follows must be understood as an esoteric path of development, as distinct from a more general "popular" psychology.

The Ka

The first level of this developmental path was the meeting with the *ka*. The *ka* was the source of a person's vital energy and can, in many contexts, be translated as "vital force." For the common people, this vital force was not felt as an emanation of their own personality, but rather was bestowed upon them from an extraneous source. This was the ancestral group that existed in the spirit world as a source of power, at one with *ka* energy. It was the ancestors who directed this energy toward the physical realm, thereby infusing not only human beings but also animals and crops with vitality. As Rundle-Clark puts it:

The ancestors, the custodians of the source of life, were the reservoir of power and vitality, sustenance and growth. Hence they were not only departed souls but still active, the keepers of life and fortune. Whatever happened, whether for good or evil, ultimately derived from them. The sprouting of corn, the increase of the herds, potency in men, success in hunting or war, were all manifestations of their power and approval.[1]

This is one of the main reasons why the tomb and the group cemetery in which it was located were such important focuses of ancient Egyptian spiritual life. For it was at the tomb that a vital interchange occurred between the dead and the living. If the dead were given food offerings and prayers, this was not simply out of some pious remembrance of who they had been. It was an acknowledgment of who they had become, namely, the custodians and directors of *ka* energy. The tomb was known as the "place of the *ka*" for this reason, and when a person died they were said to "go to their *ka*," that is, to the *ka* group with which they now became conjoined. In return for the offerings and prayers, the dead would then direct the benevolent *ka* energy toward the world of the living.

It is important that we realize that for the common people, "going to the *ka*" was an experience of becoming absorbed into the ancestral group. Individual self-consciousness was not accentuated but rather diluted by direct contact with the *ka*. The same cannot be said for the king and the social-spiritual elite close to royalty (although in the course of time their spiritual experiences certainly became less exclusive and more generally accessible). The king went to his *ka* in a state of consciousness that enabled him to assimilate it to himself rather than be assimilated by it. In the meeting with his *ka*, his own member-based self-consciousness was preserved. And it was this preservation of the member-based self-consciousness that led to the experience of the *ka* as a kind of spiritual double of the physical body. In the Pyramid Texts we read:

> *O Unas, the arm of your* ka *is before you,*
> *O Unas, the arm of your* ka *is behind you,*
> *O Unas, the leg of your* ka *is before you,*
> *O Unas, the leg of your* ka *is behind you.*[2]

Thus the royal *ka* was evoked limb by limb. This evocation involved an intensifying of the normal psychophysical awareness toward the experience of the vital or etheric forces permeating the physical organism.

Elsewhere we read that the *ka*, like the physical body, has flesh (*afu*).[3] Portrayals of the royal *ka* often simply consisted of a second person, as if the *ka*'s spiritual form was indeed an exact replica of the king's physical body and that both were originally created simultaneously. In figure 9.1 the god Khnum is portrayed creating the king and his *ka* in a single act on his potter's wheel.

Sometimes we find the king shown making offerings with his *ka* accompanying him, walking behind him like a medieval page. An example of this is given in figure 9.2, where Queen Hatshepsut (who is represented here as if she were a king, sporting a royal beard) makes perfume offerings accompanied by her *ka*, who walks behind her with the *ka* sign of two uplifted arms above its head. In this and the above illustration, we

Fig. 9.1. The god Khnum creates the king and his ka *in a single act. Luxor Temple.*

again see the justification for translating *ka* as "double," for it appears here as a second image of the queen, bearing in its right hand the *ankh* sign of life, and the feather of *maat*.

While we are used to seeing gods portrayed in strikingly concrete images, there is something strange and perplexing about seeing an invisible aspect of the human being represented so concretely. Was the *ka* really experienced in this way, as if it were external to a person? The text from the pyramid of Unas just quoted would seem to support this interpretation. Despite being an essentially human energy, the effect of which was experienced as an intensifying of normal psychophysical awareness, the *ka* itself was not internalized but rather apprehended as an entity distinct from the king. Unas is told to look for the limbs of his *ka* in front of him and behind him, as if they really were separate from his own limbs. When, therefore, we are presented with images like that of Hatshepsut and her *ka*, we must suppose that this actually does relay to us the royal experience of the *ka*.

Fig. 9.2. Queen Hatshepsut, portrayed as a king, makes offerings. Behind her is her ka. *Temple of Hatshepsut, Deir el Bahri.*

Even if the role of the *ka* was taken by a young boy on ceremonial occasions like this, it does not weaken but rather strengthens the grounds for supposing that the *ka* was regarded as an independent being, a "second person," in some sense external to the king.

It is clear from both artistic and textual sources, such as those we have just been considering, that the royal rapprochement with the *ka* did not occur only after death, as it did for the mass of the people. The king was conscious of his *ka* during life. Hence the Pyramid Texts state that the king did not travel *to* the *ka* at death but rather *with* it.[4] The king therefore lived on earth in a state of consciousness that was attainable for most people only after death; that is, in a state of consciousness infused with *ka* energy, but with the important difference that this state of consciousness was maintained by him as an individual, whereas for most people at death their individual self-consciousness became absorbed into that of the ancestral group. And to the extent that they experienced their *ka* during life, they located it outside themselves either in the ancestors or, as we shall see, in the king or some other powerful figure.

For this reason, the king had authority over *ka* energy, and was thus said to "unite the hearts" of all the people.[5] He had control over the forces of nature, as we have seen (chap. 5), because of his mastery of *ka* energy.[6] This extraordinary power of the king was due to his having travelled into the world of the dead and having gained authority there, "bestowing *ka*s and removing *ka*s/imposing obstacles and removing obstacles."[7] As Horus, the king engaged in a mythological relationship with the whole community of the dead, at whose head was the god Osiris. Just as Osiris was dependent on Horus for his reanimation in the Beyond, so also were the ancestors—especially but not exclusively the royal ancestors—dependent on the king. The kingship was positioned at a pivotal point in the reciprocal relationship between the communities of the dead and the living, and the king's role was as chief mediator between the two realms. Since the flow of *ka* energy occurred across this divide, the person who was positioned at this vital crossing point accrued to himself tremendous power.

In the eyes of the mass of the population, therefore, the king just as much as the ancestors was the repository of *ka* energy. Hence common Egyptian names from the Old Kingdom onward had the form "My *ka* belongs to the king," or "The king is my *ka*."[8] The *ka* of the king was believed to permeate the whole country and to affect each person in a most intimate way, for the king was felt as a presence in the heart. In the heart of the ancient Egyptian was the *ka* energy of the god Horus, "the dweller in hearts,"[9] and it was none other than Horus whom the king embodied. He was the *ka* of Egypt, and he was the personification of *ka* as experienced in each individual. As Frankfort puts it, "The Egyptian . . . experiences the influence of the king in his very being, in what he feels is the center of his life's energy. It is this which he calls the *ka*."[10] In commanding *ka* energy, the king experienced an enhancement of his own power as an individual, whereas the people could not rise above a collective consciousness of *ka* energy, and felt their individuality to be overwhelmed in relation to it. Thus, the king became the individual focus of the collective consciousness.

As has been indicated, however, even in the Old Kingdom the king was not alone in having attained this level of consciousness. He may have been, formally speaking, unique in this respect, but other people in the higher echelons of Egyptian society—insofar as they became aware of their inner identity with Horus—attained a similar, individualized relationship to their *ka*. It became "their" *ka* precisely because in relation to it they felt an expanded sense of selfhood. And perhaps this is why it could be—indeed, had to be—personified as if it were a second person. For relationship to it had become integral to the enhanced "Horus consciousness" of the spiritually advanced individual.

Fig. 9.3. The ka *as guardian spirit of the royal child. New Kingdom.*

As it was for the king, then, so it was for the social elite, consisting of the higher ranks of the priesthood and the "nobles," who often also held high priestly office. The maxims of the Old Kingdom magnate Ptahotep clearly indicate that people in positions such as his own acted in conscious harmony with their *ka*s,[11] and that their relationship to their followers was comparable to that of the king to the general populace. Their *ka*s supported and sustained those who were in their immediate following. As Ptahotep says: "Your sustenance will come from his [the magnate's] *ka*. The belly of one whom he loves is contented, and your back will be clothed by it. And his help will be there to sustain you. . . . He will make a good arm towards you [i.e. he will help you]."[12]

The "nobles" of Old Kingdom Egypt were very often spiritual adepts, and would have had a large number of disciples and dependents. For their dependents, the *ka* of the nobles, as much as the *ka* energy dispensed by the ancestors, was their good (or bad) fortune. But for the king and the social and spiritual elite for whom the *ka* energy had become individualized, the *ka* was more like a protective and inspirational genius or daimon. Thus the Old Kingdom king Pepi says:

> *It goes well with me and my name;*
> *I live with my* ka.
> *It expels the evil that is before me,*
> *it removes the evil that is behind me.*[13]

In figure 9.3, the *ka* is depicted as the guardian spirit of the royal child, holding it in an all-encompassing embrace. We are reminded of the Heliopolitan creation myth in which Atum's embrace of Shu and Tefnut both shielded them from the dissolving power of Nun and also instilled them with his own *ka* energy: "You put your arms around them with your *ka. /* So that your *ka* was in them."[14] Instead of Atum, here we have the *ka* itself, personified. It could be understood as the person's deeper self, residing in the divine world. This explains how it was felt to be appropriate to make offerings to the *ka* as one would to any divine being.

By the New Kingdom, relationship to a personal *ka* had become more widespread. Thus a prayer to the *ka* became a standard entry in the Book of the Dead. It began:

> *Hail to you, my* ka *of my lifetime!*
> *Behold, I have come before you,*
> *risen, animated, mighty and healthy.*
> *I have brought incense to you,*
> *and I have made myself pure with it,*
> *and with it I will purify*
> *that which comes forth from you.*[15]

Figure 9.4 shows the vignette to this prayer, from the papyrus of Nesitanebtasheru. In the illustration, despite the greater degree of personalization of the relationship to the *ka*, the *ka* is nevertheless portrayed

Fig. 9.4. Food offerings to the ka. *Papyrus of Nesitanebtasheru. Twenty-first Dynasty.*

abstractly, as two upraised arms on the pedestal in front of Nesitanebtasheru. It does not appear in fully human guise, as do the royal *ka*s of the same period. Between the arms are the food offering that she has presented to the *ka*.

Perhaps the abstractness of the *ka* symbol as it appears in this and other illustrations of the period can be understood as pointing to the fact that even when conceived as a "personal" *ka*, it nevertheless retains a basic universality. For the wealthy elite who had access to the Book of the Dead, it has still not quite become the personal daimon that it was for the king. It is the universal life-force in relation to which a heightened sense of individual power may be experienced, but that never forms part of the personality as such. It remains universal. And, from the textual evidence, it would seem that the ancient Egyptians (whether royalty, nobles, or commoners) never felt a sense of personal identification with the *ka* such as they felt with the next component of their spiritual psychology that we must consider: the *ba*.

The Ba

A very different feeling accompanies the use of the term *ba* from that which accompanies the term *ka*. Only rarely could it be translated as "vital force," for it has a more interior, more subtle connotation. The concept of the *ba* goes beyond that of life-energy, connoting a more refined, more spiritualized psychic force. E. A. Wallis Budge, in discussing the relationship of *ba* to *ka*, writes that the *ba* "dwells in the *ka*," implying that in order to reach the *ba*, we must reach into a more inward mode of existence.[16]

The *ba* is usually translated as "soul," but this is a misleading translation since the *ba* was activated only in nonordinary psychic states, when the normal sense-based and member-based consciousness was no longer functioning. Such psychic states typically characterized sleep, the after-death consciousness and the nonphysical mode of consciousness attained through initiation. The *ba*, then, was the way in which the human being manifested in these specifically spiritual circumstances. Literally, the *ba* means "a manifestation," and the term is applied to the various manifestations of the gods: the bennu bird is the *ba* of Ra, the constellation Orion or the Apis bull are *ba*s of Osiris, the sacred ibis the *ba* of Thoth, and so on.[17] But whereas the gods, who are pure spirits, can have *ba*s on the physical plane, the human *ba* is a manifestation on the spiritual plane. The use of the term, however, in its application to human beings suggests a more precise understanding of the nature of the *ba*.

From the Old Kingdom Pyramid Texts onward, one of the main characteristics of the way in which the term is used is that it is frequently connected with movement. And the kind of movement it is connected with is
movement between earth and heaven. As we have seen from a Pyramid Text
already quoted, the destiny of the *ba* is heaven, in contrast to the body: "*Ba*
to heaven, Body [*shat*] to earth."[18] The *ba* seeks out heaven—the spiritual
world in which the gods reside—like a falcon soaring toward the sun. In the
following text, it is perhaps the *ba* itself that is responsible for the growth of
soul-wings that will carry the person upward toward spiritual heights:

> *My wings have grown into those of a falcon,*
> *My two plumes are those of a sacred falcon,*
> *My* ba *has brought me,*
> *Its magic has equipped me.*[19]

Because it belongs to the eternal heaven world, one can strengthen one's
ba during life by steeping oneself in matters of the spirit. Thus the Old
Kingdom sage Ptahotep says, "The wise feed their *ba* with what endures."[20]
The nature of the *ba* is that it is drawn to what is eternal, for this is its place
of origin, its home. So we read in the Old Kingdom "Instructions to
Merikare":

> *The* ba *comes to the place it knows,*
> *It does not miss its former path,*
> *No kind of magic holds it back.*
> *It comes to those who give it water.*[21]

As in so many Old Kingdom references to the *ba*, we have the impression
that its special quality is that of travelling toward its spiritual goal. We do
not necessarily have such a strong sense of its having arrived. A person will
be described as "coming forth in the form of a living *ba*"[22]—an expression
that was used through to the New Kingdom—but the *ba* itself is but a preliminary to a yet more exalted state of consciousness. The *ba* seems to be
always on the way: it is the energy that carries a person onward and inward
to a higher level of being.

As the vehicle of ascent, it is aptly represented hieroglyphically by the
jabiru bird. Equally, it is depicted as the human-headed falcon. That the *ba*
has a human face—the face of the person to whom it belongs—points to
another fundamental difference between the *ba* and the *ka*. Whereas the *ka*
is a relatively undifferentiated universal life energy, the *ba* pertains more to

Fig. 9.5. A man and his ba. *Papyrus of Soutimes. New Kingdom.*

the individual. In figure 9.5, a man clutches his *ba* to his breast, in a manner that would be inconceivable were it his *ka*. In relation to the *ka*, there is both more detachment and more deference. And if there were to be an embrace, it would be the *ka* that would be embracing the man, not the other way round. But most notable in this picture is the similarity of the two faces. This conveys to us the fact that the *ba* is the person but in another form.

The *ba* could be defined as an individual in an out-of-body state. For most people, therefore, the experience of the *ba* was beyond the range of their normal waking consciousness. While the experience of the *ka* was more accessible, in relating to it one was relating to something to a certain extent external to oneself, to one's sense of who one was. This was the case even though the *ka* was felt to permeate and sustain the physical organism in health and well-being, and contact with it could lead to a kind of intensification of the member-based sense of self. For the *ka* itself, insofar as it could be objectively apprehended, was always distinct and separate from a person, in some way "other." The *ba*, by contrast, was how one experienced oneself when one was outside of oneself, outside of the body and the member-based self-consciousness. In the case of the *ba*, we are considering a deeper level of psychospiritual force, which does not have the same degree of intimate connection with the physical body. Through the *ba* one becomes detached from oneself, from the psychophysical self-consciousness. Whereas contact with the *ka* could lead to an enhancement of the member-based psychology, the experience of the unitary self-consciousness that the *ba* represented was incompatible with the member-based awareness that characterized normal life.

It is as well to remember that the psychology we are considering is a psychology of inner development, and concerns the deliberate cultivation of "abnormal" states of consciousness. If the experience of the *ka* involved becoming aware of the spiritual source of the life-forces underlying and permeating the physical body, the experience of the *ba* involved becoming aware of the physical body as lifeless, as a corpse. The individual self-consciousness of the *ba*-state was attained in juxtaposition to the apprehension of the body as an inert object. Whereas in life this out-of-body awareness had to be induced, at death this awareness occurred spontaneously. Figure 9.6 is one of many pictures that portray the relationship of the *ba* to the inanimate physical body. The *ba*, having separated from the body, would feel drawn to look upon the decaying remains of the physical organism below it, as if to distinguish itself from the latter. "When the *ba* rises up,"

we read in the Book of the Dead, "a man sees corruption and his bones decayed, his flesh rotting, his members disintegrating."[23] The "rising up" of the *ba* here seems necessarily to include an awareness of the psychophysical organism in total demise.

The *ba* is often portrayed loitering around the tomb. In figure 9.7, the *ba* perches on top of the tomb chapel, while in figure 9.8 it flies down the tomb shaft to visit the mummy, attracted like some moth to the dark scent of decay.

Chapter 89 of the Book of the Dead includes a prayer for the *ba* to see the lifeless body of the *khat*: "May it look

Fig. 9.6. The ba *looks upon the inanimate body below it. Papyrus of Teherera. New Kingdom.*

Fig. 9.7. The ba *perches on top of the tomb. New Kingdom papyrus.*

upon my *khat,*/May it rest on my mummy,/ May it never perish nor suffer decay."[24] Figure 9.9 is the vignette to this chapter, and shows the *ba* looking down upon the mummy of the person below it, as if an irresistible fascination compels it to return again and again to view the physical organism from the detached standpoint of an external observer.

Inasmuch as the *ba* is destined for heaven, its distinctive mode of consciousness nevertheless arises in relation to the earth, for it is continually needing to reestablish its own identity by renewing contact with the body, if only to experience itself as distinct from the body. It is as if the self-consciousness that characterizes the *ba*-state is too frail to be sustained in total independence of the body, but needs the latter as an external reference point, in order to establish its own inner sense of self.

In ancient Egypt, normal waking consciousness, as we have seen, was diffused throughout the psychophysical organism; there was no well-defined ego. The *ba* may therefore be understood as a kind of prefiguration of the modern ego consciousness. Hence, the temptation to translate it as "soul"—a temptation that should be resisted as the *ba* only came to itself in nonordinary, out-of-body states. If these states involved a degree of attachment to the body, this attachment was of the peculiar sort that has been described, namely, from the standpoint of an onlooker viewing the body from the outside. This objectification of the body was, it seems, a necessary accompaniment of the *ba*-state, at least initially. The ultimate destination of the *ba*, however, was the heavenly world to which its wings would carry it.

Before turning to consider the higher destination of the *ba*, it is necessary to dwell a little more on its relationship to the earth. We have seen that as much as it strove for heaven, the *ba* was drawn back to earth, because it derived its own sense of selfhood from its objectification of the inanimate body. Arising out of the objectifying mode of perception of the *ba* was the apprehension of the shadow or *khaibit*. Because the term *shadow* is familiar to us from Jungian psychology, we must be wary of projecting a Jungian interpretation onto the ancient Egyptian concept. Although the ancient Egyptian conception of the shadow is comparable to that of Jung, they are not the same and we should be careful not to conflate them. The nature of shadows is that they come into existence where light falls on a physical object. In symbolic terms, the psychic shadow came into being as a concomitant of the *ba*'s intermediate position between heaven and earth. Turning toward heaven, it turned toward realms of light. But turning toward earth, it necessarily became aware of the shadow that was evoked by its relationship of dependency on the physical body.

In figure 9.10, we see the *ba* of Arinefer in a double relationship to his shadow. At the bottom left of the picture, the *ba* bird walks on the ground as if shackled by the menacing black circle of the shadow; whereas above, the *ba* flies freely and seems to be calling forth the shadow, now in human form, from the tomb.

We see here two distinct possibilities for the *ba*. On the one hand, it can be drawn into too close a contact with the shadow, and become bound to the earth. On the other hand, it can bring about the liberation of the shadow from the tomb. The shadow may perhaps best be understood as

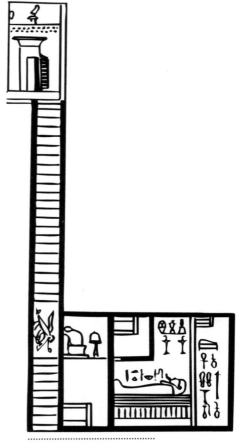

Fig. 9.8. The ba *flies down the tomb shaft. Papyrus of Nebquet. New Kingdom.*

representing all the untransformed earthly appetites and obsessions that fetter the *ba* to the physical realm and prevent it from moving on. The shadow haunts the *ba* as the product of everything in the *ba*'s awareness that is unable to transmit light. Since the destiny of the *ba* is to become wholly translucent, the shadow must be summoned forth from the tomb and thus subjected to the dissolving spiritual light to which the *ba* is attracted.

In chapter 92 of the Book of the Dead, Nebseni prays to the eye of Horus (the healing eye that gives new life to Osiris), to liberate his *ba*. He then prays for the liberation of his shadow as well:

Fig. 9.9. The ba, *carrying the* shen *sign, symbolic of eternity, hovers over its body. Papyrus of Ani. Eighteenth Dynasty.*

Fig. 9.10. The ba *and the shadow. Tomb of Arinefer, Thebes.*

When the dusk is in your sight,
you wardens of Osiris,
do not restrain my ba
or hold back my shadow (khaibit)
Open a way for my ba *and my shadow,*
so that it [the ba*] may see the Great God [i.e., Ra]*
within the shrine
on the day of judgement of bas.[25]

The Akh

If the *ba* exists between worlds, the next level of psychospiritual existence has its natural home in the heavenly realm. The *akh*, sometimes translated as "intelligence," comes into its own in regions of spiritual light. Written with the hieroglyph of the crested ibis—a bird with dark green plumage shot through with glittering gold—the word *akh* conveys notions of light: "shining," "illumination," "irradiation."[26] Budge translates *akh* as "the shining one" or "the shining form."[27] The hieroglyph of the crested ibis is shown in figure 9.11.

Whereas the divine archetypal field through which the *ba* moves belongs to the god Osiris, the lord of the intermediate region or Dwat, the archetypal field of the *akh* is the light-filled heaven, presided over by the sun god Ra. Union with Ra was considered the goal of the celestial ascent of the king in the Old Kingdom Pyramid Texts. It was achieved with the king becoming a "shining one," a star irradiating light throughout the universe, and hence a "son" of his divine "father" Ra. Thus Unas could proclaim:

Fig. 9.11. The hieroglyph of the crested ibis.

O Ra-Atum, this Unas comes to you,
an imperishable akh,
a lord over the place of the four pillars.
Your son comes to you,
this Unas comes to you.[28]

In many texts, as in this one, reference to the *akh* is combined with a sense of homecoming, of return to the source. The condition of being an *akh* is one of spiritual radiance only because one has contacted and become united with the source of spiritual light. The *akh* is radiant because it is saturated with the rays of spiritual light that emanate from the creator god. In the Book of the Dead, Ani says:

> *Praises to you, O Ra when you rise as Harmarkis!*
> *I adore you when I see your beauties*
> *and when your shining rays fall on my breast. . . .*
> *Primeval god, from whom all forms come into being,*
> *you send forth the word,*
> *and the earth is flooded with silence.*
> *O you, the only One, came into existence in heaven*
> *before ever earth and mountains existed. . . .*
> *Make my shining form* (akh) *to be glorious,*
> *O make the Osiris, my* ba *divine. . . .*
> *Shine with your rays of light upon me,*
> *Osiris Ani, who loves you.*[29]

Ani prays, "O make the Osiris, my *ba*, divine." The *akh* may be understood as the *ba* divinized, and raised to a plane of existence above that of the Osiris state. The chief difference between Osiris and Ra is that Osiris does not have the key to his own self-renewal (for this is dependent on Isis and Horus) whereas Ra does. The *akh* is the self-renewing spirit, and it is this power of inner self-regeneration that is the hallmark of its divine status. In chapter 174 of the Book of the Dead, the theme of rebirth figures prominently. The title of this chapter is "For causing the *akh* to come forth from the great door in the sky," and it contains these potent lines:

> *A god has been born*
> *now that I have been born:*
> *I see and have sight,*
> *I have my existence,*
> *I am lifted up upon my place,*
> *I have accomplished what has been decreed. . . .*
> *I am the lotus which shines in the Land of Purity,*
> *which has received me*
> *and which has become my abode*
> *at the nostrils of the Great Power.*
> *I have come into the Lake of Flame*
> *and I have set* maat *in place of wrong. . . .*[30]

The lotus was a primary symbol of the power of self-transformation and rebirth. In the Hermopolitan cosmogony Ra himself was born from the lotus bud that emerged from the Primordial Ocean (see chap. 3). To claim "I am a lotus" meant no less than to identify with the self-generating and regenerative power of Ra.

We have seen that the *ba*-condition involved a certain objectification of the physical body. As a *ba*, a person had the experience of looking at his or her body as if from an outsider's standpoint. This experience was central to the Osirian initiation. When we come to consider the *akh*, however, the final stage in the relationship to the physical body unfolds, in which the *akh* is released entirely from it. But this release involved a newfound awareness of a "spiritual body" (the *sah* or *sahu*), which henceforth became the vehicle of the *akh*'s individualized consciousness. The "germination" of the spiritual body from the physical was an important esoteric event. It is referred to in chapter 154 of the Book of the Dead, in which the person identifies with Kheprer, the god of self-renewal:

> *I am the god Kheprer,*
> *and my members shall have an everlasting existence.*
> *I shall not rot, I shall not putrefy.*
> *I shall not turn into worms,*
> *and I shall not see corruption*
> *before the eye of Shu.*
>
> *I shall have my being.*
> *I shall have my being.*
> *I shall live, I shall live.*
> *I shall germinate,*
> *I shall germinate,*
> *I shall germinate,*
> *I shall awake in peace.*[31]

Figure 9.12 accompanies this text in the papyrus of Nu.

The text suggests that the germination of the spiritual body, or *sahu*, ensures that the member-based psychology is preserved and carried over into the higher spiritual state ("my members shall have an everlasting existence"). This may explain why hands, feet, legs, and arms are referred to so frequently in the Otherworld literature. A person's "members" came to exist in a spiritual form. One way of understanding this experience of the spiritual body that accompanied the realization of the level of conscious-

Fig. 9.12. The germination of the spiritual body. New Kingdom papyrus.

ness indicated by the *akh*-condition is that it was an experience of the so-called double at a more refined level. It is difficult, however, to be certain of how the Egyptians understood the relationship between the *ka* as spiritual double, and the *sahu*, given that these terms were not used with a single, clearly defined meaning. It is sufficient here to point to the likelihood that the germination of the spiritual body from the physical corresponded both to a "re-membering" experience and to the metamorphosis of the *ba* into the *akh*. Thus the *akh* and *sahu* came into existence at the same time, and this event marked the liberation of a person from the Osirian realm of the Underworld and the tomb. Figure 9.13 shows the germination of the *sahu*, which the text explains as being due to Ra calling it forth to breathe the divine air.[32]

The simultaneous generation of the *sahu* and the *akh* is described in a chapter from the Book of the Dead entitled "The chapter of coming forth into the day, having passed through the tomb." In it, the soul-traveller says:

> *I have passed through the Underworld [Dwat],*
> *I have seen my father Osiris,*
> *I have scattered the gloom of the night. . . .*
> *I have become a sah,*
> *I have become an akh,*
> *I have become equipped [aper],*
> *Oh all you gods and akhs,*
> *make a way for me. . . .*[33]

"Becoming equipped" may be interpreted as having all one's members. In chapter 99 of the Book of the Dead, there is an interesting dialogue between the soul-traveller and the ferryman who would carry him over the river. The ferryman demands to know if the traveller is "equipped." "I am

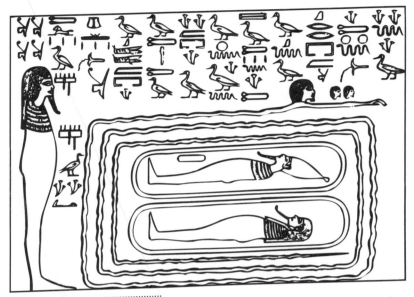

Fig. 9.13. The sahu *is called forth by Ra to breathe divine air. Exterior left panel of shrine 2 of Tutankhamon.*

equipped" responds the traveller. "Have you healed the limbs?" "I have healed the limbs." "What are those limbs?" "They are the arm and the leg," comes the reply.[34]

The healing of limbs, the restoration of the members of the dismembered body, is a theme that runs through the sacred literature of ancient Egypt. It was the climax of the Osirian initiation, which involved the experience of dismemberment. The "re-membering" of the body can thus be understood as an essential component of the "germination" of the *sahu*, and the attainment of the state of consciousness referred to in terms of becoming an *akh*. Insofar as this was achieved, one passed beyond the Osirian realm to that of Ra. This was the final rite of passage, the crossing of the heavenly threshold symbolized by the celestial river, or the gates of heaven.

In the following Old Kingdom text, from the pyramid of Teti, the *akh* is linked on the one hand to the "re-membering" of the king (and thereby to the germination of the *sahu*), while on the other hand the *akh* is associated with images of passing through celestial doors, travelling to the sky, and becoming joined with the stars. Instead of the god Ra, it is here Geb (the father of Osiris) who greets the king:

Oho! Oho! Rise up Teti!
Take your head,
collect your bones,
gather your limbs,
shake the earth from your flesh,
take your bread which does not grow moldy
and your beer that does not grow sour,
and stand at the gates which keep out the commoners.
The gatekeeper comes out to you,
he grasps your hand,
he takes you to the sky,
to your father Geb.
He rejoices at your coming,
gives you his hands,
kisses you, caresses you,
sets you at the head of the akhs,
the imperishable stars.[35]

It remains now for us to consider the journey of the soul with greater attention to the symbolic imagery of the sacred texts of ancient Egypt.

10 ORIENTATING IN THE UNDERWORLD

Psyche, Gods, and Cosmology

The states of consciousness referred to by the terms *ka*, *ba*, and *akh* were experienced in the context of a person's spiritual development. The integration of *ka* energy within an individual was instrumental to his or her liberation from the collective consciousness, and involved an enhancement of one's sense of selfhood. This development occurred in relation to the god Horus. To the degree to which one's *ka* energy was experienced as integral to one's own individual self-consciousness, one felt inwardly identified with Horus.

The state of consciousness referred to by the word *ba* arose as a concomitant of a different kind of experience of oneself—an experience involving separation from the body and normal sense-based awareness. The term *ba* denotes a mode of consciousness freed from physical constraints, but nevertheless bound up with psychic conditions, many of which might be derived from attachments to the physical world. The *ba*, therefore, existed in relation both to the physical and to the spiritual worlds. It dwelt in the region intermediate to them both, the Dwat, which was under the dominance of the god Osiris. Experience of the *ba*, therefore, came about in association with Osiris, with whom it was the destiny of the *ba* ultimately to be merged.

The word *akh* signified a state of consciousness that could only be gained when one had freed oneself from all bodily attachments, and become pscychologically "pure." Much emphasis is placed on the concept

213

of psychological purity in the literature dealing with the Underworld, for it is the precondition for being reborn as an *akh*. The *akh* signified a state of inner illumination and radiance, such as connected a person inwardly with the god Ra. In becoming aware of oneself as an *akh*, one realized one's own transcendent identity with Ra.

Ancient Egyptian esoteric psychology can therefore be understood as a path of development through which a person's relationship to the gods Horus, Osiris, and Ra was intensified, as they progressed through to ever more exalted levels of consciousness. One moved through the different spheres of influence of these gods on the journey of spiritual self-realization. In chapter 2, I tried to show that ancient Egyptian cosmology was essentially a metaphysical picture of the world. It was an ontological map disclosing different levels of being—physical, psychic, and spiritual. It can now be appreciated that the spiritual psychology we have been considering can be charted on this ontological map. To the physical world belongs the physical body subject to decay, the *khat*. What prevents it from decaying is the *ka* energy that imbues it with life. To the heavenly or spiritual world belongs the *akh*, the eternal and shining spirit. While between heaven and earth, between the material and spiritual realms, the *ba* lives and moves.

The following table presents these relationships:

Heaven	*akh*	spirit
Intermediate	*ba*	soul
	ka	vital body
Earth	*khat*	physical body

The relationship of Horus to the physical level, to the realm of manifest forms, is that he infuses this realm with life-forces, with *ka* energy. Horus, among other things, symbolizes spirit become manifest on the physical level. By contrast, the realm of Osiris is the realm of unmanifest forms and energies—the Dwat. This is the realm to which the *ba* belongs, and through which it travels in order to attain a higher level of existence as an *akh*. The *akh* comes into being in spheres of light that exist beyond the Dwat. This light is the light of pure spirit, bringing itself into being from out of the vast cosmic background of nonbeing. Here, in the heavenly world of Ra, is the source of eternal creativity, of self-generating and self-renewing spirit.

From this perspective, it follows that the journey through the Dwat was a journey undertaken in the modes of consciousness characterized by the *ka* and the *ba*; and of these two it was primarily in that of the *ba*. Quite often the two terms are used interchangeably in the Underworld literature. It is important to remember that the ancient Egyptians valued fluidity of thought over rigid conceptions, for when thought becomes fixed and rigid it no longer corresponds to lived experience.

Concepts of the Underworld

Although the Dwat is often referred to as the Underworld, it will be recalled that our word *underworld* is a misleading translation of what the Egyptians understood the Dwat to be (see chap. 2). Literally, the word *dwat* has the connotation of morning twilight, of dawn just before sunrise. It should thus be translated as "place of morning twilight" for this is its original meaning.[1] And in this original meaning there is the idea of a region that is in between night and day, darkness and light. Because it carries the connotation of morning twilight, it is not simply a state halfway between light and dark. There is the suggestion of the darkness giving way to the light, and hence the Dwat is the region through which one travels from the darkness into the light, or from the night into the day.

But the word *underworld* is not only employed to translate the Egyptian *dwat*. There are two other words that appear frequently in ancient Egyptian texts and that are generally translated as "Underworld." The first is *amentet*, which means literally "the hidden place." Like the concept *maat*, *amentet* was personified as a goddess of great beauty. She is the "Lady of the West" who receives the sun as it enters "the mysterious region" beyond manifestation. *Amentet* is an aspect of the cosmic mother goddess Hathor or Nut, who each evening swallows and each morning gives birth to the sun. What applies to the sun applies to the manifest world as a whole. *Amentet* is both the region into which forms disappear at death and arise out of when they are born. According to Plutarch, *amentet* signified for the Egyptians "the space which gives and takes."[2] If *amentet* is the hidden, or unmanifest, world within the cosmic goddess, it is an unmanifest world full of potency. In it, things exist neither purely spiritually nor as physically observable phenomena, but in an invisible yet dynamic state of metamorphosis and transformation.[3]

The third word commonly translated as "Underworld" is *neterkhert*, which translated literally means "the divine under place." The hieroglyphs do not specify exactly *what* this divine place is underneath. It could as well be under the stars as under the earth. And it is evident that the Egyptians conceived of it as *both* under the stars (that is, between heaven and earth) and under the earth. Insofar as the stars covered the flesh of the cosmic goddess Nut, the Underworld was as much within her body as underneath it, as we have seen. It was also regarded as located geographically in the west, where the sun set each evening, and equally in the east, for the sun rose out of the Underworld each morning. It was also believed that the Nile emerged from the Underworld, which gives it a southerly location. And human spirits, travelling to their celestial home among the northern stars, passed through the Underworld, which means it was also to be encountered in the north. Perhaps the most important thing about the term *neterkhert* is that it implies that there is a region "above" it or beyond it. Whether it is conceived as being above or below the earth, this side or the other side of heaven, whether it is found to the north, south, east, or west, the Underworld is always on the way to a higher realm.

We should really say that the Underworld was experienced as omnipresent. But because it was never regarded as a physical place, it was never allocated an exact physical location. Its location was psychic and mythographical, and one found oneself entering it whenever one approached the borders of normal sense-based consciousness. For this reason, when we employ the word *underworld* with reference to the ancient Egyptians, we should employ it with an acute awareness that it inadequately conveys the breadth of meanings of the original ancient Egyptian concept.

It came to be believed that everyone entered the Underworld when they died, and assumed the form of a *ka* or *ba*. Some people were also able to enter the Underworld during life. Familiarity with the regions of the Underworld was intrinsic to the knowledge of the magician and the priest, for these regions were constituted by psychic energies that it was necessary to master and transmute on the path toward spiritual attainment.

Unlike the Mesopotamian "Place of No Return," the Greek Hades, and the Israelite Sheol, the Egyptian Underworld was not a place in which those who went there were reduced to a shadowlike existence, without hope of change or movement. It was, on the contrary, a place through which one travelled, and one's journey consisted of a series of contests and trials, each of which—if one succeeded in them—resulted in an inner transformation. One became more and more oneself, more and more attuned to the divine and light-filled core of one's being, as one travelled through the Underworld. In this respect the Underworld of the Egyptians is closer to the later Christian conception of Purgatory than to the Mesopotamian, Greek, or Israelite underworlds, or to the Christian notion of Hell.

One main source of knowledge of the Egyptian Underworld is the New Kingdom Book of the Dead, to which we have already referred many times. It is by no means the only source, for the literature dealing with the Underworld is extensive, but it is the most graphic and accessible collection of texts available to us. As the following presentation of the Underworld journey will, for the most part, be based on the the Book of the Dead, some preliminary observations about it may be helpful.

First of all, the Book of the Dead is not the title by which the ancient Egyptians knew these texts. It was invented by modern Egyptologists because the texts, written upon papyrus rolls, were found placed on the bodies of the dead. The ancient Egyptians referred to these texts as the Book of Coming Forth into the Day (*pert em hru*), a title reflecting the concept of the Underworld as lying between night and day and also suggesting that it is a place from which one eventually comes forth."

The modern Book of the Dead contains nearly two hundred "chapters," all of which are numbered. This numbering is again the work of nineteenth-century Egyptologists, in particular Lepsius, who gave numbers to different sections on the basis of a rather late papyrus that was relatively complete. We possess large numbers of papyri, however, none of which contain all the chapters, but only a selection of the total range of nearly two hundred. There is, in fact, no "complete" Book of the Dead containing all the chapters. Furthermore, the ancient Egyptians did not hold to a fixed sequence of chapters, but would vary the sequence from papyrus to papyrus. What we find, then, is an apparent muddle of chapters in each papyrus. The papyrus of Ani, for example, begins with chapter 15, which is followed by chapter 30. Then we have chapter 1, after which come in succession chapters 22, 72, 17, 147, 146, and 18. The numbering of chapters is therefore purely a device to facilitate the identification of the contents of each papyrus, and in no way indicates the sequence in which the Book of the Dead is to be read.

It is, in fact, very hard to establish any "order of events" in the journey through the Underworld. And the papyri were not intended to be read in this way, but rather to provide the Underworld traveller with a range of prayers, spells, and images that would serve him or her in a variety of possible situations. The main purpose of the papyri was to enable a person to identify what "psychic space" they had arrived at, and to assist them to move through it. The idea of establishing a linear sequence was anyway

alien to the Egyptian mentality. The Underworld was travelled differently by each person, depending on the balance of psychic energies within
them.

With these qualifications in mind, we can now consider some of the
main features of the Underworld journey, in a sequence that hopefully
conveys the greatest archetypal force, but that is intended as no more than
one among many possible interpretations.

Opening the Way

The first stage of the Underworld journey is the Opening of the Door of
the Tomb so that the *ba* may be released from its incarceration there. The
tomb may be understood symbolically as the physical body and the consciousness based upon the physical senses, which according to the ancient
Egyptians, was a consciousness in which the *ba* was rendered inert. The *ba*
was believed to become active in sleep, when sensory consciousness is
completely stilled, or in "nonordinary" out-of-body states that could be
induced in initiatory rites. It also became active spontaneously at death
when normal sensory consciousness ceases. But the total release of the *ba*
from "the tomb" also depended on one's having "power in the legs." The
"opening of the door" was only the first step in a long journey of liberation, which demanded from a person diligence and resolve.

Figure 10.1 shows Ani opening the door of his tomb in order to enable
his *ba* to fly out. As the *ba* is liberated, Ani sets off on his long journey. The
illustration accompanies chapter 92 of the Book of the Dead. Chapter 92
bears the title "The Chapter for Opening the Tomb to the *Ba* and Shadow
[*khaibit*], of Coming Forth into the Day and of Getting Power in the
Legs." And it begins:

> *The place of bondage is opened,*
> *that which is shut is opened,*
> *the place of bondage is opened to my* ba. . . .
> *My steps are made long,*
> *my thighs are lifted up;*
> *I travel along the great path*
> *and my limbs are strong.*
> *I am Horus . . .*
> *and the path of* bas
> *is open to my* ba.

Given sufficient power in the legs, the Underworld traveller is able to turn away from the physical world, and sets off toward the horizon that marks the boundary between all that is familiar and that which is unknown. Figure 10.2 shows Nu, staff in hand, bravely striking out toward the Otherworld beyond the horizon. This first stage of the journey, of finding the paths that lead from the tomb to the Underworld, takes place in a region called Restau. Originally conceived as a gate between worlds, through which the sledge of the god Sokar (a god who was portrayed as an amalgam of Horus and Osiris) was ceremonially drawn, Restau was later thought of as a place of many paths, none of which were necessarily "open" to the traveller. It was therefore considered advisable to enlist the support of a guide, and of all the gods, the most dependable guide through these paths was Anubis, the jackal-headed god who was also known as Upawet, or Wepwawet, meaning "the Opener of the Ways."

Jackals used to live on the edge of the desert, in holes in the ground. They were perceived by the Egyptians to be at home on the borderland between civiliza-

Fig. 10.1. Opening the door of the tomb. Papyrus of Ani. Eighteenth Dynasty.

Fig. 10.2. Nu strikes out toward the Otherworld. Papyrus of Nu. Eighteenth Dynasty.

tion and the wild, between the Upperworld and the Lower World where they made their lairs, and between night and day since their favorite hunting time was at dusk. Statues of Anubis were characteristically painted both black and gold to symbolize the jackal's inherent duality. Anubis,

219

Fig. 10.3. Anubis leads Nakht toward the entrance of the Underworld. Papyrus of Nakht. Eighteenth Dynasty.

therefore, was—along with Horus—one of the most important helpers in the Underworld journey.

Figure 10.3, which belongs to the same chapter as figure 10.2, though from a different papyrus, shows Anubis leading Nakht by the hand toward the entrance to the Underworld. In front of it stands a tree, probably a sycamore fig *(Ficus sycomorus)* sacred to the goddess Nut.

She often appears in its branches offering refreshment of food and drink to the *ba* as it goes on its way (fig. 10.4). The benevolent presence of a feminine deity, whether in the guise of Nut, Hathor, or Maat, is an intermittent feature of the Underworld journey. Of the three, Maat is probably the most constant of the feminine divine companions on this journey. For she is the personification of moral truth and cosmic harmony, in relation to which the journey—in each of its stages—is made. If one falls out of relationship to Maat, then one cannot proceed any further. At the end of the journey, one comes before Maat in her tribunal and one is judged against her purity. The image of the judgment hall we shall come to later. But in a sense the whole journey takes place there, with Maat presiding over every decision and action that one makes.

On passing through the portal of the Underworld, the initial experience is of total darkness. This is one of the main signs to travellers that they have entered the Underworld. There is no longer any light of understanding or of hope. Everything that one associates with life and happiness is gone. The Underworld journey begins in darkness, the obliteration of all that previously gave one comfort and security in the Upperworld. The traveller says:

> *What kind of place is this*
> *into which I have come?*
> *It has no water, it has no air;*
> *it is unfathomably deep;*
> *it is black as the blackest night,*
> *and people wander in it helplessly.*
> *How can I find contentment here*
> *when it is impossible to satisfy*
> *the longings of love?*

From out of the depths of the all-encompassing darkness, the traveller hears a voice. It is the voice of the god Atum who, in the First Time, gave birth to himself out of the unfathomable abyss of Nun. Atum says:

> *I shall give you spiritual radiance*
> *in place of cakes and beer;*
> *peace of heart*
> *in place of the gratification of desire;*
> *and you shall look upon my face*
> *and you shall lack nothing.*[4]

Hearing these words of encouragement, the traveller gains new strength to continue the journey. But in the Dwat, everything is upside down and inside out. The Underworld is an inversion of the familiar world (see chap. 2). It is like a mirror world where what is apparently familiar reveals itself on closer inspection to be strangely other. Figure 10.5, from the tomb of Ramesses IX, shows the Underworld traveller encountering a topsy-turvy world. It becomes difficult to judge which way to stand, let alone which way to travel. For the laws of the Dwat are not the laws of the physical world. They are more like the laws of the dream world.

Fig. 10.4. The Underworld traveller is refreshed by the goddess of the sacred tree. Papyrus of Ani.

221

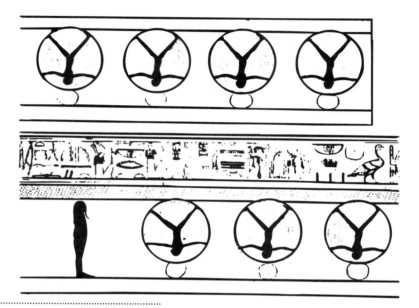

Fig. 10.5. Encountering a topsy-turvy world. Tomb of Ramesses IX, Valley of the Kings.

This experience of disorientation and confusion carries with it the specific danger of walking upside down through the Underworld. Just because what is above seems like what is below, and what is below seems like what is above, it is advisable for those travelling the paths through the Underworld to arm themselves with the necessary spells against this danger. Many of the spells in the Book of the Dead refer obliquely to it. The prophylactic chants against eating one's own excrement can be read in this light, for such an unpleasant possibility is clearly a peril attendant on losing one's fundamental orientation.[5] Figure 10.6, also from the tomb of Ramesses IX, illustrates the discomfort of those who are obliged, through ignorance or self-neglect, to make their way upside down, while those above them have discovered the secret of how to remain the right way up, and travel with ease along the paths.

Charting the Underworld

One conception of the Underworld journey, which goes back at least as far as Old Kingdom times, is that it takes place to a large extent in a very

Fig. 10.6. The danger of travelling upside down. Tomb of Ramesses IX.

boggy region, the predominant element being water. This region was referred to as the Field of Rushes (Sekhet Aaru), and it was regarded as important, from Middle Kingdom times onward, for those who travelled through it to be equipped with a map. We thus find maps painted on the bottom of the wooden coffins of Middle Kingdom nobles. Figure 10.7 is an example of one. All the gray areas on it indicate water or swamp. It is evident from the Old Kingdom Pyramid Texts that the Field of Rushes was understood as a place of purification.[6] It was traditionally regarded as being under the lordship of Osiris, but by the time of the Middle Kingdom this whole region was also known to be under the governance of the god Hotep (whose name is best translated as "Peace"). Hence the Field of Rushes was also the Field of Peace.

Turning to the map, we read that the three islands in the top register on the left are "The Place of Beating," "The Peaceful Place," and "The Great One." The inscription on the land mass beside them (on the right) states "To be the god Hotep, Lord of the Fields, with the breath of life in one's nose. One will not die." While below the three islands, the text describes the dimensions of this area as "one thousand leagues in length and in width"; and adds, "It is called Horns of the Lady of Purification." The reference to a goddess with horns is quite possibly a reference to the cow goddess Hathor, whose favorite landscape was that of the swamp, where wild

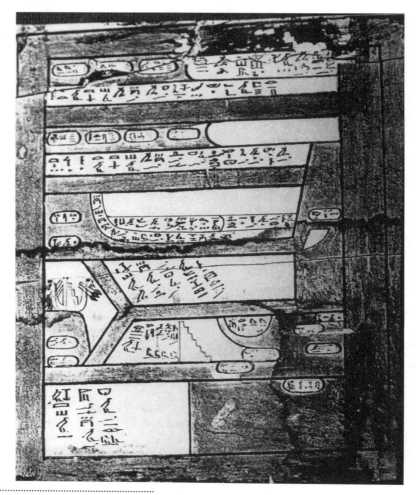

Fig. 10.7. Middle Kingdom map of the Field of Rushes. Middle Kingdom coffin.

cows foraged among the reeds and papyrus. Because Hathor was also a cosmic goddess who, like Nut, could be pictured as an image of heaven with stars on her belly, it is important to realize that the naturalistic imagery of the Field of Rushes has cosmic associations.

The next four islands bear the names "The Peaceful," "The Red One," "The Inundated," and "The Lady of the Two Lands." Again, the text underneath gives the name and dimensions of this region: "The Pool of the White Hippopotamus, one thousand leagues in length." And it adds some further information: "There are no fish or snakes in it." The reference to the white hippopotamus puts us in mind of another goddess of cosmic stature—the goddess Ipy. In the Pyramid Texts we read how Ipy suckles the king with her divine milk as he travels toward the stars.[7] The nobles of the Middle Kingdom assumed that she would perform a similar service for them.

The next inscription in the center of the map states: "Ploughing and reaping barley of Lower Egypt and emmer wheat of the estate of the God. There is no snake in it." Below left of the inscription a boat with rudders can be seen, apparently at rest on a lake with two more islands in it. Every map of this type featured a boat, moored in roughly the same place, and presumably waiting for the traveller to embark upon it. The boat was considered an essential means of transport in the celestial regions for which the traveller was destined. The area in front (to the right) of the boat is called "Storm Raiser."

Below this area is another in which it is stated that the boat is rowed by the four sons of Horus: Imsety, Hapy, Duamutef, and Qebhsenuf. This helping role is a continuation of the service they perform in the Pyramid Texts, where they are said to "bring the boat" to the king so that he can cross to the shores of the Beyond. They also "tie and make firm the rope ladder" so that the king can ascend to the stars, and indeed have a role in ensuring that he himself becomes "an imperishable star."[8]

In addition to the rope ladder, a staircase was a common means of ascent to the heaven world, and it is significant that one is featured here.[9] The staircase, along with the boat, always figures prominently in these Middle Kingdom maps of the Field of Rushes, reinforcing the impression that this is a region from which further ascent will be made.

Finally, in the bottom register is the "Sea of the Gods" where "it is cool for all the gods." This sea is so mysterious that "its length and its breadth are not told, even to Osiris."

On the whole, this Middle Kingdom map, of which there are many versions, all repeating with only minor discrepancies the same essential features, presents a relatively benign picture of the Field of Rushes. Not only are there no snakes here, but the islands and regions bear for the most part benevolent names. Furthermore, the means for subsequent travel to higher levels are provided with the boat and the staircase. The island called "Place of Beating" and the region called "Storm Raiser," however, do suggest that this could be a region of suffering and uncertain peril.

Another type of map that also appears on the inside of Middle Kingdom coffins is shown in figure 10.8. The figure depicts just one section of a larger

Fig. 10.8. The two ways. Middle Kingdom coffin.

scheme, referred to as the Book of the Two Ways, which would cover the whole floor of the coffin. This section features the "two ways," the upper one blue, the lower black. They are separated from each other by a long oblong "Lake of Fire." The blue way should be understood as a watercourse, the black as a land route. One enters at the right-hand end, where there are two gates, the Gate of Fire and the Gate of Darkness (the semicircular shape). Above the Gate of Darkness, a strange-looking ram-headed creature, mummiform and wielding a knife, is on guard. His name is "He Who Opposes the Criminal." He is but the first of a series of hostile creatures that are to be encountered whichever way one takes. Many of these creatures are not represented; their presence is simply stated in the text. In order to pass them, the traveller must both know their names and also affirm his or her own connection with higher powers. For example, in facing The Scowler, The Loud-Voiced One, The Oppressor, The Trembler, and He Who Is Hot, who crowd the second bend of the upper, blue way, the traveller says:

> *I am a Spirit, Lord of Spirits.*
> *A Spirit which I create exists as a Spirit;*
> *what I hate exists not.*
> *I am the one who circles around his lake*
> *in the fire of Ra, Lord of Light.*
> *I am he who makes the month,*
> *who announces the half-month.*
> *The Eye of Horus circles near me,*
> *Thoth crosses the sky in front of me.*
> *I pass by safely.*[10]

This pattern of challenge and response is one of the central characteristics of the Underworld journey. One meets it in the Old Kingdom Pyramid Texts, when the star traveller is challenged by the great bull of heaven, who guards the roads of the sky.[11] In order to get past the bull it is essential that one knows who one is and where one is going, and that one affirms one's ability to get there. In the section of the Book of the Two Ways we are considering, the single challenge by the bull is multiplied into a series of challenges by the guardians of the bends, each of which have nightmarish names: The Leaper, The Fiery One, She of the Knife, He Who Curses, The Swallower, The Alert One, He Who Is Acute, He Whose Face Is Dreadful, are but a sampling of the demons of the upper waterway. On the lower way, there is a marked decrease in the number of guardian demons, but though fewer they are no less formidable. They include Knife, Hippopotamus Face With Wild Strength, Repulsive Face Who Lives On Dung, and so on. As with the demons of the upper way, they are met with affirmations of one's inner resolve and purity. The main difference between the two ways, however, is less in the amount of demons attendant on each than in the relationship that the traveller adopts with either Ra or Osiris. Passage along the lower land route would seem to require an especial devotion to Ra, while the passage along the upper waterway is undertaken mostly with reference to Osiris. The distinction between these two ways is never clearly elaborated, however, and by the time of the New Kingdom it becomes absorbed into a rich diversity of images of the Underworld journey.

Nevertheless, there is a basic continuity in the conception of the Underworld as composed of many regions to be traversed. In the New Kingdom, the maps emphasize the specific qualities of the different regions. One such map, from the papyrus of the scribe Userhat (Eighteenth Dynasty) is shown in figure 10.9. The Field of Rushes is here divided into fifteen "mounds" (*aats*), and it is clear that the largely benevolent aspect of the earlier Middle Kingdom Field of Rushes has changed to something more demanding indeed. The text begins on the top right, and moves downward through the different prominences, some of which are evidently difficult places to be. For example, the U-shape on its side (center right) is a region of fire called "The Horns of Fire," while immediately below it is a "mountain, exceedingly high." The region third from the bottom on the right is ruled by the god who is ominously named "The Overthrower of Fish." As we shall see, travelling the Underworld in the form of a fish was a danger to be avoided. On the left center, the area shaped like a house has inscribed within it "Here resides the divine destroyer of souls." Immediately below it, the S-shaped region is one of

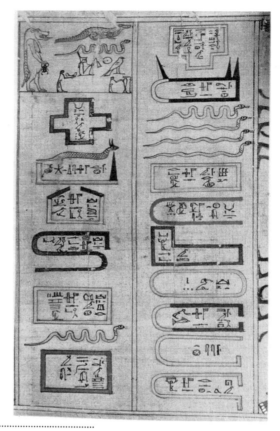

Fig. 10.9. The New Kingdom Field of Rushes. Papyrus of Userhat. Eighteenth Dynasty.

rushing waters." Looking at the map as a whole, one notices the presence of several snakes among the different mounds, which add to the general atmosphere of menace conveyed by the map.

The implication of this and other maps is that there is a range of archetypal states of soul that the *ba* goes through on its Otherworldly travels, but each state is experienced as an externalized environment. In the Underworld there is no physical environment, for it is not a physical world. Rather it is a psychic world that arises for a person out of his or her own psychic condition. Just as in a dream one finds oneself in situations and contexts that reflect one's own inner state, so in the Underworld what is presented to one as an external environment is but a reflection of one's own

228

psychic energies. The wisdom of the map-making tradition is that it charts, as psychic environments, the range of possible archetypal states of soul. One is thus enabled to understand "where one is," and to move from one region to another. Progress through the Underworld consists in a gradual purging of the *ba* of all those elements in it that are spiritually disharmonious. In this way, the "outer" environment in which it finds itself gradually changes and becomes less threatening or ugly, and more beautiful and pacific.

Not all the mounds bear negative names. There is a mound of spirits, for instance (beneath the "mountain, exceedingly high") and the whole region is introduced as "the beautiful hidden land [Amentet] where the gods live on cakes and ale." The Field of Rushes, it seems, is interpenetrated by higher worlds, and the benevolent presence of exalted spiritual beings can always be felt there, if one is open to it. It is for this reason that there also exist many New Kingdom maps of the Underworld that show it to be a kind of paradise. For it is, potentially, just that. Figure 10.10, from the papyrus of Ani[12] contains many of the features of the earlier Middle Kingdom maps—the wateriness of the Field of Rushes, the existence of islands, boats, and staircases. But it also shows Ani consorting with the gods

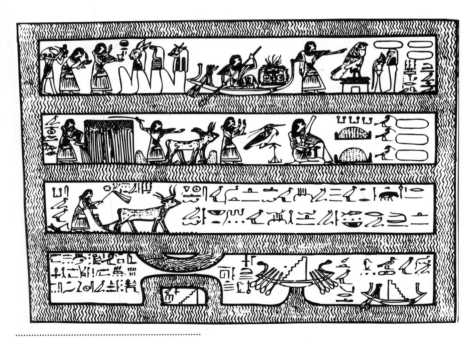

Fig. 10.10. The Field of Rushes as Paradise. Papyrus of Ani.

who dwell in this region. On the top left he makes offerings to three animal-headed deities, he paddles his boat, and he addresses a divine hawk, symbolic of Horus. Beneath the three islands, the text states: "Being at Peace in the Field of Peace, and having air for the nostrils."

On the next register Ani, here identified with Osiris, reaps an exceedingly high crop of grain and threshes it by driving oxen over it. He holds his hands up in adoration before the bennu bird of Ra, he sits holding the sacred *kherp* scepter, and at the end on the right we see three *ka* signs above two heaps of red and white grain respectively, and three *akh* birds, symbolic of shining spirits, in front of islands that they presumably live on.

On the third register, which shows Ani ploughing, we are informed that this is a region belonging to a hippopotamus and that "the river is one thousand leagues in length. Its width cannot be told. There are no fish, nor snakes, in it." Finally, in the bottom register, two boats are moored, each one with a flight of steps on it, and there are two islands, one of which has a third flight of steps. We learn that the god here is Osiris, and that this region is "the seat of the shining ones [*akhs*] . . . the blessed dead who are perfected." They are said to reap wheat three cubits high.

Maps like this one have lead some Egyptologists to equate the Field of Rushes with the Elysian Fields of the Greeks.[13] But it is important to bear in mind that such a positive experience of the Underworld assumes that one has already undergone, and been thoroughly transformed by, the purifications that are also central to the ancient Egyptian conception of the Underworld. It takes on this sunny and benevolent aspect only for those who have travelled through the darker and more shadowy encounters that beset one when one first enters this mysterious place.

Images of Travel

Having attained some impression of the range of possible Underworld environments from the foregoing maps, we can now investigate in more detail the kind of experiences that travellers have as they journey through the Underworld. Being predominantly watery, the most suitable method of traversing the Underworld is by boat. In ancient Egypt, the boat was the primary means of transport not only in the marshes but also along the length and breadth of the Nile valley, on the river and the canals adjacent to it. The waterways were the main arteries of communication, both more convenient and faster than travel by foot or donkey.

In the Underworld the waterways are traversed with an uncomfortable

Fig. 10.11. Nu travels on his boat through the Underworld. Papyrus of Nu. Eighteenth Dynasty.

awareness that underneath them there lurks the dreadful presence of the opposing serpent Apophis. In some of the New Kingdom Underworld texts, Ra's boat is shown literally sailing across the undulating back of the serpent. Figure 10.11 (from the Book of the Dead) does not show the serpent, but the text accompanying the illustration refers explicitly to the tensions felt by the traveller who, in order to reach his "father" Osiris, must travel over the back of Apophis. The text is addressed to the "bringer of the boat" whose identity is revealed in the last stanza as the traveller's own "shining spirit"— that part of oneself that can be relied upon to see one through this frightening part of the journey. Since we are not concerned here with a physical boat, the boat is best understood as an image of the spiritual or psychospiritual quality that one can rest in and depend upon to carry one through this indirect encounter with the opposing power of Apophis.

> *O you who bring the boat*
> *over the evil back of Apophis,*
> *bring me the boat,*
> *make fast the rope in peace, in peace.*

Come, come! Hurry, hurry!
for I have come to see my father Osiris,
Lord of the Red Cloth,
who has gained mastery with joy of heart.

O Lord of the Storm, the one who navigates,
O you who sail over the evil back of Apophis!
. . . O you who are in charge of the mysterious boat!
O you who fetter Apophis!
Bring me the boat,
make fast the rope for me
so that I may sail forth.

This land is baleful,
the stars have overbalanced
and fallen on their faces,
and are unable to rise up again.
I am brought along like one who has suffered shipwreck.

May my Shining Spirit, my brother, come to me,
so that I may set out for the place
which my Spirit knows.[14]

Fig. 10.12. The ferryman, He Who Sees Behind Him. Papyrus of Ani.

In some texts making contact with the bringer of the boat, the shining spirit, is fraught with difficulty. One is no longer dealing with just one entity but two. For as well as the bringer of the boat, who will also act as the ferryman who will take one across (or along) the waters, there is the "keeper of the boat." The keeper of the boat is another aspect of, perhaps a deeper level of, the shining spirit; and because deeper, more difficult of access. The keeper is sometimes described as being asleep, and must be awakened by the ferryman. In the following text, the keeper of the boat is called Aqen, while the ferryman is called Mahaf, a name that came to be understood as "He Who Sees Behind Him." He is shown in figure 10.12 as a man with his head swiveled round completely so that it is facing the opposite way to the rest of his body and to the direction in which he is travelling. The image is reminiscent of those depicting the god Osiris as the constellation Orion in the southern sky. He is frequently portrayed as a man in full stride, travelling on a boat, his face turned to look behind him (fig. 10.13). He is in fact looking back toward Isis, the divine cow, who as the star Sirius was Orion's faithful companion. Between them their son Horus perches on a papyrus stem. This is to suggest a connection between the ferryman and the god Osiris, as well as a celestial location for the navigation of the waters.

Fig. 10.13. Isis, Horus, and Osiris, as constellations in the southern sky. Temple of Hathor, Denderah.

233

In the text (referred to in chap. 9) it is made clear that it is necessary for the traveller to be whole and complete, implying that he, like Osiris, has been through a process of dismemberment. The dialogue with the ferryman begins as follows:

TRAVELLER: O Mahaf, as you are endowed with life, awaken Aqen for me, for see, I have come.

MAHAF: Who are you who comes?

TRAVELLER: I am a magician.

MAHAF: Are you complete?

TRAVELLER: I am complete.

MAHAF: Are you equipped?

TRAVELLER: I am equipped.

MAHAF: Have you healed the limbs?

TRAVELLER: I have healed the limbs.

MAHAF: What are the limbs, magician?

TRAVELLER: They are the arm and the leg.

MAHAF: Take care! Do you say that you would cross to the east side of the sky? If you cross, what will you do?

TRAVELLER: I will govern the towns, I will rule the villages, I will know the rich and give to the poor, I will prepare cakes for you when going downstream and bread when going upstream. O Mahaf, as you are endowed with life, awaken Aqen for me, for see, I have come.

Mahaf is still not satisfied, and fires more cryptic questions at the traveller, which the latter answers equally cyptically. At last he goes to waken Aqen, only to return saying, "He does not wake for me." Eventually the traveller, forgoing the aid of Mahaf, manages to get through to Aqen and rouse this profoundly somnolent being.

AQEN: What is it? I was asleep.

TRAVELLER: O Aqen, as you are endowed with life, bring me this, for see, I have come.

AQEN: Who are you who comes?

TRAVELLER: I am a magician.

AQEN: Are you complete?

TRAVELLER: I am complete.

AQEN: Are you equipped?

TRAVELLER: I am equipped.

AQEN: Have you taken care of the two limbs?
TRAVELLER: I have taken care of the two limbs.
AQEN: What are the two limbs, magician?
TRAVELLER: They are the arm and the leg. O Aqen, as you are
    endowed with life, bring me this, for see, I have come.

And so a virtually identical dialogue ensues with Aqen. But Aqen now claims that the boat is not equipped. It has no bailer, no spars, no beams, no rigging. The traveller must show that he has the power to provide all these things himself. In other words, the traveller must himself construct, or reconstruct, the "dismembered" boat. It is perhaps worth noting here that the great boats buried near the Giza pyramids were not buried whole but in pieces. These boats, presumably meant to serve as vehicles for the Otherworld journey, also had to be put together by the traveller to the Beyond.

When the labor of putting the boat together is eventually completed, there is a final and somewhat unnerving exchange between Aqen and the traveller.

AQEN: HAve you power over what I have not brought to you,
    magician? That august god will say: "Have you ferried over to
    me a man who does not know the number of his fingers?"
TRAVELLER: I know how to count my fingers; take one, take the
    second, quench it, remove it, give it to me, be friendly towards
    me; do not let go of it; have no pity on it; make the Eye
    bright; give the Eye to me.[15]

This mysterious reply relates to the myth in which the eye of Horus is plucked out by Seth, but is later restored to him more "complete" and better able to see for having been torn apart. There are a series of utterances in the Pyramid Texts that refer to this, one of which reads as follows:

> O King, take for yourself the finger of Seth,
> that causes the clear eye of Horus to see.
> O King, take for yourself the clear eye of Horus,
> that is lighted by the tip of Seth's finger.[16]

Aqen's cross-examination of the traveller is best understood as a means of ascertaining the extent to which the traveller has integrated and metamorphosed the negative power of Seth so that it promotes clarity of vision. The depth and complexity of the traveller's reply is better appreciated when it is realized that the bolt of a temple naos containing the divine image was also referred to as the "finger of Seth." Furthermore, Seth's fire-emitting phallus was likewise referred to obliquely as his "finger," which explains why the traveller should speak of "quenching" his finger.[17] The unrestrained and violent aspect of libidinal energy that Seth represents must be tamed or redirected in a positive way in order for the traveller to cross the water.

It is likely that the water here was identified with the great celestial river, the Milky Way, which figured prominently in the ancient Egyptian understanding of the celestial location of the Underworld journey. But the image of water that a traveller has to be ferried across is universal in Underworld mythology. The water represents a great obstacle that must be overcome in order to attain a higher level of consciousness, and thus to find oneself in a different psychospiritual environment. Whether one locates it in the sky or elsewhere is less important than what the crossing of the water entails for the development of consciousness. It will be remembered that the image of crossing the water by ferryboat included the acknowledgment that under the water the powerful adversary Apophis lives. The Book of the Dead could hardly rest content with such a deceptively simple account of how one traverses the realm of psychic energies as that of merely getting into a boat and paddling across. This journey was by no means easy, and the difficulties that travellers faced were represented in an array of images of encounters with monsters, demons, and wild animals, all of which were thrown up by Apophis (or the opposing power) to confront the consciousness of those who sought to make headway through this discomforting zone. It is to these encounters that we now turn.

11 THE TRAVAILS OF THE UNDERWORLD

Air, Water, and Fire

The imagery of traversing the watery regions of the Underworld by boat is complex and multileveled. We have already seen that it involves the associated ideas of a ferryman and boatkeeper, as well as the hidden presence of the opposing serpent Apophis underneath the surface of the waters. The boat itself is a powerful symbolic image of the soul's ability to sustain a journey through many trials and perils. The requirement that one be able to construct one's own boat clearly indicates that a certain degree of spiritual attainment is assumed. Boats are not simply provided for travellers; they must understand all the details of how a boat is put together and must then be able to put it together themselves. Each part of the boat has its symbolic meaning and can be understood as corresponding to specific inner qualities.

This is especially clear in the case of the sail that, hieroglyphically, signifies air, wind, or breath. The Underworld is quite often described as an airless place.[1] This is because the only air that is to be breathed there is *maat*, or truth. This alone is what sustains the spirit; hence the gods were all regarded as breathing *maat*, the divine air that pervades the universe. To the extent that one has lived on earth oblivious of the divine air, one must experience the Underworld as suffocating. In chapter 54 of the Book of the Dead, the traveller prays: "O Atum, give me the sweet breath which is in your nostrils."[2] The prayer continues with an affirmation that the traveller is the egg of the Great Cackler—a form of the the earth god Geb who, as a divine goose, lays the primeval egg from which the world hatches at the beginning of time:

> *I am the Egg which is in the Great Cackler,*
> *and I watch and guard that mighty thing*
> *which has come into being*
> *and with which the god Geb has opened the earth.*[3]

To breathe the divine air is to be reborn into the spirit world, and hence it is to recapitulate the essential first phases of creation. One must return to the egg in order to germinate afresh as a living spirit, breathing the air of the gods:[4] "As it [the egg] germinates, so do I germinate, /As it lives, so do I live, /As it breathes, so do I breathe."[5] So says Nu. There are many chapters in the Book of the Dead concerned with ensuring that the traveller has air to breathe. Figure 11.1 shows Ani holding to his nostrils the hieroglyphic sail as he utters his prayer, and hopes for his spiritual rebirth.

Breathing the air of the gods, one is able to avoid the fate of being caught in the net cast by the three baboons shown in figure 11.2. Baboons habitually gathered just before sunrise and sunset in ancient Egypt, to mark the rising and setting of the sun with their noisy chattering and dancing. They were thought of as the guardians of the gates of the eastern and western mountains through which the sun passed on his way out of and then back into the Underworld. Baboons were also the sacred animals of Thoth, the god of wisdom and power-knowledge. The fish, living in the element of water, was an image of the ignorant or undeveloped soul. According to Herodotus, fish formed no part of the diet of priests.[6] It is significant that, of the six fish hieroglyphs, four of them carry negative connotations—"abomination," "stinking," "discontent," and "corpse." If the Underworld is a watery place, then the last thing that one should attempt to

Fig. 11.1. Ani carries a sail, the hieroglyph for air, which he hopes to breathe in the Underworld. Papyrus of Ani. Eighteenth Dynasty.

Fig. 11.2. Three baboons try to catch souls that, travelling submerged in water, lose their human form and take on the form of fish. Papyrus of Nefer-Ubenef. New Kingdom.

do is to swim through it like a fish. The element water, for the Egyptians, was the element the Sethian creatures inhabited—the crocodile, the hippopotamus, the water snake. The fish itself was regarded as a Sethian creature: was it not three species of Nile fish that ate the penis of Osiris?[7] And how came Osiris to be in the Nile anyway? It was through the evil machinations of Seth, who threw him into the dark depths of the river where no light of the sun could penetrate. There Osiris languished as the "Drowned One,"[8] the one overwhelmed by water, with no air to breathe.

Figure 11.2 can be seen, then, as depicting a specific danger attendant on passing into the Underworld: that one's *ba* neither preserves its human form nor attains its birdlike manifestation, but takes the form of a fish, because one's psyche is more attuned to the element of water than air.

Certain sayings of the Ephesian philosopher Heraclitus seem peculiarly relevant here, for instance: "For souls it is death to become water," and "A dry soul is wisest and best."[9] The dry soul (*ba*) of Nefer-Ubenef is pictured kneeling, above and to the left of the baboons, as having preserved its human shape: for Nefer-Ubenef ("beautiful and shining") is a master of the elements.

Figure 11.3 shows Nakht escaping unscathed from the dreadful net. The illustration is an image of immunity from being caught up and entangled in negative energies. In chapter 153a of the Book of the Dead, the net is described as reaching from heaven to earth. Nakht shouts defiantly:

> *Oh you fishermen who go about in the abode of waters,*
> *you shall not catch me in your net*
> *in which you catch the inert ones!*
> *You shall not trap me in your net*
> *in which you trap the wanderers!*
> *. . . I have escaped from its clutches,*
> *I have risen up like Sobek [the crocodile god].*
> *Like a bird, I fly away from you—*
> *from you who fish with hidden fingers.*[10]

Nakht knows the secret of how to transform himself into a bird—the *ba* bird. But this is only one reason why he is able to escape being caught. The other reason is that he knows the names of every part of this net and he proceeds to demonstrate his knowledge to the last detail. Each part of the net is named as a member of a god—the reel is the middle finger of Sokar, the guardbeam the thigh of Shemu, the valve is the hand of Isis, and so on. Some parts are weapons of gods and others are some object belonging to a god. Nakht gives a long and complex interpretation of the esoteric correspondences of the parts of the net, and concludes with the following statement:

> *Oh you fishermen . . .*
> *you shall not catch me in your net,*
> *you shall not trap me in your net*
> *in which you trap the inert ones,*
> *and trap those who are earthbound.*
> *For I know it.*
> *I know it from its upper floats*
> *to its lower weights.*

Fig. 11.3. Nakht escapes from the net. Papyrus of Nakht. Eighteenth Dynasty.

> *Here I am.*
> *I have come with a reel in my hand,*
> *my valve in my hand.*
> *I have come and I have entered in.*
> *I smite and I catch.*[11]

Nakht knows the net so well that he proves that he has power over it. Not only is he not a fish, he claims that through his knowledge of the net he is himself a fisherman.

Water, however, is not only a symbol of negative states of consciousness that prevent one from breathing divine air, it is also a symbol of purification. Every temple in ancient Egypt had a sacred lake in which the priests would ritually wash themselves each morning before entering the temple. The purificatory aspect of water is often indicated by its being combined with the element of fire. In the Middle Kingdom map of the Two Ways (fig. 10.8), we have already encountered the "river of fire" that separates the upper way from the lower way. But in addition to rivers of fire, there were also lakes of fire in the Underworld. One such lake is depicted in figure 11.4, from the papyrus of Ani. The lake is filled with burning water—a fact that is emphasized not only by the water being colored red, but also by the hieroglyph on the four sides of the lake, which signifies "fire."

At the four corners of the lake, baboons appear once again. The reason

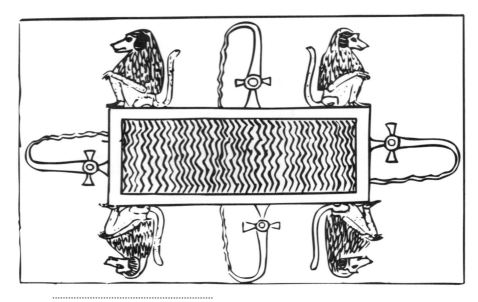

Fig. 11.4. The Lake of Fire. Papyrus of Ani.

why they are present is that the lake of fire is the setting in which Ra is born. Indeed, it is created by Ra's birth. According to ancient Egyptian creation mythology the birthplace of Ra was regarded as being the First Land that arose out of the dark Primordial Ocean of Nun. This First Land—sometimes also pictured as a lotus or an egg—was referred to as the Isle of Fire, because it was alight with Ra's dazzling presence. Such was the intensity of Ra's first appearance at the dawn of time that the waters surrounding his birthplace were also lit up and, as it were, caught fire. For the Egyptians, Ra's birth from the great ocean was an event repeated each day when, at dawn, the whole sky lights up and turns a fiery red. Just as the baboons of Thoth each morning excitedly greet the dawning sun, so they greeted the very first rising of Ra from the primordial ocean, rejoicing as his rays illuminated the surrounding darkness.

It is into this powerful primordial event that the Underworld traveller is projected when he or she comes to the Lake of Fire. Chapter 17 of the Book of the Dead warns that, "As concerning the Lake of Fire, those who attempt to cross it who are impure will fall down among the knives."[12]

The Lake of Fire threatens to cut out all that is impure in the soul, so if a person enters it wholly identified with those aspects of themselves that are unregenerate and unable to transmit the life-giving light of Ra, then they will suffer a torment similar to being hacked to pieces. Such a fate is vividly depicted in the eleventh division of the Book of What Is in the Underworld where the "enemies of Osiris" are shown both being cut up with knives and burnt. But, as Saint Catherine of Genoa was later to say, "The fire of hell is simply the light of God as experienced by those who reject it."[13] By turning oneself toward it and submitting oneself to its burning, purgatorial pain, the Lake of Fire loses its destructive aspect and becomes the essential means of inner transformation. Thus we find, in chapter 126 of the Book of the Dead, the following prayer addressed to the four baboons:

> *Homage to you, you four baboons*
> *who sit upon the bow of the boat of Ra,*
> *who make the truth of God advance,*
> *who apportion to me both my weakness and my strength,*
> *who pacify the gods with the flame that issues from your nostrils,*
> *who give holy offerings to the gods*
> *and invocation offerings to the Shining Ones,*
> *who live on* maat, *who gulp down* maat,
> *whose hearts harbour no lies,*
> *who detest falsehood:*
> *Purge the evil that is in me!*
> *Destroy all falsehood that is in me!*
> *Heal the wounds which I had on earth!*
> *Purge away all the evil that clings to me!*[14]

The Beasts That Oppose

The meeting with the baboons is but the first of a series of encounters with various animal denizens of the Underworld. Sometimes the animal forms that rise up to meet the traveller are not recognizable; they are so monstrous that nature could not find it in herself to give them physical embodiment, and yet they exist in the psychic world, for the energies of the psyche can be uglier and more bestial than those of any beast living in nature. To be accosted by such forms—whether of known animals or of unknown monsters—is to be accosted by energies that still cling to one's psychic aura, and that become objectified in the Underworld.

The journey through the Underworld is a purgatorial journey. In the course of it, the *ba* must free itself of all those elements in its nature that are inconsonant with *maat*. And this process of becoming free is pictured as involving three stages: first of all the negative energy presents itself to the traveller as an autonomous force, usually a beast of some description. This stage can of course be precipitated by the more conscious traveller who has learned how to objectify actively the blocking energy in a specific visual image. Second, the traveller and the opposing force engage in a struggle. The opposer wants to steal the traveller's heart, take away the traveller's magic power, or kill the traveller's soul—that is, to cut the *ba* off from all contact with its spiritual source. The aim of the traveller, by contrast, is not to kill or eliminate the opposer, but rather to master it. This is often symbolized in the act of "turning the head" of the beast that comes against you. And this "turning of the head" may be thought of as the third stage of the process. For in accomplishing this difficult feat, one actually wins for oneself—for one's higher purpose—all the negative energy by which one was initially opposed. This appropriation of negative energy— the transformation of one's demons into beneficent daemons, as one modern psychologist has put it[15]—is crucial to the whole notion of journeying through the Underworld, in contrast to merely stagnating in it.

In figure 11.5, three crocodiles suddenly appear on the path, and challenge the Underworld traveller (in this case Nakht), threatening to steal his magic power and destroy his soul. How are we to understand this image of the three crocodiles? One of the characteristics of this creature is that it can lurk in the depths of a river or canal, and one can have no idea that it is there. You may think that you are completely safe, and that there is no danger at all, because you cannot see any sign of the crocodile's presence. The crocodile has this capacity to conceal itself beyond the range of human awareness, and this is what makes it so terrifying. It is an animal that can strike from complete concealment. Once in the grip of its deadly jaws, one's fate is determined: there is no reprieve.

This aspect of the crocodile's nature is most significant for travellers of the Underworld. For in the Underworld one encounters crocodiles on the psychic plane that lie in wait in the depths of the unconscious, and whose object is to drag down the unwary traveller. The fate of the soul is then, like the fate of the body on the physical plane, to drown in dark waters and to become fodder for this merciless creature.

The crocodile's main desire is to consume the magic that is the soul's principal possession. Travellers must therefore arm themselves with a knife and shout out these words of power:

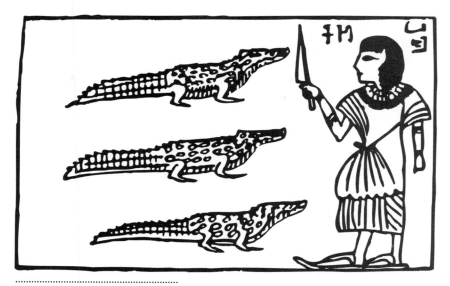

Fig. 11.5. Three crocodiles appear on the path. Papyrus of Nakht.

> *Get back! Give way!*
> *Get back you crocodile fiend!*
> *You shall not come against me*
> *for my magic lives in me!*
>
> *May I not have to speak your name*
> *to the Great God who has allowed you to appear.*[16]

The traveller then proves that he knows the name of each crocodile. In so doing he brings the light of conscious knowledge to bear on the dark and fearful powers that oppose him. Were this conscious knowledge then to be held at the level of the divine consciousness of Ra, which is what the traveller threatens to do by "speaking" the name to the Great God, the crocodile opponents would be completely vanquished. For no crocodile can withstand Ra's burning radiance. The ability to discern the true nature of the enemy, and then to name it, is perhaps symbolized by the long knife that Nakht holds. It is the knife of discernment, of clear consciousness that is blunted neither by fear nor desire, but is, as it were, sharpened by devotion to truth, or *maat*. The crocodiles blurt out: "Your face is turned towards *maat*." Nakht then pronounces the words of an incantation in which he himself appropriates the essence of the crocodilian foes that would steal his magic. As he chants his words of power, he becomes visibly bigger than his opponents, who seem to shrink before him.

> *As the sky encloses the stars*
> *and as magic* [heka] *encloses all that is within its power,*
> *so does my mouth enclose the magic which is in it.*
> *My teeth are knives of flint,*
> *and my back teeth are fangs filled with venom.*
> *O you crocodile who would swallow my magic,*
> *you shall not take it away!*
> *No crocodile that lives on magic*
> *shall take my magic away!*[17]

In figure 11.6, another traveller demonstrates the technique of turning the heads of the crocodiles so that they face the other way. This is an impossible position for crocodiles to adopt on the physical plane, but several illustrations from ancient papyri attest to its possibility on the psychic plane. The crocodiles shown here come at the traveller from each of the four directions. To deal with them, he must identify himself with a specific deity. Facing west, he identifies himself with Seth, the god to whom the crocodile is sacred, and who has authority over all crocodiles. Facing east, he is Osiris, the god who triumphs over death. Facing south, he is Soped, a star god connected with Sirius, and renowned for his sharp teeth. Facing north, he identifies with Atum, the inexhaustible fount of creative energy.

Chapter 32 of the Book of the Dead "for beating back the crocodile" ends with the following beautiful affirmation:

Fig. 11.6. Turning the heads of crocodiles that come from each of the four cardinal points. Twenty-sixth Dynasty papyrus.

That which exists is in the hollow of my hand,
that which does not yet exist is in my belly.
I am clothed and equipped with your magic, O Ra. . . .
My face is open,
my heart is upon its seat,
and the uraeus serpent is with me day by day.
I am Ra, who through himself protects himself,
and nothing shall cast me down.[18]

In addition to crocodiles, one may also be attacked by wild pigs in the Underworld. Figure 11.7 shows Nakht again, now armed apparently with a long spear, turning the head of a wild pig. As in figure 11.6, the spear is in fact a harpoon, the weapon that Horus victoriously uses against Seth in their conflict. In the Book of the Dead, chapter 12, it is stated that Seth assailed Horus in the form of a black pig, causing serious injury to Horus's eye—that is, to his faculty of vision. In the illustration, the pig is not killed, but the force of his attack is deflected by the skillful use of the harpoon. It will be noticed that the snake is also held fettered by a rope. If one cannot turn the head of the opposing animal, then tying it up would seem to be the next best thing.

With snakes, however, there are more effective means of harnessing

Fig. 11.7. Deflecting the assault of the raging pig. Papyrus of Nakht.

Fig. 11.8. Overpowering the snake. Papyrus of Ani.

their energy than literally tying them up. In figure 11.8, Ani overpowers a snake with a forked snake-catching stick, with which he traps its head while he places one foot on its tail. This vignette is from chapter 10 of the Book of the Dead, but the text that should probably accompany it is that of chapter 39, "For Repelling The Rerek Snake," who is identified in this chapter with Apophis, the eternal opponent of Ra. The further stage of turning the serpent round so that it faces the other way is illustrated in certain papyri of the Book of the Dead. In figure 11.9, for instance, the serpent is turned round and made to go in the direction from which it came, while in the accompanying text the traveller recites the following spell:

Get back! Crawl away!
Depart from me you snake!
Go and be drowned in the Waters of Nun,
at the place where your father
has commanded that you shall be slain.
Depart from the divine birth-place of Ra!
You tremble with fear,
for I am Ra at whom all tremble.
Get back, you fiend, before the arrows of his light!
Ra has overthrown your words.
The gods have turned your face backwards,
Mafdet [a panther goddess] has torn open your breast,
Selket [a scorpion goddess] has fettered you,
Maat has completed your destruction.[19]

The incantation continues with the traveller identifying the snake with Apophis and himself with Ra, or the servant of Ra, and hence with the archetypal situation described in the Book of What Is in the Underworld, which we have already considered in the context of the battle of Kadesh (chap. 5) and Egyptian state magic (chap. 7). As we have seen, in this esoteric New Kingdom text the great serpent seeks to prevent the progress of Ra's journey through the Underworld regions. The serpent is first lassoed and knives are inserted into key points of its body. It is then turned around so that it faces the direction in which Ra wishes to travel. Finally, in the climactic twelfth division of the Book of What Is in the Underworld, Ra is drawn through the serpent's body, entering the tail end, and is "reborn" through the serpent's mouth. The imagery that is to be found in the Book of the Dead concerning the control and redirection of the serpent energy should therefore be understood in the context of the subsequent event of Ra's rebirth—which is in fact alluded to in the text of chapter 39 just quoted. The rebirth of Ra corresponds to the initiation of the Underworld traveller into the exalted state of consciousness that characterizes those who achieve an inner identification with the *akh* or "shining spirit" in themselves. The chapter ends with all the gods intervening on the side of the traveller, offering exhortations and words of encouragement.

Fig. 11.9. Turning the serpent around. Papyrus of Nefer-Ubenef.

Fig. 11.10. The Slayer of the Heart. Papyrus of Nefer-Ubenef.

Figure 11.10 shows a further encounter with an opposing force—this time it takes the form of a monstrous apparition, half animal, half human, who brandishes a knife threateningly in front of the traveller. For the ancient Egyptians, the heart is the organ in the body symbolically associated with one's spiritual identity (chap. 8). The heart is always essentially pure. It lives on *maat*. In this illustration the purity of the seated man vividly contrasts with the ugly, licentious, and vicious-looking creature, whose form seems to express the utter debasement of the human instincts. Such monsters, personifying unintegrated animal drives, can steal, wound, or kill the heart. Once again, it is the Horus principle that will protect the traveller from this particular type of psychic attack. But this is achieved not by killing the creature, but by appropriating its power. In chapter 29 of the Book of the Dead, the traveller insists that he is himself the Slayer Of The Heart, thus depriving the monstrous opponent of its raison d'être:

> *My heart is with me*
> *and it shall never come to pass*
> *that it shall be taken away.*
>
> *I am the Lord Of Hearts.*
> *I am the Slayer Of The Heart.*
>
> *I live on Truth* [maat]*,*
> *and I have my being in Truth.*
> *I am Horus, who dwells in the heart,*
> *who dwells in the center of the body.*
>
> *I live by saying what is in my heart,*
> *and it shall not be taken away from me.*
> *My heart is mine,*
> *and it shall not be wounded.*
> *No terror shall subdue me. . . .*
>
> *I have committed no sin against the gods;*
> *I shall not suffer defeat;*
> *I shall be victorious.*[20]

There are many spells in the Book of the Dead to ensure the security of the heart. It was not simply that a person needed to protect the heart from opposing forces coming against it from the level of unintegrated or degenerate instincts. The heart itself, because of its innate purity, could stand against a person in the final judgment of the soul. In the relationship to the heart, therefore, hung the fate of a person's soul: the critical point was whether one's sense of self-identity was centered in the heart. If it was not, then the heart itself could reject the person as a stranger, as not belonging to it, when that person came to the Judgment Hall. Seen from this point of view, the journey through the Underworld was essentially a journey toward the heart, toward the vital and eternal core of the self.

In figure 11.11, Anubis offers the heart of Nebseni to his *ba*. It is significant that Anubis, the guide of souls through the Underworld, has the role of enabling the soul to come together with its heart. In the text accompanying the illustration, the traveller prays that he and his heart will be united in the House of Hearts—the Judgment Hall. The reference to the "Lake of Flowers" in what

Fig. 11.11. Anubis offers the heart of Nebseni to Nebseni's ba. *Papyrus of Nebseni. Eighteenth Dynasty.*

follows may be to the lotus-filled lake of rebirth that is sometimes depicted in Egyptian wall reliefs and paintings.

May my heart be with me in the House of Hearts!
May my heart be with me in the House of Hearts!
May my heart be with me, and may it remain there,
or I shall not eat of the cakes of Osiris
on the eastern side of the Lake of Flowers. . . .

My awareness is centered in my heart,
I have power in my heart,
I have power in my arms,
I have power in my legs,
I have power to do whatever I desire.

My ba *is not fettered by my body*
at the gates of the Underworld [Amentet],
but I shall enter in peace
and I shall come forth in peace.[21]

251

The Gates of the Underworld

The images of the journey through the Underworld that we have been considering so far all presuppose the naturalistic environment of the Field of Rushes discussed in chapter 10. The perils of the elements, and of the animals and demonic figures that oppose travellers, are perils that seem to be set within a naturalistic landscape, similar perhaps to that of Egypt itself. But the Underworld was also pictured using a different kind of imagery. This belongs not to the natural landscape but to a world of interior architectural spaces: the pylons, gateways, and halls of the temple.

As in the human being, so in the heart of the temple—in its most interior space—was the sanctuary where the god resided. To reach the inner sanctuary and come before the god, one had to pass through a series of barriers, the outermost being the massive walls of the outer pylon, in the middle of which was a narrow entranceway (see figure 11.12). Throughout ancient Egyptian history, the population at large never set foot inside this outer pylon. The whole of the temple was sacred space to which only the priesthood had access. To this day, the experience one has of approaching an Egyptian temple, such as that of Luxor, down the long avenue of impassively questioning sphinxes, as the pylon walls tower up above you, is to feel increasingly small and humble. One is approaching the house of the god, and the double pylon is the symbolic barrier between profane consciousness, caught up in mundane concerns, and consciousness directed toward the sacred.

"How deeply shaken the people who stood there must have been," writes Gottfried Richter,

> for the experience that the Egyptian temple addresses to those who approach it is this: they must first encounter a gigantic wall and then go through it, forcing their way into an interior that may well harbour enormous and entirely hidden dangers.[22]

Once through the outer pylon, one finds oneself in a large open courtyard. Beyond, there are further pylons, each of which, in ancient times, would have had great cedar doors hung at their entrances, closed against the incomer. And beyond the series of pylons and courtyards were pillared hallways, vestibules, and sanctuaries, every one of which would have been protected by similar heavy wooden doors inlaid with bronze, which had to be swung open in order for the visitor to enter them. No threshold in an Egyptian temple could be crossed unconsciously. The journey toward the

Fig. 11.12. The approach to the temple of Luxor.

interior was a journey made with a growing awareness that one was coming into a world to which one did not belong as a mere mortal human being. It was only by virtue of that which was divine in oneself that one dared to advance toward the sanctuary where the god dwelt. The final threshold, which took one into the sanctuary, was a threshold that none but the high priest could cross. Only the most advanced initiate could come face to face with the god.

Usually, in ancient times, one entered the temple only as part of a group that would have slowly moved forward, bearing sacred emblems amid the smoke of incense, the shaking of the sistrum, and the chanting of hymns. The crossing of each threshold was a ritualized event, involving the solemn breaking of the seals of the doors before they were opened. But in the Underworld, one made this journey alone. The supportive presence of the group was no longer there. There was no incense. No music. No procession that one was part of. Each individual was thrown entirely onto his or her own resources. Hence the imagery of travelling through pylons and doorways in the Underworld has an added potency, which it is easy to miss.

Fig. 11.13. The halls and doorways of the temple to Horus at Edfu.

Simply to be *alone* in the great Underworld temple of Osiris was in itself an extraordinary and awesome predicament to be in (fig. 11.13).

A doorway or gate implies two things. First of all, it implies that one has come up against a barrier that prevents one from progressing from the space one currently occupies to the more sacred space on the other side of the barrier (more sacred because one is advancing toward the interior of the temple). It is not just the gate that is the barrier, it is of course the whole wall in which the gate is set. The gate actually constitutes the way through the barrier. So the second implication of this imagery is that there *is* a way through the barrier. The question then is: how does one get the gate to open, so that one can pass through it? It is not simply a question of turning a handle. The gate has guardian spirits, or may itself be animated. So it is necessary to negotiate with these spirits so that they allow one to enter.

Finding oneself before a closed gate is comparable to finding one's path blocked by an opposing animal. In the case of being confronted by an animal, one cannot make any progress until one has mastered the opposing force, and skillfully "turned its head" so that its energies work for, rather than against, one. In both cases, the barrier or opposing force is essentially whatever it is in one's own psyche that prevents one from being fully attuned to *maat*. And the meaning of progress is here a greater and greater at-one-ment with *maat*, and hence the whole divine world. There remains, however, an important difference of emphasis in the two types of imagery. If the traveller is confronted by a crocodile or wild pig, he or she is not in any clearly defined sacred location: just somewhere in the Dwat, traversing the Field of Rushes. But if the traveller encounters a closed gate that bars the way into a hall, he or she is already in "the house of the god." There is thus an intensified focus upon the climactic event of coming to meet the divine.

Figure 11.14, from the papyrus of Ani, shows the first of a series of ten gates of ten pylons that Ani must pass. The gateway itself is animated. It is a feminine deity. But this deity is not the creature shown in the illustration. The latter is the gatekeeper. Ani must approach the gateway and then shout out:

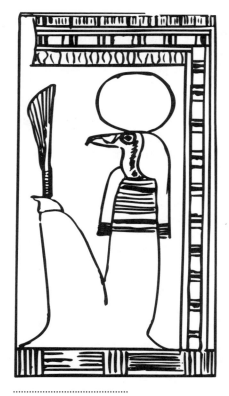

Fig. 11.14. The animated gate of an Underworld pylon. The creature shown is its bird-headed gatekeeper, who holds a small broom in its hand. Papyrus of Ani.

> *Make a way for me, for I know you*
> *and I know your name,*
> *and I know the name of the god who guards you.*
> *"Lady Of Terrors With Lofty Walls,*
> *Great Lady, Mistress Of Destruction,*
> *Whose Words Drive Back The Destroyers,*
> *And Rescue the Traveller From Afar."*
> *The name of the gatekeeper is "Terrible One"*[23]

Having correctly named both the animating spirit of the gate and the gatekeeper, Ani demonstrates his awareness of the process that he is embarked upon. It is evidently terrifying. To come face to face with the

255

"Lady of Terrors" who is the "Mistress Of Destruction" could not but be a deeply unsettling experience.

It is worth considering a little further what is actually involved here. The fact that the deity animating the gate is feminine may well be because the two towers of each pylon were equated by the ancient Egyptians with the two sisters of Osiris—Isis and Nephthys.[24] The two pylon towers form together a concretized image of the hieroglyph of the horizon, and Isis and Nephthys were thought of as assisting in raising the sun above the horizon each dawn.[25] In other words, they assisted in the rebirth of the sun just as they assisted in the rebirth of their brother Osiris. All rebirth presupposes a previous death, however, and this is why the first Underworld pylon is called "Lady of Terrors . . . Great Lady, Mistress of Destruction," for it is here that the Underworld traveller faces his or her own utter annihilation.

Fig. 11.15. The manifestation of Atum-Ra between the twin peaks of the mountain of the horizon. Twenty-first Dynasty coffin.

The concept of the horizon is one of the most profound in ancient Egyptian symbolic thought, and the series of images and texts concerned with passing through the pylon gateways are probably best understood in relation to it. In ancient Egyptian symbolism, the two mountains of the horizon, between which the sun rose, were conceived of as twin peaks of the cosmic mountain—the Primordial Hill or First Land—that was split in two when Atum-Ra first manifested as light (fig. 11.15). The two mountains are in fact an eastern and a western mountain and are named Bakhu and Manu, respectively. They correspond to, or at least approximate, the mountain ranges on the eastern and western sides of the Nile valley. The actual physical sun never therefore rises between them, but rather behind the eastern mountain (Bakhu), and then sets behind the western mountain (Manu).

The image of the sun rising between the two mountains therefore refers to the prior spiritual event of Atum-Ra's self-manifestation at the beginning of time.

But it also refers to an event that was enacted within the temple, namely, the manifestation of the divine on earth, between the eastern and western ranges that marked the boundaries of Egypt. In strictly human terms, the manifestation of the divine in the human being required that the soul die and be reborn again: die to that which was mortal and perishable in its nature, and be born again with an awareness of that which is divine in human nature. And this precisely is the meaning that passing through the gates of the pylons holds in the Book of the Dead. Each time the threshold of a pylon entrance is crossed, one dies symbolically to the outer or mundane world, and one is reborn to the environment into which one steps. The passage through the pylons involves coming ever closer to the indwelling god, Osiris, whose temple one is entering. And since this temple is a soul temple rather than a physical temple, the process of drawing closer to Osiris is a process of inner metamorphosis, in which the traveller really enters into the Osirian myth of death, dismemberment, and reconstitution.

At the first pylon, therefore, one crosses a threshold that entails meeting the "Lady of Terrors" who is also "Mistress of Destruction." The gateway to the second pylon is no less of an ordeal. Here the traveller comes up against "The Mistress Of The World, Who Devours With Fire, Lady of Mortals, Who Is Greater Than All Human Beings." Her doorkeeper is called "He Who Fashions The End."[26] The traveller is here precipitated into the experience of being devoured by fire. Many of the subsequent gateways contain references to fire, to burning, and to being cut up, themes that also form an important part of the more esoteric New Kingdom Book of Gates.

But at the sixth pylon, there is a reference to being healed and reconstituted. The doorkeeper of the sixth pylon is called "He Who Has Been Joined Together." At the next pylon, the goddess, or animating spirit, of the pylon is called "She Who Clothes The Feeble One, Weeping For What It Loves, And Shrouding The Body." The eighth pylon, however, suggests another violently painful experience. The goddess is called "Blazing Fire, Unquenchable Flame, Whose Flames Reach Far, Slaughtering Without Warning, Whom None May Pass Because Of The Pain She Causes"[27] (fig. 11.16).

But after this, at the ninth pylon, the "godlike form" is raised up, the Feeble One (Osiris) is clothed.[28] The doorkeeper of the ninth pylon has the

Fig. 11.16. The eighth pylon. Papyrus of Ani.

name "He Who Makes Himself." This is perhaps an allusion to the rebirth of the *ba* in the image of the divine. If one can successfully endure the travails of passing through the initially destructive thresholds of initiatory experience, then the promise of rebirth, of raising up the godlike form, will be fulfilled.

The Osirian nature of the process of passing through the gates of the Underworld is articulated in more detail in the second series of texts and images concerning the doorways to the halls, as described in chapters 144 (papyrus of Nu) and 147 (papyrus of Ani) of the Book of the Dead. In figure 11.17 from the papyrus of Ani, three guardians of the doorway are shown. On the left is a hare-headed doorkeeper, whose job it is to open and shut the gate. In the middle is a serpent-headed watcher, who guards the door. And on the right is a crocodile-headed herald, who announces those who pass through the doorway. The hare holds an ear of wheat in its hands, while the others both wield knives. Above the door—which is the first of seven to the seven halls that Ani must go through—are the symbols of power (the *was* scepter), life (the *ankh* cross), and stability (the *djed* column).

In order to negotiate his way past the three guardian spirits, Ani must prove that he knows their names. The gatekeeper is called "He Whose Face Is Turned Backwards, Of Many Forms." This is a name that immediately puts us in mind of the ferryman, and indeed of Osiris himself. The watcher is called "Eavesdropper." The announcer or herald is called "Loud Voice." Unless one can show that one knows their names, these spirits will prevent one from advancing any further, for it is not possible to pass through the gates of the Underworld unconsciously.

But in addition to knowing their names, the traveller must also make a series of affirmations, in much the same manner as we have seen in the Book of the Two Ways in chapter 10. Ani says:

> I am the Mighty One who creates his own light.
> I have come to you, Osiris, I adore you,

purified from all that is foul within you.
Truly, I say, O Osiris, I am divinized.
Do not let me be driven back,
do not let me be driven against the wall of flame.
I have opened the way in Restau,
I have eased the pain of Osiris. . . .
I have made a path for him in the great valley
and he has a path.
How Osiris shines![29]

The journey that Ani makes through these halls is a journey undertaken in relation to Osiris. Ani himself is formally referred to as "Osiris Ani." From a spiritual perspective, what he goes through is not simply a series of halls but a series of states of consciousness, each of which reflects—as with the gateways to the pylons—a condition of Osiris in the cycle of his death, putrefaction, and rebirth. Before the first hallway Ani describes how "Osiris goes round heaven sailing in the presence of *Ra*." This is significant because this is also how Osiris is described when Ani comes before the doorway to the seventh and last hall. Osiris begins, in other words, as he will end. But between the first and seventh halls, Osiris (or Osiris Ani) must endure his own disintegration and reconstitution, with all that this entails.

Before the second hall, Ani invokes the strength of Thoth, the god who reconciles the antagonistic energies of Horus and Seth, who are locked in conflict while Osiris is dead. At the third hallway, he identifies himself with Geb, the judge of Horus and Seth and thus

Fig. 11.17. *The first of the seven gates to the halls of the Underworld. Papyrus of Ani.*

the key figure in the resurrection of Osiris who, at this stage, must be in the grip of the forces of death and disintegration. Before the fourth hall, Ani identifies himself with "the mighty bull," the animal renowned throughout the ancient world for its sexual and generative power, which now begins to stir in Osiris. At the fifth hall, Ani gathers together all the fragments of Osiris, decisively drives away Apophis, and "brings the backbone," symbolic of Osiris's resurrection. At the sixth, Ani has become the "avenger" of Osiris—that is, he has become Horus, possessed of the magic power both to triumph over Seth and to heal Osiris. Finally, at the seventh of the doorways to the seven halls, Osiris is now wholly purified, and restored to the condition that he enjoyed before the first hall, "going round heaven" in the presence of Ra, and "knowing all things."

The passage both through the gates of the pylons and the doorways of the halls, therefore, should be understood in terms of the soul or *ba* entering fully into the Osirian process, in order to become merged with the god. For these gates and pylons, these doorways and halls, belong to the temple of Osiris himself: as one progresses through them one draws ever closer to the god.

12 THE END OF THE UNDERWORLD JOURNEY

The Hall of Maat

At last the traveller comes to a doorway guarded by none other than the god Anubis.[1] It was Anubis in his form of Upuat (the "Opener of the Ways") who first acted as the guide to the entrance to the Underworld. Now the doorway facing the traveller is the entrance to the Hall of Maat. Could it be that the whole journey through the Underworld up to this point has been nothing more than an approach to this one entrance, and that every doorway up until now has been but an image of this great doorway to the Hall of Maat? And every guardian an image of Anubis?

In the papyrus of Ani, Ani begins by telling Anubis of his familiarity with the domain of Seth:

> I have been in the place where the acacia tree does not grow,
> where the tree thick with leaves does not exist,
> and where the ground yields neither herbs nor grass.
> And I have entered into the place of secret and hidden things, and I
>   have spoken with the god Seth.[2]

He then makes a declaration to Anubis concerning his spiritual accomplishments. This declaration seems to involve a series of references to initiatory rites in which he has participated, in all probability in the role of Horus.

I have travelled to the boundaries of the soul (ba).
The Lord of Djedu [i.e., Osiris] has permitted me
to come forth as a Bennu bird,
that I may have the power of speech.

I have passed through the river flood,
I have made offerings with incense. . . .
I have been in Abydos in the Temple of Satet[3]
I have submerged the boat of my enemies. . . .

I have been in Djedu [Busiris],
concerning which I am constrained to silence.
I have set the divine image [Sekhem] on its two feet. . . .
I have seen the Dweller in the Holy Place. . . .
I have entered Restau,
I have beheld the Hidden Things that are there.

Finally Ani tells Anubis that "Seth has revealed to me the things concerning himself. I have said 'May the balancing of the scales by you be within our hearts.'"[4] "You" here refers to Anubis. The balancing of the scales is the major event that occurs in the Hall of Maat, which Ani is about to enter. The passages quoted seem to suggest that what is to be balanced in the scales are the energies of Seth on the one hand, and those of Horus on the other insofar as these have been internalized within Ani's heart.

Before being allowed to enter the Hall of Maat, the traveller must demonstrate a thorough knowledge of the door by which access to the hall is gained. In some papyri this is a lengthy process, in which the traveller is required to name every single part of the door—doorposts, bolts, lintels, cross timbers, and so on. The name of each part of the door points to what this door actually is. The doorposts, for example, are called "Plummet of Truth" in the papyrus of Nebseni, and the bolts "Tongue of the Balance of the Place of Maat"—both clear references to the balance that features in the weighing scenes that take place within the Hall of Maat.[5] Even having correctly named these different parts of the door, the traveller, in the very act of stepping across the threshold into the Hall of Maat, is challenged by the floor onto which he is about to step.

"I will not let you tread on me!" says the floor,
"Why not?" says the traveller, "I am pure."
"Because I do not know the names of your two feet
with which you would tread on me."[6]

Only having correctly named his two feet by their secret and holy names does the traveller finally come to stand in the great Hall of Maat.

Although the Hall of Maat belongs to the imagery of the temple, for it is the vestibule to the sanctuary of Osiris, the energies present within it are landscape energies. Forty-two gods, each representing one of the forty-two regions of Egypt, fill the hall. It is as if the hall itself were the landscape of Egypt, actualized in the divine persons who line its whole length. The traveller has the realization that the Underworld is not so much an "other" world in a separate domain from the physical, but is rather the inner, metaphysical landscape that underlies the physical landscape of Egypt. Here the spiritual forces that are gathered to test and to judge the *ba* are none other than the very same spiritual forces that are active within the Egyptian landscape, distilled into the enigmatic personalities of the forty-two gods.

These gods are sternly silent. In figure 12.1, from the papyrus of Nebseni, the hall with the forty-two gods is shown. They stand upright along the center of the hall, facing two seated figures of the goddess Maat. In her right hand, she holds the scepter of truth, in her left hand the *ankh* cross of life. On her head is her emblem of the ostrich feather, which the forty-two gods also wear on their heads.

Many papyri emphasize the fact that the forty-two gods are all completely attuned to Maat by showing them either wearing her feather or carrying it. In figure 12.2, some of the gods from another New Kingdom papyrus are shown carrying the feather.

It will be recalled that Maat was regarded as the divine substance upon which the gods feed (see chapter 5), and hence both their source of nour-

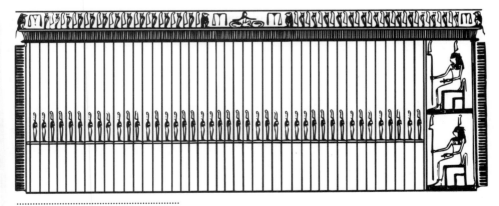

Fig. 12.1. The Hall of Maat. Papyrus of Nebseni. Eighteenth Dynasty.

Fig. 12.2. Gods in the Hall of Maat shown carrying the feather of Maat. Papyrus of Hor. Ptolemaic period.

ishment and their source of life. Maat is the divine bread that refreshes and sustains those who are in harmony with her being; but to those who are not in accord with her, the experience of Maat is like swallowing fire.[7] The Judgment Hall is the interior space, entering which one comes directly before that which nourishes the divine in oneself. To the extent that one has transformed one's nature so that it is brought into alignment with the essential divine core of oneself, becoming conscious of having entered the presence of Maat must feel like a homecoming. But to the extent that one is out of alignment with one's divine core, the experience is of searing pain, for Maat's gaze is like a knife that cuts through all false identifications.

It is required of the traveller to address each god in turn, and to make a twofold declaration. The first part of this declaration, usually referred to as the "negative confession," consists in declaring that one has not committed any of a range of possible misdemeanors. The traveller says to the representative of Heliopolis:

> *Homage to the One Whose Strides Are Long,*
> *who comes forth from Heliopolis:*
> *I have not done anything false.*

And to the god of Kheraba (a city near Memphis):

> *Homage to the One Who Embraces Fire,*
> *who comes forth from Kheraba:*
> *I have not robbed with violence.*[8]

264

It is as if each god were concerned as much with an area of moral geography as with physical geography. In the Underworld, the moral nature of the forces that shape the landscape is laid bare. The whole Underworld journey could be understood as taking place nowhere else than in Egypt, in the psychic or psychospiritual interior of Egypt, the "Land of the Gods."

The traveller addresses the god of Hermopolis:

> *Homage to the Divine Nose,*
> *who comes forth from Hermopolis:*
> *I have not done violence to any man.*

And then the god of Qernet, the region between Aswan and Philae:

> *Homage to The Devourer of the Shade,*
> *who comes forth from Qernet:*
> *I have not done murder; I have done no harm.*[9]

And so each god who presides over a certain region of the psychic interior of Egypt is addressed. The list of iniquities that the traveller has not committed is extensive. It includes theft, cheating, sexual misconduct, lying, fraud, and "eating one's heart" (meaning, perhaps, being dishonest). It also includes various wrongdoings against nature, such as laying waste to fertile land and polluting water. Also included are sacrilegious acts such as wrongly killing sacred animals, blaspheming or cursing the gods, and defiling sacred images. In the classic papyri of the Eighteenth Dynasty (such as the papyri of Nu, Nebseni, and Ani), forty-two wrongdoings are listed, corresponding with each of the forty-two gods.

The second part of the twofold declaration is, in contrast to the negative confession, a positive declaration. It is a declaration of all that one has done that is good and true and in total accord with Maat. It begins with a statement that the traveller, like any god, lives on Maat and feeds on Maat. The implication here is that the *ba* has become so inwardly "straight" that the *akh* or "shining spirit" irradiates all its impulses. The traveller's will is the will of the divine. Addressing the gods altogether, the following words are spoken:

> *I have given bread to the hungry,*
> *and water to the thirsty,*
> *clothes to the naked*
> *and a boat to the boatless.*

I have made offerings to the gods,
and sacrifices to the Shining Ones. . . .
I am pure of mouth and pure of hands,
one to whom it is said "You are doubly welcome"
by those who see me. . . .
I have come here to bear witness to the truth [maat],
and to place the balance on its support
within the Sacred Land [Aqert].[10]

The Achievement of Balance

The reference at the end of the last quotation, from the papyrus of Nu, to "placing the balance on its support" brings us to the central episode of the whole Underworld journey. It should not be too hastily interpreted simply in terms of the famous "weighing of the heart" so often depicted in funerary illustrations. The papyrus of Nu nowhere mentions the heart being weighed, but rather speaks only of the balance being placed on its supporting pole. In the papyrus of Nu, there is no indication as to what exactly is in the scales of the balance; the act of placing the balance on its support in itself seems to carry the whole significance of this Underworld ritual. Neither is the text supported by any illustration showing the heart being weighed.[11]

The notion of balancing the scales upon their support as an act carrying intrinsic meaning would seem to be confirmed from a variety of other sources. The papyrus of Nu was produced in the early part of the Eighteenth Dynasty. It is one of the earliest papyri of the Book of the Dead. In the late Eighteenth Dynasty Book of Gates, division 5, a judgment scene is depicted as taking place in the Hall of Osiris (fig. 12.3). Osiris is seated upon a throne, while in front of him a mummiform figure stands bearing the balance on his shoulders. The figure is perhaps a personification of the supporting pole, but notice that the scales of the balance contain no recognizable images, but only the merest gesture toward some abstract content. Behind the man with the balance, two scenes are shown. Below him, on nine steps, are nine blessed or transfigured human spirits. But above them Seth, in the form of a wild pig, is escorted away from the presence of Osiris on a boat, by two stick-wielding baboons. The baboons are presumably representatives of Thoth. In the right-hand corner Anubis overlooks these strange events.

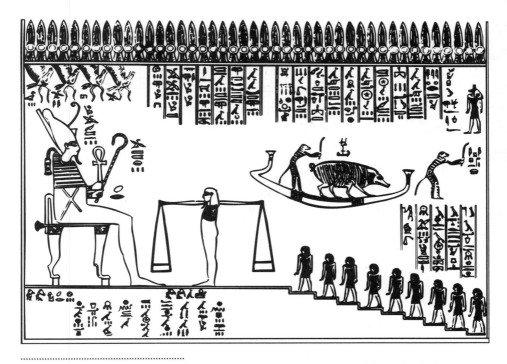

Fig. 12.3. Establishing the balance between the friends and the enemies of Osiris. Book of Gates, division 5. Tomb of Ramesses VI.

As it is very often Anubis who adjusts the balance in Underworld weighing scenes, his presence here is apposite. For what is portrayed would appear to be the establishing of the right relationships among Osiris, the Transfigured Spirits on the staircase, and Seth. Immediately underneath Osiris, the text states that his enemies are "under the soles of his feet," while "the gods and spirits are in front of him." Although the enemies are not portrayed, their stated position under Osiris's feet means that they are to one side of the balance, while the Transfigured Spirits are to the other side. The mummiform figure bearing the balance is thus literally holding the balance between the transfigured spirits and the enemies of Osiris.

In the weighing scene in figure 12.4, Horus takes the role of the adjustor of the balance, and is altering the position of the plummet. This illustration is from a Twenty-first Dynasty papyrus, and there can be no doubt that the scales are manifestly empty. Beside them, Thoth is shown

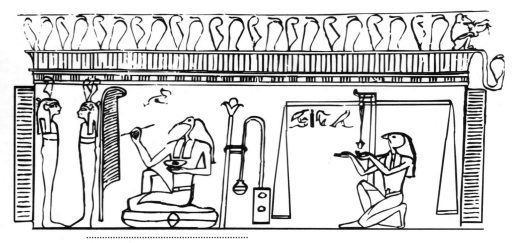

Fig. 12.4. A balance with empty scales. Papyrus of Khonsu-em-Heb. Twenty-first Dynasty.

inscribing the feather of Maat. There are many other depictions of the balance with empty scales from Twenty-first Dynasty and later papyri.[12] Could it be, then, that the notion of balance, or of attaining equilibrium between opposing forces, was symbolically and metaphysically fundamental to the ideal of being attuned to Maat? And that what was actually weighed in the scales carried less significance than the achievement of balance as an end in itself?

In chapter 1 we saw how the ancient Egyptians' conception of their country being "two lands" derived from something beyond the geopolitical division of the country into the Delta region to the north and the Nile valley to the south. The conception was ultimately metaphysical, for it expressed, as Henri Frankfort has said:

> the deeply rooted Egyptian tendency to understand the world in dualistic terms as a series of contrasts balanced in unchanging equilibrium. The universe as a whole was referred to as "heaven and earth." Within this concept, "earth" was again conceived dualistically as "north and south," the "portions of Horus and the portions of Seth," "the two lands" or "the two (Nile) banks."[13]

It is especially interesting that the sanctuary at Memphis, the capital built by the legendary founder of the Egyptian state, Menes, was called "Balance of the Two Lands." This balance was held by the king who was referred to as "The Two Lords" throughout Egyptian history. Concerning this epithet, Frankfort makes the following comment:

> "The Two Lords" were the perennial antagonists, Horus and Seth. The king was identified with both of these gods but not in the sense that he was considered the incarnation of the one and also the incarnation of the other. He embodied them as a pair, as opposites in equilibrium. Hence the ancient title of the queen of Egypt: "She who sees Horus and Seth."[14]

Horus and Seth are often depicted binding together the symbolic plants of the north and south—the papyrus and the lotus—around the hieroglyph denoting union (fig. 12.5). This hieroglyph is thought to represent two lungs attached to the windpipe, or trachea, a perfect symbol of duality functioning in harmonious unity.

The two gods, represented by their standards, can also be seen in figure 12.6, which shows the culminating rite of the Sed festival, in which the kingship was symbolically renewed. On the right, Seth offers to King Sesostris III, who is seated wearing the white crown of the south, the notched palm branch signifying "many years," that is, a long reign. On the left, Horus offers the king, now wearing the red crown of the north, the same sign again. In representations such as these, one is struck by the care taken to maintain perfect symmetry in the composition. For example, in figure 12.6 the hieroglyphs immediately in front of the king on either side, including the cartouches, are inscribed so that they are mirror images of each other.

The idea of balance, then, and in particular the idea of balancing the archetypal principles of polarity and opposition expressed by Horus and Seth, formed a very deep current in

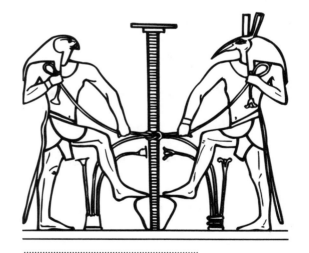

Fig. 12.5. Horus and Seth bind together the plants of the north (papyrus) and south (lotus). Bas-relief from the tablet of Senusret I. Twelfth Dynasty.

Fig. 12.6. The crowning of the king at the Sed festival. Lintel from Nag el-Madamud, depicting the coronation of Sunusret III. Twelfth Dynasty.

ancient Egyptian thinking. It is therefore not to be wondered at that it held a prominent place in the the judgment of the soul. Indeed, according to J. G. Griffiths, the prototype on which the judgment of the soul was based was the original judgment of Horus and Seth, the outcome of which was their reconciliation through the mediation of Thoth.[5] That this judgment occurs in the Hall of the Two Truths (or the Two Maats)—the vestibule to the sanctuary of Osiris—impresses upon us the more forcefully that the aim of the Underworld journey was to reach a state of inner equilibrium through an acceptance and balancing of duality, and in particular a reconciliation in one's own nature of the opposing forces of Horus and Seth.

Figure 12.7 is a particularly beautiful rendering of the achievement of such a reconciliation. It shows a balance without any supporting pole, being upheld by Anubis and Horus. In the scales are a figure of Maat, cupped in Horus's right hand, and a representation of the person in Anubis's left hand. Between them is a stylized portrayal of a human figure standing upright. The god Anubis is ambivalent at the best of times. We have already seen (chap. 10) how Anubis acquired the role of guide to the pathways of the Underworld because of his inherent duality. This derives from the beginning of ancient Egyptian history, when Pe (the

capital of the south, the domain of
Seth) had the jackal as its emblem,
as opposed to Nekhen in the north
(the cult center of Horus) whose
emblem was the falcon. This
implies a close affinity between the
jackal and Seth, which can also be
seen in other contexts. Anubis, for
instance, was "Lord of the Desert"
as was Seth; he was son of
Nephthys, the dark sister of Isis
and nominal consort of Seth. It is
significant that by Ptolemaic times
the distinction between Anubis and
Seth was no longer clearly maintained, for it reveals the latent tendency to conflate the two gods.[16] In
the late Papyrus Jumilhac, for
instance, Seth is able to transform
himself into Anubis.[17] Anubis can

Fig. 12.7. *Anubis and Horus support the balance.
From a tomb painting at Akhmin, Middle Egypt.
Roman Period.*

be understood as the god whose nature harbors a certain fluidity between
the forces of light and dark, Upperworld and Underworld, life and death.
In him, one can experience a kind of meeting ground between the opposing principles of Horus and Seth. In figure 12.7, there is a suggestion, in
Anubis holding the scale containing the person, that that person has been
guided by Anubis toward this meeting ground of the dark and light energies that the god embodies. And, precisely insofar as they are integrated,
that person achieves balance with Maat, who is "held" by Horus. There
is in fact an implied relationship between Anubis and Horus here that is
expressed more explicitly in the many papyri that show Anubis leading
the Underworld traveller to the weighing scene and, this having been
successfully carried out, Horus then introduces the traveller to Osiris (see
figures 12.9 and 12.10). In terms of balance, Horus is closer to the
Godhead, to the still point of truth, whereas Anubis is a god in movement
between contrasting states of being.

In many papyri showing a whole person being weighed, what they are
weighed against is often not the figure of Maat but their own heart. Figure
12.8 is one example. The heart here, as always, is represented by a small pot
or vase. This of course gives a different perspective on the idea of achieving balance. The heart was regarded as that part of a person that is essen-

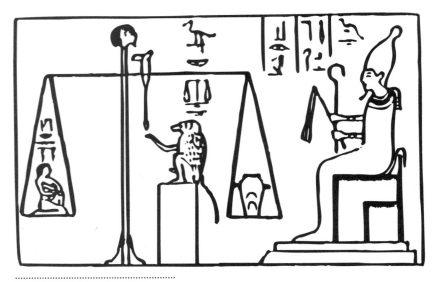

Fig. 12.8. A person is weighed against his heart. Papyrus of Nebseni.

tially pure. The heart is the organ of the body in which Horus dwells, and which is therefore intrinsically attuned to Maat.[18] But how, then, are we to understand the figure who sits in the other scale?

The idea of weighing the whole person against their heart cannot be dissociated from the ancient Egyptian understanding of different parts of the physical body—limbs, internal organs, sense organs, and so on—as each having a certain psychic weight.[19] The ancient Egyptian psychological and moral ideal was for all these members, and the desires, thoughts, feelings, and passions associated with them, to be perfectly balanced with, or in tune with, the central organ of the heart. The critical question for everyone concerning the outcome of the Underworld journey was, "Have I brought all my members, and thereby all my psychological functions, into attunement with the deepest wishes of my heart?" If the answer to this question was affirmative, then the heart would recognize them as belonging to itself and the balance would be equalized.

Such a question gave rise to inevitable anxiety when it came to the judgment in the vestibule of the god Osiris. The text that accompanies figure 12.8 takes the form of a prayer that the traveller addresses to the heart:

My heart, my mother!
My heart, my mother!
O my heart of my time upon earth!
May nothing stand up to oppose me in judgement
in the presence of the Keeper of the Balance.
Let it not be said of me or of what I have done:
"He has done things against Maat."
May nothing be against me
in the presence of the great god, the Lord of Amentet.[20]

The Keeper of the Balance in figure 12.8 is Thoth who, according to myth, was not only the reconciler of Horus and Seth but was also, according to one account, born of their union.[21] Once again, therefore, there is an implication that underlying the equilibrium attained between the person and their heart there is a more fundamental balancing of the energies of Horus and Seth.

When we come to illustrations that show the heart being weighed against Maat, it is important that we bear in mind these other variations on what is in the balance. Sometimes there is nothing at all in the scales. Sometimes there is something but it is a purely abstract symbol of weights. Then there is the possibility of a person being weighed against Maat, or against their own heart. If the convention became to show the heart being weighed against Maat, these other possibilities were never lost but can often be found as variants on the more general theme of achieving balance.

In the illustrations that show the heart being weighed against Maat, represented either by her symbol of a single ostrich feather or by the goddess herself, the heart becomes the representative of the whole person. The question is: has the heart itself become balanced? In the papyrus of Ani, we have seen that Ani addresses the following plea to Anubis: "May the balancing of the scales by you be within our hearts."[22] The well-balanced heart is the heart in which the forces of the psyche have been brought into harmony with the person's spiritual essence—which the heart symbolizes. The heart, in other words, has completely incorporated these forces, and can claim them as its own. And because of the intrinsic purity of its own nature, this event really marks the completion of the Underworld journey. The soul has come to rest in its heart, and because the heart rests in Maat, it must be in tune with Maat. It will not be weighed down by unintegrated or wayward impulses that do not properly belong to it. It will, in fact, be perfectly balanced with Maat.

Fig. 12.9. The Weighing of the Heart. Papyrus of Hunefer. Nineteenth Dynasty.

Figure 12.9 is a classic example of the weighing of the heart, from the fourteenth-century B.C. papyrus of Hunefer. Anubis leads Hunefer to the balance, and then proceeds to weigh his heart against the feather symbolizing Maat. Beside Anubis the monstrous figure of Ammit, one-third crocodile, one-third lion and one-third hippopotamus, can be seen. Ammit's head is turned toward Thoth, who records the verdict of the weighing. Should the heart and Maat not be in accord, Ammit, "the eater of the heart," will swallow the person whose heart has thus betrayed them. In this illustration, as in many others, Anubis leads Hunefer to the balance (and himself makes adjustments to the plummet) while on the other side Horus takes over and leads Hunefer into the presence of Osiris. It is as if beyond a certain point Anubis cannot go. A god less ambivalent must take over.

The Awakened Osiris

And so the traveller reaches the destination of the long journey through the Underworld. Coming before Osiris at last, the following words may be addressed to the great god:

> *Here I am in your presence, O Lord of the West.*
> *There is no wrongdoing in my body.*
> *I have not told lies.*
> *There has been no second fault.*

Grant that I may be one of the favoured ones
who are in your following, O Osiris.
Grant that I may be greatly favoured
by you, the good god.
Grant that I may be loved
by you, the Lord of the Two Lands.
Grant that I may be vindicated
before you, O Osiris.[23]

In figure 12.10, Osiris wears the *atef* crown—a special form of the white crown of Upper Egypt, with two ostrich feathers to either side. The ostrich feathers connect the crown with the goddess Maat. Very often the crown is surmounted by the sun disk, pointing to the link between Osiris and Ra. In chapter 183 of the Book of the Dead, the *atef* is described as the "crown of Ra." Wearing it, all the gods come bowing before the triumphant, resurrected Osiris offering Maat to him.[24] The flesh of Osiris is green, signifying that his whole body is endued with fertilizing power. Here is an Osiris who is no longer passive victim of the abuses of Seth, but is awakened to new life.

The awakening of Osiris is, mythologically, the function of Horus who,

Fig. 12.10. Hunefer comes before the triumphant Osiris. Papyrus of Hunefer.

descending into the Underworld where the stricken Osiris lies helplessly, offers to him his healing eye, embraces him with a life-instilling embrace, and raises him from his state of inertness.[25] The journey through the Underworld, as we have seen, was a journey undertaken by the soul largely in the role of Horus, engaged in overcoming the Sethian forces that were pitted against it. These forces were bent on preventing the soul from attaining the rebirth that it can only achieve through Osiris. In figure 12.10, then, we are presented with the paradox of the relationship between Horus and Osiris. On the one hand Osiris is the goal of the Underworld journey, for he alone is the means of the *ba*'s self-transcendence. But on the other hand Osiris is incapable of aiding the *ba* in its rebirth until the *ba* itself, as Horus, has healed and raised up Osiris. There is, in other words, a complete interdependence of the two gods on each other. It should also be borne in mind that had not Seth, in his role as demonic initiator, caused Osiris to experience death, there would be no possibility of the *ba*'s rebirth either. In ancient Egyptian mythological thinking, the negative has an important, even crucial, role to play in the total scheme of things.

Figure 12.10, therefore, shows us two events. The Horus principle has led the Underworld traveller—in this case Hunefer—through the dangers and perils of a realm that had threatened to ensnare him in energies that were incompatible with his essential self. Through overcoming these opposing forces and thereby becoming ever more truly aligned with the divine spirit within himself, Hunefer is at last brought into the presence of Osiris, the personification of the principle of renewal. But precisely because he has triumphed over all that would oppose him, he beholds Osiris as triumphant—he meets in Osiris a mirror image of himself, or of that energy within himself that is the key to his own rebirth. His journey through the Underworld has thus involved the gradual release of Osiris from the paralyzing grip of Seth, and has culminated in the intense experience of Osiris as awakened.

It is significant that Osiris in figure 12.10 is seated on a throne that rests on water. This is a visual reference to the waters of Nun from which Atum emerged as the First Land in the aboriginal act of self-creation. From the water grows a lotus flower, symbol of rebirth, upon which stand the children of Horus. The awakened Osiris is an Osiris who has realized his inner connection with the supreme Godhead, the self-creating spirit at the source of all the gods. Hunefer here comes before an Osiris who is virtually conjoined with Atum in the original act of self-emergence. It is an experience of becoming aware of the means of his own spiritual renewal.

According to the myth of Osiris, it is only when Horus has "raised up"

Osiris that the latter becomes capable of fathering a son. Isis appears in the form of a kite, and conceives from Osiris a child, who is of course none other than Horus. Osiris—strictly speaking, Osiris merged with Isis—is thus the essential middle term in Horus's rebirth. In figure 12.11, Horus can be seen arising directly out of Osiris's thighs, implying that the Isis principle is here incorporated within the recumbent figure of Osiris. On the left it is Atum who presides over Horus's

Fig. 12.11. Horus is born from the side of Osiris. Tomb of Ramesses VI, Valley of the Kings.

rebirth, which approximates to Atum's own act of self-generation. While scenes like this can always be interpreted in terms of the soul's afterlife experiences, they relate more pertinently to a level of mystical experience that the ancient Egyptians clearly believed was capable of being attained in this life. One of the reasons why ancient Egyptian religion has been so frequently misunderstood is because the gods have been conceived as almost entirely removed from the domain of human experience. Once it is grasped that the gods are interwoven with states of consciousness, and that they accompany and guide the development of consciousness, the religion of ancient Egypt assumes something of its original power. The Book of the Dead and the many other texts that concern the Underworld are not the products of some wishful fantasy about life after death, but are guides to the unfolding of ever more refined and elevated levels of spiritual awareness.

One of the most pervasive of ancient symbols for the revivification of Osiris was the raising of the *djed* column—an event mythologically performed by Horus, usually with the assistance of Isis. The *djed* column, among other things, symbolized the backbone of the god Osiris. The raising of the column thus symbolized the raising of the god from the state of inertia and inactivity into which he had fallen as a consequence of coming under the detrimental sway of Seth. That Horus (in ritual, the king) should perform the deed of raising the *djed* is doubly interesting. For it confirms both the fact that the Osiris principle represented by the *djed* is dormant until Horus, with the assistance of Isis, intervenes; and that, once raised, the *djed* magically inaugurates a new life for Horus. Hence the raising of

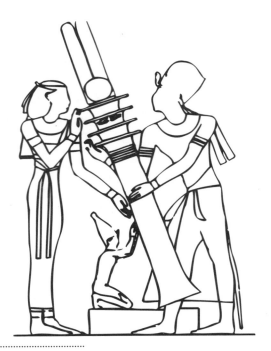

Fig. 12.12. Seti I raising the djed *column. Temple of Seti I, Abydos.*

the *djed* was a ceremony crucial to the renewal of the kingship (fig. 12.12).

In figure 12.13, the raised and animated *djed*, wearing the regalia of the *atef* crown—ostrich plumes on either side of a sun disk—is flanked by Isis and Nephthys, whose hands are raised in a gesture that suggests concentrated attention. Above it, the solar boat floats on celestial water. It contains a second *djed* protected now by two cobras. Rising out of it, the winged scarab beetle Kheprer flies, as if having burst out of its chrysalis. Above Kheprer is the solar disk. Here, then, the raised *djed* evokes the imagery of cosmogenesis, of the coming into being of a wholly new level of existence. If Horus is reborn through Osiris, his rebirth entails the mobilization of the energies of Atum, Ra, and Kheprer—the principal energies through which the divine brings itself into being.

The illustration is by no means unique. There exist many similar images, both in the Book of the Dead and in various New Kingdom magical papyri, that can be viewed as meditations upon this point of contact between the awakened Osiris and the solar principle, which in ancient Egyptian thought is primarily the principle of self-creation. This point of

Fig. 12.13. The point of contact between the awakened Osiris and the solar principle. Papyrus of Khonsu-Renep. New Kingdom.

contact is where the cult of Osiris leads into the cult of Ra. As soon as the *ba* attains to the experience of coming to the fount of its own existence, to the self-replenishing energy of pure spirit, symbolized by Ra (in whom is incorporated Atum and Kheprer), the *ba* has reached the possibility of self-transcendence. Realizing its own inner resplendence, it knows its deepest nature to be a shining spirit, or *akh*.

The "solar" nature of this event is shown in figure 12.14, which echoes figure 12.11 (they are both very close to each other in the tomb of Ramesses VI). Horus here rises up from the body of an apparently androgynous Osiris, flanked by Isis and Nephthys. Horus is hawk-headed and full of vigor. Just beside his head is the solar disk. The reborn Horus is a sun child. It is for this reason that Horus and Ra are iconographically so similar that it is often virtually impossible to distinguish them. Indeed, in the reborn Horus we are brought to the horizon where heaven and earth meet, where the divine and the human are interfused.

Fig. 12.14. The rebirth of Horus from Osiris. Tomb of Ramesses VI.

The human being as reborn Horus realizes an inner identity with Ra. Figure 12.15 succinctly reveals the complexity of the rebirth theme. On the ground—as it were, below the horizon—lies the mummiform body of Osiris, who is being awakened to new life by the rays issuing from the upside-down falcon head of Horus. Above the falcon head the sun boat sets off bearing the figure of the child Horus in the sun disk, which rests on the hieroglyphic symbol of the horizon. The child Horus is equally Ra rising in the east as Ra-Horakhti ("Ra-Horus-in-the-Horizon"). The child is adored by Thoth, and the heavenly boat is guided by Isis. In similar illustrations, the place of Horus the child is taken by a resurrected Osiris or Kheprer.[26] Here the solar disk is shown above the sun child's head, with great falcon wings outstretched to either side. In terms of human consciousness, what has now been achieved is the radiance of spirit characteristic of the *akh*. The human being has become a shining one. The *ba* has been divinized through having been brought into union with the source of its existence—the self-creating, self-renewing spirit.[27] The realm of Osiris has been effectively transcended, and now the primary experience is that of being merged with the cosmic light that emanates from Ra.

In the Old Kingdom Pyramid Texts, there is a prayer that refers to this mystical experience:

> *May I shine as Ra,*
> *having put aside all that is false.*
> *Through me, may Maat stand behind Ra.*
>
> *May I shine every day,*
> *as one who is in the horizon of the sky.*[28]

Fig. 12.15. The awakening of Osiris leads to the inward identification of the reborn Horus and Ra. Coffin of Hent-Taui. New Kingdom.

This prayer fulfilled, the Underworld traveller has truly "come forth into the day," a phrase that could equally well be translated as "come through to the light." And having come through to the light, the Underworld journey is now over, for the goal of the journey has been achieved.

EPILOGUE

....

The spiritual world of the ancient Egyptians existed in an era remote in time from our own, but it nevertheless forms part of the evolutionary arc that Western consciousness has traced in its historical development. It is a stratum of our collective experience, and we are the richer for acknowledging this ancient civilization as belonging to our collective history and therefore as part of our wider cultural identity. We are embarked upon an evolutionary journey, however, that has taken us away from the type of consciousness that prevailed in ancient times, and it is important that we understand and accept this journey in order that we come to a right relationship with ancient Egyptian culture.

Two pitfalls in particular are to be avoided. One is that we succumb to a nostalgic longing for a bygone age and a mode of awareness that is no longer appropriate for us today. While it may be that we should be doing our utmost to nurture an awareness of the spiritual powers or *neters*, if this renewed awareness is at the cost of the freedom and psychic autonomy, and hence moral responsibility, that defines the modern sense of self, then we undo the most important gains of the Western historical journey. The opposite pitfall to this is that we overvalue our own culture so much that we either project our modern presuppositions onto the ancients, assuming that they thought and felt in much the same way as we do, or else we look askance at the ancient culture, rejecting it as submersed in primitive beliefs and superstitions that we have long since outgrown.

Modern Egyptology has to a large extent been trapped by this latter pitfall because of its reluctance to focus on the structures of ancient consciousness in favor of concentrating on what is more tangible and concrete. Despite the growing number of religious texts that have been translated, Egyptologists have been interested less in the religious experiences that produced the texts than in the formalities of custom and ritual. The lack of interest in ancient modes of consciousness has meant that often the way in which the ancient Egyptians saw their world has been misunderstood. For example, modern scholarship can describe ancient Egyptian cosmology as if it were the outcome of a similar aspiration to that which lies behind modern cosmology but has simply been proved false, thereby ignoring the question of how such a cosmology could be true for the ancient Egyptians. Ancient Egyptian history is studied as if it were possible to extrapolate our modern reality principle backward in time ad infinitum, without any conception that the very nature of a historical event might have been different in ancient times from what it is today. In much modern Egyptology there is both a lack of psychological sophistication and an ignorance both of metaphysics and esotericism, which has the inevitable consequence that the spirituality of the ancient Egyptians must remain a closed book.

By giving our attention to the experiential life and consciousness of the ancient Egyptians, influenced neither by a desire to return to their world, nor in the thrall of modern presuppositions about what is important and interesting, true or false, real or illusory, the significance of ancient Egypt to us today may begin to be felt. For we then have the possibility of engaging in dialogue with a culture and a mentality that flourished at an earlier phase in our own spiritual evolution. It is a culture and mentality from which we grew estranged as we developed a different kind of soul-life in which the need to distinguish self from other, inner from outer, subjective from objective, became ever more paramount. But today, as the boundaries of the modern soul are pressed back, revealing an inner realm of objective psychic facts and spiritual archetypes, a growing affinity between ourselves and the world of the ancient Egyptians becomes apparent. And thus we may become aware of a deeper tide of history, which ebbs and flows at levels of the collective consciousness far more subtle than the surface unfolding of historical events.

Since Napoleon's army marched into Egypt in 1798, the ancient civilization has become more and more accessible to us. Accompanying Napoleon's army was a large contingent of scholars, draughtsmen, and artists who, despite the defeat of the French, were permitted to remain in control of research on the ground and eventually produced the formidable *Description de l'Egypte* between 1809 and 1830. Once the hieroglyphic system of writing had been understood (Champollion's discovery of the key to its decipherment was in 1822), the way was open for the experiential life of the ancient Egyptians slowly to become available to the modern world.

It was not, perhaps, entirely accidental that at the time when Napoleon opened up ancient Egypt, Europe was being opened up in other ways. In France, this occurred primarily in the social and political upheavals that swept through that country. The last decades of the eighteenth century were an extraordinary period of European history during which there was a shedding of old political and social forms and the birth of new ones— even new nations. For this was the time of the founding both of the new French Republic and of the United States of America.

But something else was stirring in the European psyche that did not so much find its expression in the political and social domain as in the sphere of the arts. In other countries, notably England and Germany, the redis- covery of ancient Egypt coincided with the birth of the Romantic move- ment. The Romantic movement heralded the dawning of a new sensibili- ty, through which the animating forces within nature were once again rec- ognized. And they were recognized by a newly appreciated human faculty that became the watchword of the Romantics: the Imagination. In the writings of poets and thinkers such as Wordsworth, Coleridge, Blake, and Shelley in England, and Schelling, Schiller, Novalis, and Goethe in Germany, there is a freshness and passion that marks the beginning of a new phase in European culture. The Romantics clearly distinguished the Imagination from mere subjective fantasy or reverie. It is to be understood as a higher faculty of cognition, higher because, by means of it, it is possi- ble to become aware of otherwise imperceptible forces in nature. Through the Imagination, one is able to see into that "inner space" with which the ancient Egyptians were all too familiar, and in which move the spiritual powers that the ancients knew as gods.

This is not to say that the imaginative consciousness of the Romantics was the same as the ancient Egyptian consciousness. For by the late eigh- teenth century, there had come to exist a sense of self-identity, and an ideal of self-determination, quite different from that which existed in ancient Egypt, though—as we have seen—it was prefigured in the initiatory path of development outlined in chapter 9. By the eighteenth century, the aver- age European had become totally accustomed to functioning with a type of self-possessed consciousness that assumes a degree of personal autonomy that would have been considered sacrilegious to the ancient mind.

The synchronicity of Napoleon's military and scholarly invasion of Egypt with the birth of the Romantic movement in Europe may of course be dis- missed as arbitrary and meaningless. It is the modern historian's duty, after all, to shun the very notion of meaningful coincidence in history. And yet the unfolding of the destinies of civilizations, like that of human beings, is based on such synchronicities. The Romantics owed much to the alchemical and Hermetic traditions that resurfaced during the Renaissance, and that ultimately derived from Egypt. Freemasonry was one of these esoteric traditions, and exercised considerable influence on the cultural, intellectual, and political life of the eighteenth century. The fact that Napoleon was a Freemason, and had an intense desire to discover the sources of Masonic lore—which he believed lay in ancient Egypt—probably served as a stronger motive for his invasion of Egypt than the more prosaic wish to extend his empire. Napoleon was by no means alone in his belief that ancient Egyptian spirituality had a direct bearing on the modern inner quest.

It is well known that George Washington and most of the founding fathers of the United States were Masons. Nothing better symbolizes the significance that ancient Egypt was felt to have for the transformation of Western consciousness at the dawning of this new age than the design of the new seal of the United States, which subsequently appeared (as it does to this day) on the one-dollar note. The design in fact preceded Napoleon's invasion of Egypt by some twenty-two years. It shows a pyramid with a missing capstone, which we may assume is the pyramid of Khufu (or Cheops as he is more commonly known). Above the pyramid, the capstone miraculously reappears in a blaze of light. In the middle of the capstone is an eye. Underneath the pyramid is written a motto in Latin: Novus Ordo Seclorum, which means "A New Order of the Ages."

There is a story behind this mysterious design. Originally, the Great Pyramid of Khufu had its capstone in place. It was gold-plated, and on each of its four sides a blue eye of Horus was painted. When the sun struck the pyramid, a beam of light was reflected from this golden blue eye that could be seen for miles around. As the age of Egypt came to a close, the priesthood removed the capstone and buried it secretly. No one knows where. But, according to the story, it will one day be rediscovered, and will be replaced on top of the pyramid. When that day comes, a "new order of the ages" will be established, which will correspond to a general spiritual reawakening.

It is just a story, but it has a peculiar potency, for it affirms—as does the prophecy of Hermes Trismegistus recounted in the preface—that the history of the West is inwardly linked to ancient Egypt. We have been brought up to regard history as following a linear track, in accord with our modern sense of time as the ever onward march of years and centuries. We tend to deny that there could be any connecting threads between one epoch and another. And yet we all know how important was the rediscovery of ancient Greek civilization at the end of the Middle Ages. The impact of Greek science, art, philosophy, and mythology at that time led to the extraordinary flowering of European culture called the Renaissance. But we cannot attribute the Renaissance simply to the impact of classical civilization on late medieval Europe: it also had to be received and taken hold of by people who were ready to utilize it. The rediscovery of ancient Greece coincided with a movement in the European soul already under way. Changes in consciousness were already occurring that enabled people to be inspired and nourished by the influx of classicism in one century, where a century before it might have left them cold.

Today Western culture is at a comparable stage of transition. But we are ready now to realign ourselves culturally and spiritually upon an axis that is no longer Judeo-Greek. For the monotheistic and rationalistic imperatives have run their course, and no longer command our horizons as they used to. The spirituality of ancient Egypt appeals to us today because it resonates with a deep impulse in our modern culture for spiritual regeneration. What was already heralded in the Romantic movement at the time of Egypt's rediscovery, is now—two hundred years later—beginning to take on substance. The time is ripe for us to recognize that we are moving into a new historical and cultural phase, the axis of which links us more to the ancient Egyptian than to the Judeo-Greek world.

There exists today in the nascent spiritual resurgence of our culture a growing sympathy with the spirituality of ancient Egypt. For the soul of the West is turning toward areas of experience that ancient Egypt has much to teach us about. There is the possibility therefore of a new Renaissance comparable to that which accompanied the rediscovery of ancient Greece. It is not a question of returning to the ancient mode of consciousness but of rediscovering in our own way that other half of reality of which the Egyptians were so intensely aware. It is a question ultimately of rediscovering that other half of ourselves that in the centuries intervening between then and now became lost and obscured. And like the daughter of Urthona in William Blake's prophetic poem *America*, a poem concerned with the renaissance of freedom and imagination in a new order of the ages, we may say as she said to the spirit of the new age,

> *I know thee*
> *I have found thee*
> *and I will not let you go:*
> *Thou art the image of God*
> *who dwells in darkness of Africa,*
> *and thou art fallen*
> *to give me life in regions of dark death.*

NOTES

Works frequently cited are identified by the following abbreviations:

AEL Miriam Lichtheim, ed. *Ancient Egyptian Literature*. Vols. 1–3. Berkeley: University of California Press, 1975–76.

BD E. A. Wallis Budge. *The Egyptian Book of the Dead* (*The Papyrus of Ani*): *Egyptian Text, Transliteration and Translation*. 1898. Reprint, New York: Dover, 1967. Numbers in the notes refer to chapters. (Not all translations used are Budge's; many references are solely to the Egyptian in the text.)

CT R. O. Faulkner. *The Coffin Texts*. Warminster: Aris and Phillips, 1978. Numbers in the notes refer to spells. (Not all the translations used are Faulkner's.)

JEA *Journal of Egyptian Archaeology*. London. 1914–.

KAG Henri Frankfort. *Kingship and the Gods*. Chicago: University of Chicago Press, 1948.

MAS R. T. Rundle Clark. *Myth and Symbol in Ancient Egypt*. New York: Harper Torchbooks, 1966.

PT R. O. Faulkner. *The Pyramid Texts*. Oxford: Oxford University Press, 1969. Numbers in the notes refer to sections. (Not all the translations used are Faulkner's.)

Urk K. Sethe and W. Helck, eds. *Urkunden des Ägyptischen Altertums*. 4 vols. Berlin, 1955.

Preface

1. "Asclepius" 3.29, *Corpus Hermeticum*.

CHAPTER 1 A Metaphysical Landscape

1. *CT* 76, quoted in *MAS*, p. 83.

2. Though of comparatively late date, this Eighteenth Dynasty hymn retains the imagery and style of more ancient popular hymns. See Alexandre Moret's comments on this hymn in *The Nile and Egyptian Civilization* (London: Routledge and Kegan Paul, 1972), p. 36. The quotation here from the "Short Hymn the Aten" is adapted from the translation by Miriam Lichtheim in *AEL*, vol. 2, p. 98.

3. Herodotus, *Histories* 2.4, trans. Aubrey de Sélincourt (Harmondsworth: Penguin, 1972).

4. Arthur Versluis, *The Egyptian Mysteries* (London: Arkana, 1988), p. 73. See also *KAG*, p. 19.

5. *KAG*, p. 19. Frankfort writes of the "deeply rooted Egyptian tendency to understand the world in dualistic terms as a series of pairs of contrasts balanced in unchanging equilibrium." These deep roots are in the Egyptian landscape.

6. *KAG*, p. 21.

7. See Jeremy Naydler, *The Future of the Ancient World* (Oxford: Abzu Press, 1994), p. 11ff.

8. Moret, *The Nile and Egyptian Civilization*, p. 33.

9. Marshall Adams, *The Book of the Master* (London: Putnam and Sons, 1898), p. 43ff.

10. Margaret Murray, *The Splendour That Was Egypt* (London: New English Library, 1962), p. 267ff.

11. Diodorus Siculus, *The Library of History*, 1.36, quoted in Moret, *The Nile and Egyptian Civilization*, p. 31n.

12. *Histories*, 2.100.

13. *PT* 1553–54.

14. *MAS*, p. 99.

15. "The Hymn to Hapi," adapted from the translation in A. Erman, ed., *The Ancient Egyptians: A Sourcebook of Their Writings* (New York: Harper Torchbooks, 1966), p. 146ff.

16. Diodorus Siculus, *Library of History*, 1.36.

17. *MAS*, p. 100.

18. In "The Great Hymn to the Aten" it is written: "You make the Great River in the Dwat and bring it where you will in order to sustain mankind." In *AEL* 2, p. 98–99.

19. John A. Wilson, "Egypt," in H. Frankfort et al., *Before Philosophy* (Harmondsworth: Pelican Books, 1949), p. 51.

20. Rudolph Steiner, *World History in the Light of Anthroposophy* (London: Rudolph Steiner Press, 1977), p. 11.

CHAPTER 2 Interpenetrating Worlds

1. Although certain philosophers, notably Immanuel Kant, have claimed that it is possible.

2. Jeremy Naydler, *Perceptions of the Divine in Nature*, part 1, "The Heart of the Lily" (Oxford: Abzu Press, 1993).

3. As Egypt was described in "Asclepius" 3.29, *Corpus Hermeticum*.

4. *Urk*, vol. 4, 146, 14.

5. *Spiritual Body, Celestial Earth* (Princeton: Princeton University Press, 1990), p. 4. The passage in full reads: "To come face to face with the Earth not as a conglomeration of physical facts but in the person of its Angel is an essentially psychic event which can 'take place' neither in the world of impersonal abstract concepts nor on the plane of mere sen-

sory data. The Earth has to be perceived not by the senses, but through a primordial Image and, inasmuch as this Image carries the features of a personal figure, it will prove to 'symbolize with' the very Image of itself which the soul carries in its innermost depths. The perception of the Earth Angel will come about in an intermediate universe which is neither that of the Essences of philosophy nor that of the sensory data on which the work of positive science is based, but which is a universe of archetype-Images, experienced as so many personal presences."

6. *PT* 782.

7. *CT* 80.

8. See chapter 10, for a discussion of the concept of the Underworld.

9. "The Book of Gates," division 12, in Alexandre Piankoff, *The Tomb of Ramesses VI* (New York: Pantheon Books, Bollingen Series, 1954).

10. Ibid.

11. *CT* 76, 79, 80.

12. *PT* 1040.

13. *BD* 17.

14. Inscription from the ceiling of Seti I's cenotaph at Abydos. Translation adapted from James P. Allen, *Genesis in Egypt: The Philosophy of Ancient Egyptian Creation Accounts* (New Haven: Yale University Press, 1988).

CHAPTER 3 Myths of Cosmogenesis

1. In modern times, the German philosopher G. W. F. Hegel, and the visionary founder of Anthroposophy, Rudolf Steiner, are two outstanding thinkers who have given rigorous and detailed accounts of the procees of spiritual evolution—Hegel in a purely abstract sequence of philosophical ideas, Steiner in a series of concrete imaginative concepts. See Hegel's *Logic*, part 1 of the *Encyclopaedia of the Philosophical Sciences*, 1830, translated by William Wallace (Oxford: Clarendon Press, 1975) and Rudolf Steiner's *Occult Science: An Outline* (London: Rudolf Steiner Press, 1969).

2. *PT* 1146.

3. For a discussion of the name Atum, see Allen, *Genesis in Egypt*, p. 9.

4. *CT* 80, trans. *MAS*, p. 38.

5. *CT* 321, trans. *MAS*, p. 51.

6. *PT* 1587.

7. *BD* 85.

8. *BD* 17.

9. *PT* 1248.

10. *CT* 136.

11. *PT* 1652–53.

12. *CT* 80.

13. *CT* 245, trans. *MAS*, p. 44.

14. Quoted in E. A. Wallis Budge: *Egyptian Religion* (London: Routledge and Kegan Paul, 1975), p. 26.

15. *PT* 785.

16. A fifth child is sometimes added—Horus the Elder (Har Wer in Egyptian, or Haroeris in Greek), a mighty sky god.

17. Harris Magical Papyrus, recto, col. 6, 10–12.

18. Quoted in E. A. Wallis Budge, *The Gods of the Egyptians* (New York: Dover, 1969), vol. 1, p. 400.

19. *BD*, introduction, p. cxviii.

20. *De Isis et Osiride*, 117.3.

21. G. Maspero, *The Dawn of Civilization* (London, 1894), p. 146.

22. Budge, *The Gods of the Egyptians*, vol. 1, p. 407.

23. Haremhab's "Hymn to Thoth" in *AEL*, vol. 2, p. 102.

24. *PT* 466.

25. In the so-called Shu Texts (*CT* 75–81).

26. *BD*, p. cxviii. See also George St. Clair, *Creation Records* (London, 1898), p. 192–95.

27. See *MAS*, p. 254, for a discussion of this picture and its significance.

28. Edfu inscription 6, 11–12 quoted in Lucy Lamy, *Egyptian Mysteries* (London: Thames and Hudson, 1981), p. 10.

29. A full translation of this text is given in *AEL*, vol. 1, p. 51–57.

30. Shabaka Text 54, *AEL*, vol. 1, p. 54.

31. Budge, *The Gods of the Egyptians*, vol. 1, p. 500–501.

32. Ibid., p. 500.

33. Ibid., p. 501.

34. "Hymn to Ptah-Tatenen" quoted in Budge, *The Gods of the Egyptians*, vol. 1, p. 510.

35. Shabaka Text 53, trans. John A. Wilson in J. B. Pritchard, ed., *The Ancient Near East* (Princeton: Princeton University Press, 1958), p. 1.

36. As translated in *MAS*, p. 61.

37. Shabaka Text 53–54.

38. Shabaka Text 55.

39. Shabaka Text 58.

40. Shabaka Text 54.

41. "Hymn to Ptah-Tatenen" in Budge, *The Gods of the Egyptians*, vol. 1, p. 511.

42. Shabaka Text 57.

43. Shabaka Text 59–61.

CHAPTER 4 The Marking of Time

1. See E. A. Burtt, *The Metaphysical Foundations of Modern Physical Science* (London: Routledge and Kegan Paul, 1932), chap. 3.

2. Sir Alan Gardiner, *Egyptian Grammar* (Oxford: Oxford University Press, 1957), p. 206.

3. Budge, *The Gods of the Egyptians*, vol. 2, p. 300–302.

4. Serge Sauneron, *The Priests of Ancient Egypt* (New York: Grove Press, 1960), p. 99.

5. In fact, some sixty distinct images of Ra's journey of transformation are recorded in the Coffin Texts, of which twelve are preserved in the Book of the Dead, in the "Chapters of Transformation" (chapters 76–88). See Paul Barguet's illuminating commentary in *Les Livres des Morts* (Paris: Les Editions du Cerf, 1967), p. 98.

6. *Sacred Science* (Rochester, Vt.: Inner Traditions International, 1982), p. 177n. Schwaller de Lubicz based his calculations on the *Annuaire de Flammarion* (1953), in which the pre-

cessional period is said to diminish by 11.4 years per century.

7. 18 x 1461 = 26,268. In 3000 B.C. the observable precession would have been calculated at 26,280 years. Today it is 25,780 years.

8. *Sacred Science*, p. 28.

9. From the "Aretalogy of Kyme" in Louis V. Zabkar, *Hymns to Isis in Her Temple at Philae* (Hanover, N.H., and London: University Press of New England, 1988), p. 140.

10. *PT* 965.

11. Plutarch, *De Isis et Osiride*, 38.

12. Ibid.

13. Mircea Eliade, *The Sacred and the Profane* (London: Harcourt Brace Jovanovich, 1959), p. 95.

14. Herodotus, *Histories*: 2.59ff.

15. Ibid., 60–61.

16. Heliodorus, *Aethiopica* 9.9.

17. Translation based on *AEL*, vol. 1, p. 208–9.

18. Maspero, *The Dawn of Civilization*, p. 39.

19. *PT* 585–89.

20. *De Isis et Osiride*, 38. Plutarch himself ascribes this festival to the month of Athyr several months later, when the inundation would have covered the land. According to Frankfort, however, the ceremonies he describes originally occurred at the end of the season of Shomu. See *KAG*, p. 391.

21. *PT* 584, 612, 1008, 1255–56, 1799, 2144.

22. *Aethiopica*, 9.9.

23. Inscription, Temple of Denderah, quoted in *KAG*, p. 185.

24. *MAS*, p. 100–101.

25. *De Isis et Osiride*, 70.

26. J. G. Frazer, *The New Golden Bough*, ed. T. H. Gaster (New York: S. G. Phillips, 1959), part 4, p. 258.

27. See chapter 10.

28. *KAG*, p. 291.

29. E. O. James, *Myth and Ritual in the Ancient Near East* (London, 1932), p. 50. A. M. Blackmann, "Myth and Ritual in Ancient Egypt," in S. H. Hooke, ed., *Myth and Ritual* (Oxford: Oxford University Press, 1933), p. 19–20.

30. *KAG*, p. 291.

31. R. A. Parker, *The Calendars of Ancient Egypt* (Chicago: University of Chicago Press, 1951), p. 60.

32. Manfred Lurker, *The Gods and Symbols of Ancient Egypt* (London: Thames and Hudson, 1980), p. 46–47.

33. Blackmann, "Myth and Ritual in Ancient Egypt," p. 22.

34. Ibid., p. 21.

35. G. Hart, *A Dictionary of Egyptian Gods and Goddesses* (London: Routledge and Kegan Paul, 1986), p. 184.

36. Parker, *The Calendars of Ancient Egypt*, p. 39, 58.

37. Lurker, *Gods and Symbols*, p. 100.

38. Parker, *Calendars*, p. 39–40.

39. Hart, *Dictionary*, p. 123.

40. Blackmann, "Myth and Ritual," p. 27.

41. *KAG*, p. 188. See also E. O. James, *Myth and Ritual*, p. 53.

42. Diodorus Siculus, 1.14.2.

43. Hart, *Dictionary*, p. 122.

44. *KAG*, p. 190.

45. For the relationship of the harvest festival to the regenerative cycle see Alison Roberts, *Hathor Rising: The Serpent Power of Ancient Egypt* (Totnes, England: Northgate, 1995), p. 82–86.

46. *KAG*, p. 186. See also *PT* 308–9.

47. *CT* 100.

48. Blackmann, "Myth and Ritual," p. 29.

CHAPTER 5 The Marriage of Myth and History

1. *MAS*, p. 263.

2. Eliade, *The Sacred and the Profane*, p. 69.

3. Ibid.

4. *PT* 1463. See also *PT* 1040.

5. *PT* 1775b.

6. *CT* 80 (Faulkner trans.).

7. *PT* 1775; *CT* 113. The regular offerings of Maat to the gods in the temples confirm that she was regarded as the food of the gods.

8. Inscription of the Speos Artemidos, in J. H. Breasted, *Ancient Records* (New York: Russell and Russell, 1906; reissued 1962), 2.299.

9. Donald B. Redford, *Pharaonic King Lists: Annals and Day Books* (Missuaga: Benben Publications, 1986), p. 259.

10. Ibid., p. 260ff.

11. Restoration Stela in *Urk*, 4.2026.

12. *Urk*, 4.1725.5, the words of Amenophis III.

13. *Urk*, 7.27.

14. Inscription of the Speos Artemidos in Breasted, *Ancient Records* (London, 1912), 2.299.

15. *KAG*, p. 51–52; also H. Frankfort's *Ancient Egyptian Religion* (London: Harper and Row, 1961), p. 54–55; S. Morenz, *Egyptian Religion* (London: Methuen, 1973), p. 113ff; and Redford, *Pharaonic King Lists*, p. 259–75.

16. Quoted in Morenz, *Egyptian Religion*, p. 133.

17. See, for example, the "Instructions of Ptahotep" and "Instruction for the Vizier Kagemni," both translated in *AEL*, vol. 1.

18. "The Book of Gates" in Piankoff, *The Tomb of Ramesses VI*, p. 145.

19. For the significance of the cosmic week see chap. 4. See also F. G. Fleay, *Egyptian Chronology* (London: David Nutt, 1899), p. 93.

20. Patrick O'Mara, *The Chronology of the Palermo and Turin Canons* (La Canada, Calif.: Paulette Publishing Co., 1980), p. 35.

21. Fleay, *Egyptian Chronology*, p. 98.

22. This principle is adhered to not only in the Manethonic chronology, but also in the Turin Canon of the New Kingdom, the Saite scheme recorded by Herodotus, and the Eratosthenes scheme preserved by Eusebius. See Fleay, *Egyptian Chronology*, p. 98–123.

23. O'Mara, *Chronology of the Palermo and Turin Canons*, p. 19–20.

24. Ibid., p. 21.

25. For further examples, see O'Mara, *Chronology*, chap. 2.

26. *PT* 882. See also *PT* 480.

27. *PT* 458.

28. *PT* 632.

29. O'Mara, *Chronology*, p. 27–32.

30. Ibid., p. 35.

31. Ibid., p. 40–42.

32. See, for example, Theophrastus, *De lapidibus*, 24; Tatian, *Oratio adversus Graecos*, 38.

33. *Histories*, 2.77.

34. Redford, *Pharaonic King Lists*.

35. *KAG*, p. 45.

36. Ibid., p. 58.

37. Ibid., p. 102.

38. Papyrus Sallier, 1.8.9. Translation adapted from Blackmann's translation in Erman, *The Ancient Egyptians*, p. 278–79.

39. *KAG*, p. 149.

40. James, *Myth and Ritual*, p. 88. *KAG*, p. 148, 150–51.

41. Papyrus Anastasi 2.5.6, trans. in Erman, *The Ancient Egyptians*, p. 280.

42. Sir Alan Gardiner, in *Egypt of the Pharaohs* (Oxford: Oxford University Press, 1966), writes: "In the Old Kingdom, official records of the Pharaonic achievement are completely absent; the kings were gods, too lofty and too powerful to care for recitals of their doings to be communicated to their subjects . . ." (p. 55).

43. Redford, *Pharaonic King Lists*, p. 136.

44. Ibid.

45. The king was not only "son of Ra." Kings were also referred to as "son of Geb" (*PT* 483), or of Atum (*PT* 395). For example, *PT* 826, 1431; *PT* utterances 402, 405, 570; *PT* utterances 22, 25, 26, 27, 28, etc.

46. John A. Wilson, *The Culture of Ancient Egypt* (Chicago: University of Chicago Press, 1956), p. 131 and p. 267–8.

47. *KAG*, p. 32–33; also see chap. 11.

48. Redford, *Pharaonic King Lists*, p. 22.

49. Ibid., p. 19–20. Commenting on the list of Tjuloy, Redford writes: "While it is not quite correct to imply that any royal ancestors would fill the requirements of this type of scene, absolute historical accuracy did not have priority" (p. 23–24).

50. Gardiner, *Egypt of the Pharaohs*, p. 57.

51. Frankfort, *Ancient Egyptian Religion*, p. 48.

52. Middle Kingdom text quoted in Gardiner, *Egypt of the Pharaohs*, p. 37.

53. Ibid.

54. "The Battle of Megiddo" in *AEL*, vol. 2, p. 33.

55. *KAG*, p. 9.

56. Wilson, *Culture of Ancient Egypt*, p. 195, 200.

57. "Battle of Kadesh Inscription" in *AEL*, vol. 2, p. 65.

58. Ibid., p. 65–66.

59. Ibid.

60. Ibid., p. 67.

61. Ibid., p. 70.

62. For the following interpretation I am indebted to R. A. Schwaller de Lubicz, who discusses the battle of Kadesh in his *Sacred Science*, p. 126–37.

63. Ibid., p. 130.

64. Ibid., p. 133.

65. *The Sacred and the Profane*, p. 95.

CHAPTER 6 The Theology of Magic

1. *The Catholic Encyclopaedia* (New York, 1911), vol. 11, p. 199.

2. For a full discussion of the *Corpus Hermeticum* and its impact on European thought in the Renaissance, see Frances A. Yates, *Giordano Bruno and the Hermetic Tradition* (London: Routledge and Kegan Paul, 1964). See also Arthur Versluis, *The Philosophy of Magic* (London: Arkana, 1986), p. 10ff.

3. Versluis, *Philosophy of Magic*, p. 4.

4. Ibid.

5. Matt. 2:1.

6. A. E. Waite, *The Occult Sciences* (London, 1911), p. 11. For Waite, "esoteric wisdom," "occult knowledge," and "transcendental philosophy" are interconvertible terms all signifying magic (p. 3).

7. "Philosophia Sagax" in F. Hartmann, *Paracelsus: Life and Prophecies* (New York: Rudolph Steiner Publications, 1973), p. 103–4.

8. Plato, *Timaeus*, 22B.

9. A. H. Gardiner, "Egyptian Magic" in *Hastings' Encyclopaedia of Religion and Ethics*, (Edinburgh, 1925) p. 263.

10. *CT* 261.

11. Ibid.

12. *MAS*, p. 254.

13. See chapter 3.

14. Christian Jacq, *Egyptian Magic* (Warminster: Arris and Phillips, 1985), p. 4.

15. *PT* 1324.

16. *PT* 403, 411.

17. *PT* 1318.

18. *BD* 24.

19. Wadi Hamâmat Inscriptions, in Gardiner, "The House of Life," *JEA* 24 (1938): p. 157.

20. Ibid., p. 178, 159.

21. For example, *BD* 72, rubric; Piankoff, The Book of What Is in the Underworld, division 1, *The Tomb of Ramesses VI*, p. 239.

22. Tomb of Ti, Saqqara.

23. J. A. West, *The Traveller's Key to Ancient Egypt* (London: Columbus Books, 1985), p. 171.

24. Tomb of Oukhotep, quoted in J. A. West, *Serpent in the Sky* (London: Wildwood House, 1979), p. 94.

25. Tomb of Rekhmire, Thebes.

26. Papyrus Westcar. In Erman, *The Ancient Egyptians*, p. 40–44.

27. Bob Brier, *Ancient Egyptian Magic* (New York: Quill, 1981), p. 34.

28. Exod. 20:4–5.

29. For a fuller discussion of the significance of the spiritual and physical migration of the Israelites from polytheistic Egypt, see Jeremy Naydler, *Christ and the Gods* (Oxford: Abzu Press, 1994), p. 9–16.

30. Psalm 115.

31. Owen Barfield, *Saving the Appearances* (London: Faber, 1957), p. 111.

32. Robin Lane Fox, *Pagans and Christians* (London: Penguin, 1986), p. 166.

33. C. G. Jung, *Psychology and Religion* (New Haven: Yale University Press, 1977), p. 100–103. For Jung's views on the evolution of consciousness, see also the essay "Archaic Man" in *Modern Man in Search of a Soul* (London: Routledge and Kegan Paul, 1961).

34. "Asclepius" 3, *Corpus Hermeticum* (Bath: Solos Press, 1992), p. 136.

35. Plotinus, *Enneads*, trans. Stephen MacKenna (London: Faber, 1956), 4.3.11.

36. *BD* 6.

37. Plato, *Cratylus*, especially 424–27.

38. Ibid., 397c.

39. Shabaka Text 54.

40. Iamblichus, *On the Mysteries of the Egyptians, Chaldeans and Assyrians*, trans. Thomas Taylor (London, 1821), p. 295–96.

41. Ibid.

42. R. A. Schwaller de Lubicz, *Symbol and the Symbolic* (New York: Inner Traditions International, 1981), p. 47.

43. *PT* 1655. For a discussion of the text, see Schwaller de Lubicz, *Sacred Science*, p. 191–92.

44. *Urk.* 4, 1820, 12–14; 4, 1897, 12.

45. Diodorus Siculus 1.70ff.

46. Papyrus Sallier 1.8.9. Translation adapted from Blackmann in Erman, *The Ancient Egyptians*, p. 279.

47. Frankfort, *Before Philosophy*, p. 34.

CHAPTER 7 The Practice of Magic

1. For more on the First Time, see chapter 5.

2. *KAG*, p. 150–51.

3. Papyrus Anastasi. Translation adapted from Erman, *The Ancient Egyptians*, p. 280.

4. James, *Myth and Ritual in the Ancient Near East*, p. 88.

5. Jacq, *Egyptian Magic*, p. 97. For the meaning of these ritual acts, see Robert Kriech Ritner, *The Mechanics of Ancient Egyptian Magical Practice* (Chicago: University of Chicago Press, 1993).

6. *BD* 39.

7. Quoted in Jacq, *Egyptian Magic*, p. 110.

8. Ibid., p. 69–70.

9. Murray, *The Splendour That Was Egypt*, p. 139.

10. "The Bremmer-Rhind Papyrus 1," trans. R. O. Faulkner in *JEA* 22 (1936): p. 121–40.

11. *BD* 76–88.

12. "The Kadesh Battle Inscriptions of Ramesses II" in *AEL* 2, p. 67.

13. "The Annals of Thutmosis III" in *AEL* 2, p. 32.

14. Naydler, *The Future of the Ancient World*, p. 15ff.

15. *PT* 148–49.

16. *BD* 42.

17. A. Wiedemann, *The Realms of the Egyptian Dead* (London, 1901), p. 14–15.

18. The study and interpretation of ancient Egyptian pharmacology is still far from complete. It would seem that many remedies were selected on homeopathic principles. The Papyrus Ebers, which is one of the most important sources of our knowledge of Egyptian medicine, contains a remedy for diarrhea containing figs, grapes, and elderberries. This is one example from several that could be cited that would seem to exemplify the utilization of homeopathic principles.

   Many of the substances referred to in the Papyrus Ebers are virtually unintelligible, leading Paul Ghalioungui to comment, in his study *House of Life: Magic and Medical Science in Ancient Egypt* (Amsterdam: B. M. Israel, 1973), "In our appraisal of this bulky pharmacology, many reservations are called for by the nature of the names that are often secret appellations, or do not disclose their composition, just like patent names: 'costly ointment,' 'skull fighter,' 'my hand holds, my hand grasps,' 'Thoth's feather,' etc." (p. 140). Other names were simply vernacular names, like our "mare's tail" or "foxglove." The modern horror at the inclusion of such ingredients as "rat's tail," "fly's dirt" and "fly's blood" in the Papyrus Ebers's concoctions may well be misplaced according to Ghalioungui, who suggests they were in fact vernacular names of herbs. Again, other drugs that have long been considered absurd because they employed mold, animal dung, and Nile mud are now known to have antibiotic properties.

19. Papyrus Ebers 763.

20. Quoted in Gardiner, "Egyptian Magic," p. 267.

21. Ibid., p. 264.

22. For example, *BD* 31–37.

23. Jacq, *Egyptian Magic*, p. 3.

24. *PT* 393–404.

25. Reproduced in Budge, *The Gods of the Ancient Egyptians*, vol. 2, p. 210ff.

26. Translation adapted from ibid., p. 239.

27. Frankfort, *Before Philosophy*, p. 34.

28. Quoted in Jacq, *Egyptian Magic*, p. 103.

29. Ibid.

30. Matt. 8:26.

31. For a short comparative study of the ancient animistic approach to the weather and the perspectives of modern meteorology, see Naydler, *Perceptions of the Divine in Nature*, part 2, "Baal-Hadad at Bracknell."

32. S. Sauneron, *The Priests of Ancient Egypt*, p. 167. Eunapius, *Vitae Sophistorum, Aedesius* 463 Didot, in J. G. Frazer, *The New Golden Bough*, p. 85. Frazer collects together many examples of wind magic from all over the world, every one of which arises out of an animistic view of the wind.

33. See "Hymn on the Accession of King Merenptah" in Erman, *The Ancient Egyptians*, p. 279. Amenemhet I quoted in *KAG*, p. 57.

34. *KAG*, p. 58–59.

35. Exod. 14:21–22.

36. Erman, *The Ancient Egyptians*, p. 38–40.

37. Exod. 7:9, 11–12.

38. Theodore Roszak, *Where the Wasteland Ends* (London: Faber, 1972), p. 473.

CHAPTER 8 The Soul Incarnate

1. See Naydler, *The Future of the Ancient World*, for a fuller discussion of this subject.

2. *BD* 92.

3. Building inscriptions of King Sesostris I (Middle Kingdom), *AEL*, vol. 1, p. 127.

4. Instructions of King Amenemhet I (Middle Kingdom), *AEL*, vol. 1, p. 36.

5. *BD* 89.

6. Hymn of Merikare, trans. W. K. Simpson, *The Literature of Ancient Egypt* (New Haven: Yale University Press, 1973), p. 83.

7. Stele of Sehetep-ib-re, *AEL*, vol. 1, p. 128.

8. For example, *PT* 484, where the king worships God "on his nose."

9. See the "Instructions Addressed to Kagemni," 5.1, *AEL*, vol. 1, p. 60; and "The Instructions of Ptahotep," *AEL*, vol. 1, p. 63.

10. Adapted from *BD*, "Commentary," p. 267.

11. *BD* 21–23.

12. *BD*, "Commentary," p. 266ff.

13. *PT* 320.

14. *PT* 53.

15. "Story of Sinuhe," line 279, trans. Simpson, *Literature of Ancient Egypt*, p. 72.

16. For the complex symbolism of the *wedjat* and the relationship between it and the *iret* (the term normally used for the eye) see *MAS* 218–30.

17. Maxims of Ptahotep, introduction, line 40, epilogue, line 546, *AEL*, vol. 1, p. 63, 74.

18. Maxims of Ptahotep, 23, 20.

19. "Instructions to Kagemni," *AEL*, vol. 1, p. 60. Maxims of Ptahotep, 14.

20. *PT* 1318.

21. Maxims of Ptahotep, 27.

22. "Instructions of Amenemope," 3.13, *AEL*, vol. 2, p. 149.

23. Maxims of Ptahotep, 14.

24. "Instructions of Amenemope," 14.10.

25. Maxims of Ptahotep, 11.

26. *BD* 30B.

27. "Tale of the Eloquent Peasant," B205, *AEL*, vol. 1, p. 177. Maxims of Ptahotep, 4 and 8.

28. Ibid., 39.

29. Stele of Intef, son of Sent (Middle Kingdom), *AEL*, vol. 1, p. 122.

30. As a seat of memory, see Maxims of Ptahotep, introduction, *AEL*, vol. 1, p. 63, where it is

said that "the void heart . . . cannot recall the past." As a seat of intention, see *PT* 311, where Unas's "foot" (i.e., will) is not hindered and his "heart" is unopposed.

31. Maxims of Ptahotep, 44 (line 618). "Autobiography of Ankhtifi," *AEL*, vol. 1, p. 86.

32. *BD* 30B.

33. "Instructions of Amenemope," 1.9.

34. *BD* 26.

35. Ibid., 43.

36. *BD*, p. lviii.

37. *PT* 474.

38. As Faulkner does in, for instance, *PT* 474.

39. Bruno Snell, *The Discovery of the Mind* (New York: Dover, 1982), p. 5ff.

40. R. B. Onians, *The Orgins of European Thought* (Cambridge: Cambridge University Press, 1951), is one of the best sources for the early Greek understanding of the soul.

41. M. Jastrow, *Religion of Babylonia and Assyria* (Boston, 1898), p. 323ff.

42. As has been unconvincingly argued by Julian Jaynes, *The Origins of Consciousness in the Breakdown of the Bicameral Mind* (New York: Penguin, 1982).

43. *PT* 364–65.

44. Ibid., 318.

CHAPTER 9 The Soul Discarnate

1. *MAS*, p. 119.

2. *PT* 18.

3. Ibid., 372.

4. Ibid., 17.

5. Ibid., 267; see also 157.

6. See also *PT* 507–10.

7. Ibid., 311. See also 161, where the bestowal and removal of *ka*s is linked to the "reckoning" of hearts.

8. *KAG*, p. 68.

9. *BD* 29B (Budge), 29A (Faulkner).

10. *KAG*, p. 69.

11. Maxims of Ptahotep, 7.

12. Maxims of Ptahotep, 27.

13. *PT* 908.

14. *PT* 1652. See also chapter 3.

15. *BD* 105.

16. *BD*, p. lxiv.

17. *KAG*, p. 64.

18. *PT* 474.

19. *PT* 250.

20. Maxims of Ptahotep, *AEL*, vol. 1, p. 73.

21. "Instructions to Merikare," *AEL*, vol. 1, p. 103.

22. *BD*, p. lxiv.

23. *BD* 154.

24. *BD* 89.

25. *BD* 92.

26. Lamy, *Egyptian Mysteries*, p. 24–25.

27. *BD*, p. lxvii.

28. *PT* 152. The four pillars demarcate the four points of the compass, hence the boundaries of the universe.

29. *BD* 15.

30. From the papyrus of Muthegepti, *BD* 174.

31. *BD* 154.

32. See *BD*, p. lix.

33. *BD* 9.

34. *BD* 99.

35. *PT* 654–56. Compare with *BD* 133, "For Making the Akh Strong."

CHAPTER 10 Orientating in the Underworld

1. A. Gardiner, *Egyptian Grammar* (Oxford: Oxford University Press, 1973), p. 487.

2. Plutarch, *De Isis et Osiride*, 29.7.

3. *MAS*, p. 165.

4. *BD* 175.

5. *BD* 51, 52, 53, and 189. See also *CT* 771, 772, and 894.

6. See Frankfort, *Ancient Egyptian Religion*, p. 112–13.

7. *PT* 381.

8. *PT* 1228; 2078–79; 2101–2.

9. *PT* 365, 1090, 1108.

10. *CT* 1042.

11. *PT* 914–17.

12. *BD* 110, papyrus of Ani.

13. For example, Budge, *Egyptian Religion*, p. 176ff.

14. *BD* 99, papyrus of Nu.

15. *BD* 99, trans. R. O. Faulkner, *The Ancient Egyptian Book of the Dead* (London: British Museum, 1972), p. 92–95. See also *CT* 397.

16. *PT* 48.

17. For a discussion of the symbolism of the "finger of Seth" in relation to the eye of Horus, see H. T. Velde, *Seth: God of Confusion* (London: E. J. Brill, 1967), p. 49–53.

CHAPTER 11 The Travails of the Underworld

1. For example, *BD* 175.

2. *BD* 54, papyrus of Ani; *BD* 56, papyrus of Nu.

3. *BD* 54, papyrus of Ani.

4. On the concept of germination, see chapter 9.

5. *BD* 56, papyrus of Nu.

6. Herodotus, *Histories*, 2.37. See also Plutarch, *De Isis et Osiride*, 7.

7. Plutarch, *De Isis et Osiride*, 18.

8. See *KAG*, p. 191–92.

9. Heraclitus, frags. 36 and 118 Diels.

10. *BD* 153a, papyrus of Nakht.

11. Ibid. See also *CT* 473–77.

12. *BD* 17, section 22.

13. For a discussion of St. Catherine's doctrines on Hell, Purgatory, and Heaven, see Von Hugel, *The Mystical Element of Religion*, vol. 1, (London: 1908), p. 281–94.

14. *BD* 126.

15. Rollo May, *Love and Will* (London: Fontana, 1974), p. 123ff.

16. *BD* 31.

17. *BD* 31; see also *CT* 342.

18. *BD* 32.

19. *BD* 39.

20. *BD* 29b.

21. *BD* 26.

22. Gottfried Richter, *Art and Human Consciousness* (Edinburgh: Floris Books, 1985), p. 12–15.

23. BD 146.

24. This was the case at Edfu, for example. For the symbolism of the pylon, see R. H. Wilkinson, *Reading Egyptian Art* (London: Thames and Hudson, 1992), p. 135.

25. See R. E. Finnestad, *Image of the World and Symbol of the Creator* (Wiesbaden: Otto Harrassowitz, 1985), p. 9; Wilkinson, *Reading Egyptian Art*, p. 135.

26. BD 146.

27. Ibid.

28. Ibid.

29. *BD* 147, papyrus of Ani.

CHAPTER 12 The End of the Underworld Journey

1. *BD* 125, papyrus of Ani.

2. Ibid.

3. In *PT* 1116, Satet is described as purifying the king with four jars, probably containing floodwater from the Nile at the time of its inundation. Satet was a goddess of the Elephantine associated with the Nile flood.

4. *BD* 125, papyrus of Ani.

5. Ibid.

6. Ibid.

7. See chapter 5, p. 97.

8. *BD* 125, papyrus of Ani.

9. Ibid.

10. *BD* 125, papyrus of Nu.

11. No illustration of the weighing of the heart accompanies the passage quoted (sheet 24), and it is highly unlikely that any vignette appeared in the damaged first sheet of the papyrus, which contains a figure of Osiris and a tree. There is room for a representation of Nu in the damaged section, but hardly room for a weighing scene. The papyrus of Nu (BM 10, 477) is in the British Museum.

12. Examples in Christine Seeber, *Untersuchungen zur Darstellung des Totengerichts im Alten Ägypten* (Berlin: Deutscher Kunsterling, 1976). See also the papyrus of Anhai (Twenty-third Dynasty) that contains two illustrations depicting weighing scenes, one of which shows the scales empty.

13. *KAG*, p. 19.

14. *KAG*, p. 21.

15. J. G. Griffiths, *The Conflict of Horus and Seth* (Liverpool: Liverpool University Press, 1960), p. 54.

16. See Terence DuQuesne, *A Coptic Initiatory Invocation* (Thame, England: Darengo, 1991), p. 47–48.

17. Ibid.

18. *BD* 29B; see chapter 9.

19. See chapter 9.

20. *BD* 30B.

21. *BD* 139. See also Griffiths, *The Conflict of Horus and Seth*, p. 82ff; 43.

22. *BD* 125.

23. *BD* 30B rubric.

24. *BD* 183, line 32; lines 32–33.

25. R. T. Rundle Clark, *Myth and Symbol in Ancient Egypt* (London: Thames and Hudson, 1978), p. 130ff.

26. See, for example, N. Rambova, "The Symbolism of the Papyri" in Alexandre Piankoff, *Mythological Papyri* (New York: Bollingen Foundation, 1964).

27. See chapter 9, p. 208.

28. *PT* 1582.

ILLUSTRATION CREDITS

Figs. 2.1, 2.8, 3.3, 3.8, 3.14, 8.7, 11.2 from W. Max Müller, *Egyptian Mythology* (Boston: Marshall Jones, 1918).

Figs. 2.2, 2.5, 2.12, 2.16, 3.12, 12.13, 12.15 from A. Piankoff and N. Rambova, *Mythological Papyri* (New York: Bollingen Foundation, 1957). Reproduced by permission of Princeton University Press.

Figs. 2.3, 2.7, 2.9, 3.13, 4.3, 4.5, 4.9, 5.2, 5.3, 6.1, 6.2, 6.5, 7.2, 8.1, 8.6, 9.1, 9.3, 9.10, 9.11, 10.3, 10.8, 11.15, 12.5, 12.9, 12.10, 12.11, 12.14 drawings by Barry Cottrell.

Figs. 2.4, 2.6, 3.6, 4.12, 4.20, 7.9, 7.10 from E. A. Wallis Budge, *The Gods of the Egyptians*, vols. 1 and 2 (New York: Dover, 1969).

Figs. 2.10, 5.9 from J. H. Breasted, *A History of Ancient Egypt* (London, 1912).

Fig. 2.11 from Roy Willis, *World Mythology* (New York: Duncan Baird Publishers, 1993).

Figs. 2.13, 10.5, 10.6 from Guiolmant, *Le Tombeau de Ramsès IX* (Paris, 1907).

Figs. 2.14, 2.15, 3.16, 6.8 from R. A. Schwaller de Lubicz, *The Egyptian Miracle* (Rochester, Vt.: Inner Traditions International, 1985).

Fig. 2.17 courtesy of the Committee of the Egypt Exploration Society.

Figs. 3.1, 3.9, 3.10, 3.15, 4.14, 6.12, 7.6, 7.7, 7.8, 8.2, 8.4, 8.5, 8.9, 8.10, 8.11, 9.7, 9.8, 9.9, 9.12, 10.1, 10.2, 10.4, 10.10, 10.11, 10.12, 11.1, 11.4, 11.5, 11.6, 11.7, 11.8, 11.9, 11.10, 11.11, 11.14, 11.16, 11.17, 12.1, 12.8 from E. A. Wallis Budge, *The Book of the Dead* (London: Routledge and Kegan Paul, 1985).

Fig. 3.2 from E. A. Wallis Budge, *From Fetish to God in Ancient Egypt* (London: Oxford University Press, 1934).

Figs. 3.4, 3.5, 3.7, 6.3, 8.3, 9.4, 9.6, 11.3, 11.12, 11.13, 12.2 drawings/photos by Jeremy Naydler.

Figs. 3.11, 4.4, 5.6, 6.7, 7.11, 9.5, 10.13 from G. Maspero, *The Dawn of Civilization* (London, 1894).

Fig. 4.1 from Brian Loomes, *Complete British Clocks* (London: David and Charles, 1978), with kind permission of the author.

Fig. 4.2 from Donald de Carle, *Watches and their Value* (London: N.A.G. Press, 1978).

Fig. 4.6 from Paul Barget, *Les Livres des Morts* (Paris: Editions du Cerf, 1967).

Fig. 4.7 from A. Piankoff, *Tomb of Ramesses VI* (Princeton, N.J.: Princeton University Press, 1954).

Figs. 4.8, 4.13, 4.21, 4.22, 5.8, 5.11, 5.12, 5.13, 6.10 from R. A. Schwaller de Lubicz, *Sacred Science* (Rochester Vt.: Inner Traditions International, 1982).

Fig. 4.10 from R. T. Rundle Clark, *Myth and Symbol in Ancient Egypt* (London: Thames and Hudson, 1959).

Figs. 4.11, 4.24, 7.1, 8.8 from A. Erman, *Life in Ancient Egypt* (New York: Dover, 1971).

Fig. 4.15 from E. A. Wallis Budge, *Osiris: The Egyptian Religion of the Resurrection* (London, 1911).

Figs. 4.16, 7.3 from Louvre Museum, photo copyright Réunion des Musées Nationaux.

Figs. 4.17, 12.12 from R. David, *A Guide to Religious Ritual at Abydos* (Warminster: Aris and Phillips, 1981), with kind permission of the publishers.

Figs. 4.18, 4.19 from W. R. Cooper, *The Serpent Myths of Ancient Egypt* (London, 1873).

Fig. 4.23 from Denon, *Voyage en Egypte* (Paris, 1802).

Fig. 5.1 from Lucy Lamy, *Egyptian Mysteries* (London: Thames and Hudson, 1981).

Figs. 5.4, 5.7, 5.10 from A. Gardiner, *Egypt of the Pharaohs* (1966). Reproduced by permission of Oxford University Press.

Fig. 5.5 courtesy of Bavarian State Collection, Munich.

Figs. 6.4, 6.9 from A. Gardiner, *Journal of Egyptian Archaeology* vol. 24 (1938). Reproduced by permission of the Committee of the Egypt Exploration Society.

Fig. 6.6 courtesy of Museum of Fine Arts, Boston.

Fig. 6.11 from Fr. Lexa, *La Magie dans l'Egypte ancienne III* (Paris, 1925).

Figs. 7.4, 7.5 from H. von Schäfer, *Ägyptischer Kunst* (Leipzig, 1919).

Fig. 7.12 from *The Holy Bible*, (London: Eyre and Spottiswoode, 1957).

Fig. 9.2 from A. Wiedemann, *The Ancient Egyptian Doctrine of the Immortality of the Soul* (London, 1895).

Fig. 9.13 from A. Piankoff, *The Shrines of Tutankhamon* (Princeton, N.J.: Princeton University Press, 1955).

Fig. 10.7 from A. Piankoff, *The Wandering of the Soul* (New York: Bollingen Foundation, 1974). Reproduced by permission of Princeton University Press.

Fig. 10.9 copyright British Museum.

Fig. 12.3 from Champollion, *Monuments de l'Egypte*, vol. 3 (Paris, 1850).

Figs. 12.4, 12.7 from C. Seeber, *Untersuchungen zur Darstellung des Totengerichts im Alten Ägypten* (Munich and Berlin: Deutscher Kunstverlag, 1976).

Fig. 12.6 copyright Egyptian Museum in Cairo.

INDEX